COUNTERNARRATIVES

SUNY series, Teacher Preparation and Development
Alan R. Tom, editor

COUNTERNARRATIVES

*Studies of Teacher Education
and Becoming and Being a Teacher*

Robert V. Bullough Jr.

State University of New York Press

Published by
State University of New York Press, Albany

© 2008 State University of New York

For information, contact State University of New York Press, Albany, NY
www.sunypress.edu

Production by Diane Ganeles
Marketing by Anne M. Valentine

Library of Congress Cataloging-in-Publication Data

Bullough, Robert V., 1949–
    Counternarratives : studies of teacher education and becoming and being a
teacher / Robert V. Bullough, Jr.
        p. cm. — (Suny series, teacher preparation and development)
    Includes bibliographical references and index.
    ISBN 978-0-7914-7313-9 (hardcover : alk. paper)
    ISBN 978-0-7914-7314-6 (pbk. : alk. paper)
    1. Teachers—Training of—United States. 2. First year teachers—United States.
I. Title.

LB1715.B8453 2008
370.81'1—dc22
                                                                2007010150

10 9 8 7 6 5 4 3 2 1

For my parents,
my first and best teachers

Contents

Acknowledgments

Over the years I have been very fortunate to have had many helpful and generous colleagues—as a teacher, in graduate school, then at the University of Utah, and now in the Center for the Improvement of Teacher Education and Schooling (CITES) and the McKay School of Education, Brigham Young University. My debts of gratitude are numerous and extensive. I am especially appreciative of the support given me by former Dean Robert S. Patterson, who enticed me to the McKay School by his expansive vision and goodness, Dean K. Richard Young, M. Winston Egan, chair of the Department of Teacher Education, Steven Baugh, director of CITES, and Cecil Clark, now emeritus. The McKay School is a most unusual place, where one individual's success is celebrated by all. In addition to stretching my ability and expanding my understanding in sometimes surprising ways, the many projects undertaken through CITES have had the added benefit of building and sustaining several friendships. I have learned a great deal from and am deeply grateful for several friends: Janet Young, Roni Jo Draper, Leigh Smith, Kendra Hall, Lynnette Erickson, Jim Birrell, Nancy Livingston, Paul Wangemann, Myra Tollestrup, and Joyce Terry. Additionally, I never shall be able to assuage my indebtedness to Stefinee Pinnegar, Clifford Mayes, and Al Merkley of the McKay School, Kerrie Baughman, Paul R. Klohr, Emeritus Professor, Ohio State University, and Craig Kridel, of the University of South Carolina and coauthor of *Stories of the Eight-Year Study* (Kridel and Bullough 2007). Lastly, some debts are hopelessly deep, as is the case with my debt to my wife, Dawn Ann, a dedicated and an inspiring elementary schoolteacher.

I am grateful to State University of New York Press for support in producing this collection and to several coauthors and publishers for permission to include previously published works. Chapter 1: Reprinted from *Teaching & Teacher Education* 17(7), R. V. Bullough Jr., "Pedagogical Content Knowledge circa 1907 and 1987: A Study in the History of an Idea," pp. 655–66, 2001, with permission from Elsevier. Chapter 2: Reprinted from *Teaching & Teacher Education* 16(2), R. V. Bullough Jr., "Teacher Education Reform as a Story of Possibility: Lessons Learned, Lessons Forgotten—The American Council on Education's Commission on Teacher Education (1939–1942), pp. 131–45, 2000, with permission from Elsevier. Chapter 3: Reprinted from *The Missing Links in Teacher Education: Innovative Approaches to Designing*

Teacher Education Programs, edited by G. Hoban, R. V. Bullough Jr., "The Quest for Identity in Teaching and Teacher Education," pp. 237–58, with permission from Springer. Chapter 4: Reprinted from *Teaching & Teacher Education* 21(2), R. V. Bullough Jr., "Being and Becoming a Mentor: School-based Teacher Educators and Teacher Educator Identity," pp. 143–55, with permission from Elsevier. Chapter 5: Reprinted from *Educational Action Research Journal* 12(3), R. V. Bullough Jr., R. J. Draper, L. B. Erickson, L. K. Smith, and J. R. Young, "Life on the Borderlands: Action Research and Clinical Teacher Education Faculty," pp. 433–53, with permission from Taylor and Francis (http://www.tandf.co.uk). Chapter 6: Reprinted from *Teacher Development* 6(3), R. V. Bullough Jr. and J. R. Young, "Learning to Teach as an Intern: The Emotions and the Self," pp. 217–431, with permission from Taylor and Francis (http://www.tandf.co.uk). Chapter 7: Reprinted from the *Journal of Teacher Education* 44(2), R. V. Bullough Jr. and K. Baughman, "Continuity and Change in Teacher Development: First Year Teacher after Five Years," pp. 86–95, with permission from Sage. Chapter 8: Reprinted from *Teaching & Teacher Education* 11(5), R. V. Bullough Jr. and K. Baughman, "Changing Contexts and Expertise in Teaching: First-Year Teacher after Seven Years," pp. 461–77, with permission from Elsevier. Chapter 9: Reprinted from *Teachers and Teaching: Theory and Practice* 12(2), R. V. Bullough Jr., D. A. Bullough, and P. Blackwell Mayes, "Teacher Dreams, Emotions, and the Work of Teaching," pp. 223–38, with permission from Taylor and Francis (http://www.tandf.co.uk). Chapter 10: Reprinted from *Teaching & Teacher Education* 9(4), R. V. Bullough Jr., "Case Records as Personal Teaching Texts for Study in Preservice Teacher Education," pp. 385–96, with permission from Elsevier. Chapter 11: Reprinted from the *Journal of Teacher Education* 42(1), R. V. Bullough Jr., "Exploring Personal Teaching Metaphors in Preservice Teacher Education," pp, 43–51, with permission from Sage. Chapter 12: Reprinted from *Teaching & Teacher Education* 19(1), R. V. Bullough Jr., J. R. Young, J. R. Birrell, D. C. Clark, M. W. Egan, L. B. Erickson, M. Frankovich, J. Brunetti and M. Welling, "Teaching with a Peer: A Comparison of Two Models of Student Teaching," pp. 35–51, with permission from Elsevier.

Introduction

Counternarratives is more than simply a collection of studies of teaching and teacher education. It represents a portion of a professional journey into the problems of teacher education and offers a reminder that educational improvement is always and everywhere dependent on the well-being of the individual teacher.

Ours is a difficult time for teachers and teacher educators. Over the past several years much criticism, often biting and unbridled, has been directed toward education and teacher education. Teachers are under constant attack, and well-funded efforts are under way to dismantle the American public school system. Although many teacher educators are quite certain their practice makes a positive difference in the lives of aspiring teachers, we have failed to convince but few of the worth of that work. The value and quality of research done within education and teacher education also have been severely criticized (National Research Council 2004), and conclusions asserting that rather little is known about the education of teachers abound (Cochran-Smith and Zeichner 2005). The view is now widely shared that what is needed is an education science that will not only prove the value of public schooling and, perhaps, but not probably, of teacher education, and, by establishing causal links among variables, provide compelling evidence of best practices for replication across diverse educational sites (Shavelson and Towne 2002).

In her American Educational Research Association (AERA) presidential address, Marilyn Cochran-Smith (2005) argued that "from the late 1990s to the present, a new teacher education has been called for and, to a great extent, has actually emerged. This new teacher education, and now dominant set of narratives, has three closely coupled pieces: it is constructed as a public policy problem, based on research and evidence, and driven by outcomes" (4). This set of narratives underpins development of what might tongue in cheek best be described as "Baby Big Education Science," offering normative tales of system intransigence, teacher incompetence, and program ineffectiveness that now dominate discourse.

Seeking to further develop evidence-based teacher education, but displaying a measure of generosity, the AERA Panel on Research and Teacher Education's main recommendation was that

> research about teacher education needs now to be undertaken using methods that will increase our knowledge about important features of teacher education and its connections to the outcomes that are important in a democratic society. We recommend attention to the full variety of research approaches available, recognizing that multidisciplinary and multimethodological approaches are necessary. (Cochran-Smith and Zeichner 2005, 31)

This is a relatively generous view of research, one acknowledging the need for education research to mature (see Mayer 2006) and acknowledging the potential value of diverse kinds of studies to the improvement of teaching and teacher education.

Unfortunately, this generous view of education research may get lost as the wider discourse is controlled by special interest groups with their "think" tanks, and especially impatient and unforgiving politicians for whom subtleties are of little interest and replicability of results and randomized trials are gold standards for research. Driven by a deep, although consistently denied, distrust of educators, school change is widely thought best achieved through mandated standards, punitive accountability measures, and expanded competition without regard for human variability. Emerging federal funding priorities and practices certainly support this conclusion—fewer funded studies, given more money and involving very large data sets, linked to a small number of comparatively privileged institutions working to influence policy to assure their continued prominence and funding.

For many teacher educators, perhaps most, the message seems to be stick to practice, leave theory generation and policy matters to others, and await your fate. As Johnson, Johnson, Farenga, and Ness (2005) observe, "This latest standards movement has left teachers to recognize that they have little control over their own fate" (104). With Voltaire's *Candide*, we should contentedly tend our gardens.

A Chastened Ambition: "Better" not "Best" Practice

Years ago, David Tyack published the now classic *The One Best System* (1974), within which he detailed the quest for a single institutional solution to the complex problems of urban education. He concluded by arguing, in part, that "Effective reform today will require reassessment of some cherished convictions about the possibility of finding a one best system" (290). Despite the warning, everywhere, most especially including accreditation visits, one now hears earnest talk about "best practice" in education. Compared to creating a single best system of education, aiming for best practice seems harmless, a reflection of a much-chastened ambition. Nevertheless, both aims are ensconced in a shared set of assumptions of just the sort Tyack argued needed reconsidering, assumptions that belie the complexity of the processes of teaching and learning and ignore the persistent and inevitable uncertainties of educating the young.

Looking ahead, a few best teaching practices may emerge, and these will most certainly depend for their lives upon the strength of the linkage to raising student standardized test scores (Lasley, Siedentop, and Yinger 2006). But, more likely, and assuming the ability to overcome very serious technical problems with value added studies (Martineau 2006; Schmidt, Houang and McKnight 2005), a few "better practices" or "promising practices" will be identified, *better* based ultimately upon their value within specific contexts characterized by a few variables and in relationship to a set of highly contestable propositions about what is most worth doing, being, learning, and becoming. These will, of course, like all educational practices, be wholly dependent for their impact upon the artistry and skill of the teacher when reading and then responding to a shifting and dynamic learning environment. Given the complexity of teaching and learning, where the aim is education and not training, a proper sense of humility would prohibit using the term *best practice* and also and especially temper enthusiasm for the quest.

Representing conflicts in value and interests, and speaking of "stages," Tyack and Cuban (1995) observed that policy talk operates in cycles—beginning with the need to diagnose problems, talk moves into "policy action," and finally, through a variety of means, toward implementation, by far the most difficult and complex stage (40). They further observe that the three stages frequently are disconnected, and that discourse and practice diverge, often sharply. Typically, a crisis thrusts them more closely together as one or another value vanquishes other values, takes center stage, and enjoys a season of rhetorical prominence while dominating problem diagnosis. Initially, the organization and structure of an education science find their purpose in shaping the discourse of the first two policy cycles. These cycles aim at agreement on definitions and actions. By creating a sense of perpetual crisis, legislated accountability measures seek to tightly join all three stages and to achieve standardized practice.

Crises, engineered or genuine, galvanize agreement, although tensions inevitably remain simmering, waiting to boil over. But a state of perpetual crisis like our own has additional effects, including growth of a widespread sense of futility among those who, having been excluded from policy discussions and always found wanting, are nonetheless charged with and held accountable for implementation. Thus at American Association of Colleges of Teacher Education meetings, one sees education deans shuffling through hotel hallways wearing long faces just as one hears from school administrators a great deal of grumbling about the original design of the No Child Left Behind legislation and its directives (but not publicly espoused intent). Futility turns to anger, as in their haste, policy makers and their allies offer sweeping solutions to problems often not well understood and, misunderstanding human motivation, rely upon increasing standardization and threats and punishments to encourage change. Innovation does not thrive under threat, but certain kinds of research do. Behind the scenes, struggle is internalized, and resistance forms quietly. Being sensible, a measured and self-protective conservatism emerges among educators, and the impulse to innovate browns and withers.

Hopefully the education science that is emerging will helpfully inform and direct federal and state education policy makers. This, of course, assumes that when thinking about education and teacher education policy makers actually are interested in data-driven decision making, respectful of contextual differences, and most especially committed to getting the questions and the data sources right. This assumption, and hope, underpins the work of both the AERA Panel and the National Academy of Education-sponsored volume *Preparing Teachers for a Changing World* (Darling-Hammond and Bransford 2005). Clearly, much rests on the ability of researchers to wisely educate and better influence policy makers. Not only resource allocation and governance are at stake but also definitions of what counts as data and as questions worthy of inquiry (topics over which there is a good deal of disagreement). Consider: Remarkably little attention is now given to how poverty and well-being affect student learning in favor of an overly narrow focus on the presumed powers of teachers and schools to overcome the effects of inequality (Rothstein 2004). The point was nicely made nearly half a century ago when H. Gordon Hullfish and Philip Smith (1961) wrote: "Remember that miseducative conditions in a culture will cancel out the educative efforts of schools" (255).

Context and Counternarratives

To a certain degree living and working within complex institutions like schools and universities will inevitably bring a measure of double-mindedness. It certainly has for me. But double-mindedness is becoming a necessary way of life among educators. Of course, tension, contradiction, and paradox abound in teaching (Kennedy 2006) and probably always have. Sometimes teachers know the good but, as Shakespeare reminds us, they, like others, simply lack the energy, commitment, or moral imagination to do what they know should be done: "It is a good divine that follows his own instructions: I can easier teach twenty what were good to be done, than be one of the twenty to follow mine own teaching" (*Merchant of Venice*, Act I, Scene II). Yet conditions are changing and something greater is now at stake. St. James's warning comes to mind: "Double-minded man is unstable in all his ways" (James 1:8).

A new managerialism has emerged that emphasizes what Stephen Ball (2003) has described as "performativity," where educators are "valued for their productivity alone," and authentic social relations are replaced by "judgmental relations" (224). Performativity invites "fabrications . . . versions of an organization (or person) which [do] not exist. . . . [Rather] they are produced purposefully in order 'to be accountable'" (ibid.). And, inauthenticity results. Clearly, education suffers when teachers must live dividedly and deeply so, when they consistently find themselves needing to engage in actions contrary to their most fundamental beliefs about teaching and learning in order to satisfy one or another set of externally imposed mandates. Some years ago I described this condition at its extreme as producing a sort of "professional schizophrenia" (Bullough 1982), a condition resulting from feeling or being compelled to work against what one believes and of being pulled in multiple directions by conflicting but always insistent claims. Under such conditions, work slowly becomes joyless. It is little wonder that there is a growing shortage of aspiring teachers. The word is getting out, and teachers are spreading it.

As every teacher knows, to teach is to live on and find pleasure living on the edge, in a shifting, tightly packed, and often very noisy life space, one forever opening and closing in unpredictable and often delightful ways. Exposed and vulnerable, teachers offer themselves to those they teach, and they testify of themselves and of what is of most worth, and as they do so they anxiously look for the signs of recognition and engagement but find also signs of rejection. As David Patterson comments: "Those of us who are teachers cannot stand before a class without standing for something . . . teaching is testimony" (1991, 16). Despite their vulnerability, consistency of commitment and action is expected of teachers, especially by the young, who scan constantly the moral horizon hoping to gain their bearings. As a moral relationship, the nature of teaching places teachers on that horizon, and so it is offstage where teachers compromise and backstage where they keep their inner disappointments and concerns hidden from view. Insofar as the dominant narratives support performativity, they give little hope for the resolution of inner dividedness, and divisions necessarily widen. So, one wonders, of what does the deeply double-minded teacher testify?

This is where the need for *Counternarratives* arises, for stories that recognize and respond to the complexity of teaching while honoring the hopes and dreams and legitimizing the problems and concerns of teachers working in specific contexts and with specific students. Such narratives embrace the lives lived beneath the much-desired generalizations promised by education science and the systems that encourage "fabrications."

On Teacher Education

For teacher educators, like teachers, the otherwise expected challenges of teaching are made much more difficult by the context of teacher education and the highly charged and very public debates raging over purpose and value. Here too arises the need for *Counternarratives*. Friends and foes alike frequently and roundly criticize teacher education, and not always with knowledge and understanding. Among the friends, no critic has been more insightful nor more understanding than has John Goodlad. In *Teachers for Our Nation's Schools* (1990), he accurately and painfully portrayed the problems of teacher education in research institutions, persistent problems I have come to know well over the past thirty years. Writing in 1990, he concluded that in research universities the norms of the arts and sciences dominated, and in the pursuit of an illusive prestige, education faculty often distanced themselves from teacher education and the concerns of teachers. Adjunct faculty bore most of the burden of teacher education. External agencies set teacher education policies, and there was comparatively little "curricular autonomy" (Goodlad 1990, 93). Relationships with students often were strained, and placements were made for practice teaching with comparatively little regard for cooperating teacher quality. Preparation programs did little to influence the beliefs and expectations about teaching that beginning teachers brought with them: "Their preparation programs are simply not powerful or long enough to dissuade them from what has already been absorbed from role models" (Goodlad 1990, 149). Little attention was given to socializing students to a professional ideal, and surprisingly little attention given to the moral and ethical issues that Goodlad thought ought to command the interest of educators. Where foundations courses existed, they were separated from methods classes. The values of individualism dominated: "They come through their preparation as individuals [and are] likely to take responsibility only for their individual classrooms and assume that someone else will take care of the rest" (Goodlad 1990, 265–66). Students entered and left their programs with a "very practical orientation—an orientation that leads them to judge all education courses by utilitarian, instrumental criteria" (Goodlad 1990, 213). Accordingly, the "socialization process appeared to nurture the ability to acquire teaching skills through experience rather than the ability to think through unpredictable circumstances" (Goodlad 1990, 215). Technique mattered, and learning to fit into and survive within "an operational role in the classroom" mattered most (Goodlad 1990, 251).

These were, and to a degree still are, the problems of teacher education (Levine 2006). Fortunately, there has been considerable although uneven improvement particularly because of growing interest in and commitment to building public school/university partnerships (Goodlad, Mantle-Bromley, and Goodlad 2004; Smith and Fenstermacher 1999) and to paying much greater attention to the social systems, like cohorts (Mather and Hanley 1999; Darling 2001) and mentoring (Giles and Wilson 2004; Young, Bullough,

Draper, Smith and Erickson 2005), that support and enhance student learning and community building. Nevertheless, to a degree these have been weaknesses of the programs within which I have taught.

Confronting Self

In the early 1980s I lead my first secondary cohort at the University of Utah. This proved to be an extraordinarily difficult teaching assignment, but one I was required to accept despite a desire to associate more directly with foundational studies and minimize my involvement in teacher education. I planned and then, with the help of a graduate assistant, coordinated and taught the courses that formed a year-long and full-time program for a group of about twenty-two teacher education students. Together these students completed curriculum and methods classes and practice teaching and participated in a weekly problem-solving seminar tightly linked to the work they were doing in the schools. At that time I did not think of myself as a teacher educator and was one of those education faculty members Goodlad identified as distancing themselves from teacher education and the concerns of teachers. I was deeply conflicted. Most particularly, the few connections that then existed between my scholarship and my teaching practice were flimsy and strained.

Spending a year with a group of students forced me to attend to their personal and developmental issues and concerns. Sometimes, as Guskey (2002) has noted, changes in practice must precede changes in belief. While working with these students I began to face myself and reconsider my commitments. I asked, but had only unsatisfactory answers for, the "who" question Parker Palmer poses: "Who is the self that teaches? How does the quality of my selfhood form—or deform—the way I relate to my students, my subject, my colleagues, my world?" (1998, 4). I noticed that some students seemed to ignore what I taught while others grabbed hold of it easily, as though what I had to say confirmed but failed to challenge beliefs. While struggling with this issue, I began exploring the role of life history as the backdrop against which students become teachers. Paul Klohr planted that seed when I was a graduate student at Ohio State, a seed that grew in the hands of the reconceptualists in curriculum theory (Pinar 1975) and has since sprouted abundant fruit (Day, Stobart, Sammons, and Kington 2006; Goodson 1992; Goodson and Sikes 2001; Richardson 1996).

My second cohort began a change in me. Quickly I bonded with this group that was composed of smart, interesting, and sometimes confrontational and often very funny people. I found myself heavily invested in their learning and in their school successes. Almost despite myself, their disappointments became my disappointments. I worked very hard with, and on behalf of, this group, but when the year ended, I felt a measure of disappointment, although I did not quite know why. I needed to dig deeper and more fully confront myself (see Day 1999, ch. 2); I needed to become a student of teaching (Bullough and Gitlin 1995; Dewey 1904). That summer I contacted a member of the cohort, Kerrie Baughman, and we began the series of studies that led to the publication of *First-Year Teacher: A Case Study* (Bullough 1989). Kerrie proved to be one of my best teachers. I also completed a series of essays that formed *The Forgotten Dream of American Public Education* (Bullough 1988), which was an attempt to settle my thinking and to present foundational issues in ways accessible to beginning teachers and others interested in education.

Other studies followed, and gradually the problems of teacher education became much more personal and more intriguing. Research is, after all, the best form of professional development: Principles emerge from practice; we practice our principles, and in practicing and confronting our limitations often we discover just what those principles are, and in the process something profound about who we are and what we most value is revealed. And we change as a result. Attempting to listen more carefully to my students, I began gathering data from my classes and used the data to rethink my actions—course content, instruction, and organization. With my students I openly explored what we were doing and why, and I solicited feedback and criticism from them (see Featherstone, Munby, and Russell 1997; Cook-Sather 2002). Exit interviews were conducted and written evaluations invited and taken very seriously. A series of articles grew from this work, some touching on life history and others on teaching metaphors (Chapter 11) as a means for helping beginning teachers think productively about themselves as teachers. Still others explored what I came to call personal teaching texts (PTTs), case records of a sort, as a means for building program coherence and for helping beginning teachers take greater responsibility for their development (Chapter 10). The initial focus on metaphors came from spending a year and a half in Kerrie's classroom and coming to realize how central nurturing and mothering were to how she thought about teaching. Only later would I realize that others were working along similar lines. The results of this work eventually were brought together in a single volume, *Becoming a Student of Teaching: Methodologies for Exploring Self and School Context* (1995), written with Andrew Gitlin. By 1990, I had become a teacher educator and found myself needing to work on the problems of teacher education.

Local Studies

Twelve chapters follow, divided into the following four sections, "Historical Studies," "Studies of Becoming and Being a Teacher Educator," "Studies of Becoming and Being a Teacher," and "Program Studies." Each chapter was previously published between 1991 and 2006. An Afterword follows, in which I share a set of principles for teacher education drawn from an analysis of the studies presented here and from reflecting on my experience as a teacher and teacher educator. Every chapter offers a counternarrative, presenting a view of teaching and teacher education and of learning to teach, which in various ways challenges the now-dominant narratives. They represent comparatively small stories, but, as I will argue, it is within such stories that life finds its fullest, although not only, meaning. The Afterword represents an attempt to speak and reach beyond the local studies presented. My hope is that readers will engage in a "critical conversation" (Loughran 2006, 165) with the text, comparing and contrasting experiences, beliefs, and practices. The first two chapters, "Pedagogical Content Knowledge circa 1907 and 1987," and "Teacher Education Reform as a Story of Possibility: Lessons Learned, Lessons Forgotten," are historical. They are included not only because they are reminders that knowing the past is often helpful for thinking about the future, but also because they underscore how the past quietly shapes the present and often without the awareness of those who have been shaped, sometimes twisted, by it. Moreover, these two chapters underscore how misguided many critics are in their claims that teacher education offers little value to improving the education of the young. The problem is often a failure of memory. There is a desperate need for teacher educators to reclaim our collective past and to begin to build a shared memory, in part because memory is necessary to building programs of research of the sort Shulman (2002) has described. Perhaps more importantly, both resistance and innovation frequently begin in the recovery of memory, a reclaiming of the past. With the exception of these two chapters forming Part 1, the collection is composed of local studies, results of "practical inquiry" (Richardson 1994), or self-study (Allender 2001; Loughran 2006; Loughran, Hamilton, LaBosky, and Russell 2004; Samaras 2002).

There are two answers to the question "Why local studies?" One is easy, the other is hard. The easy answer is that local studies are what I like to do, give me pleasure, have been encouraged by the institutions I have served, and have enabled program improvement. My experience echoes the words of Samuel Johnson, in response to James Boswell's comment that his journal was filled with "all sorts of little incidents," Johnson remarked: "'Sir . . . there is nothing too little for so little a creature as man. It is by studying little things that we attain the great knowledge of having as little misery and as much happiness as possible'" (Pottle 1950, 305). Being fully purposeful, local studies moderate feelings of futility by revealing unrealized possibilities within current practices. The hard answer points toward a complex set of issues, contextual and conceptual, leading toward the conclusion that quality education is heavily dependent on teacher research (Cochran-Smith and Lytle 1999) and self-study (Hamilton and Pinnegar 2000).

Those of us who see our arena of action as the local, who seek better practices from the study of our own practice and work context, may not recognize our research as connected to the concerns of policy makers or of Baby Big Education Science. Yet clearly it is, just as it is linked to the wider practice and study of teacher education. Local studies open up for discussion what Darling-Hammond (2006) has described as the "black box of the [teacher education] program—inside the courses and clinical experiences that candidates encounter—and . . . how [the] experiences programs design for candidates cumulatively add up to a set of knowledge, skills, and dispositions that determines what teachers actually do in the classroom" (303). However, connections must not be taken for granted—they must be made, especially if they are to have any influence on policy. Policy and policy makers operate at multiple levels, and spheres of influence range outward. To extend their reach and increase their influence, local studies need to be connected, and this requires paying careful attention to literature reviews and to the need to describe clearly the research methods used, underpinning assumptions, the settings within which studies are conducted, and failures as well as successes. In addition, local researchers need to recognize that to answer the "so what" question necessarily means moving outside of and beyond a specific location, cautiously perhaps, to engage with others who share similar concerns but who work elsewhere. This points toward the need for the much-neglected work of synthesis (Zeichner 2007). In this way, larger narratives are formed around which like-minded communities may coalesce. To invite engagement and comparison, local studies need to be made transparent (Loughran, Berry, and Tudball 2005), such that *your better practice* can be compared to *my practice* with relatively little guesswork and with a reasonable degree of precision. And to this end, concepts need to be defined and used consistently (Zeichner 2007). Comparisons of this kind invite reimagining of practice and encourage cycles of testing and refinement which, in any case, is the only sound basis for developing and sustaining quality programs and for program improvement.

This said, when facing powerful forces supporting increasing standardization and the nearly overwhelming demands of continuous and very public assessment, local studies have a value that often is ignored and seldom appreciated. Stephen J. Gould (1996) nicely makes the point: "[O]ur culture encodes a strong bias either to neglect or ignore variation. We tend to focus instead on measures of central tendency, and as a result we make some terrible mistakes, often with considerable practical import" (44). Some years ago, John Goodlad (1994) expressed a profoundly important insight about the motivation of educators: "Good teachers are driven in their daily work by neither the goals of improving the nation's economic competitiveness nor that of enhancing the school's test scores. Instead, they are driven by a desire to teach satisfyingly, to have all their students excited about learning, to have their daily work square with their conception of what this work should be and do" (203). He further argued that exceptional schools become that way "primarily by paying close attention to their own educational business and largely ignoring the changing exhortations of a national reform crusade" (ibid.). Quality is undermined when, under pressure of an "ethics of competition and performance," creative compliance and opacity become dominating educator concerns (Ball 2003, 218). Goodlad's argument holds true for teacher education as well: Exemplary programs arise from inspiring and thoughtful teachers whose work is supported by good, well-designed, and *honest* local research, studies that speak directly and forcefully to the challenges of the students taught and the programs within which they study.

Local studies have revelatory and disciplinary functions; comparing results reveals where central tendencies collapse and where prejudices lie hidden. As Paul Feyerabend (1975) argues, "All methodologies, even the most obvious ones, have their limits" (32), and limits are located through comparison. Moreover, by attending carefully to outliers, theories are tested, perhaps revealing something profound, "that the eccentric can be used to explain the central, rather than the other way around!" (Toulmin 2001, 30). Put differently, local studies "account for the particular" (Kelchtermans and Hamilton 2004, 803) and encourage (drawing on Garrison 1997) "outlaw" thinking, non-normative discourse that enables the raising of questions that reside outside of established methodological parameters and taken-for-granted system imperatives.

The future of teacher education most certainly rests on our ability to sustain a generous view of research. Quality experimental studies are desperately needed to successfully make the argument for the value of public education and teacher education to doubting policy makers and to making a case for the trustworthiness of educators. But so too are quality local studies needed that speak directly to the challenges of improving practice and policy—small stories that test larger narratives. Local studies serve as a direct means for generating, exploring, and testing theories and established policies and practices and for building and extending the conversation about quality teaching and teacher education. This said, perhaps above all else the value of local studies is to serve as reminders that beneath central tendencies and the much-publicized efforts to raise standardized test scores are living people, individuals working in extraordinarily complex settings and striving to make sense of their lives and work as best as they can to live undividedly, and for whom teaching is first, foremost, and always a personal and profoundly moral relationship (Ayers 1993). Research that does not support and strengthen such relationships will most certainly fail over time and likely do a good deal of harm along the way.

PART 1

Historical Studies

CHAPTER 1

Pedagogical Content Knowledge circa 1907 and 1987: A Study in the History of an Idea (2001)

Introduction

Since the 1980s in the United States teacher education has undergone consistent scrutiny and frequent attack by politicians and policy makers concerned with the quality of public education. Responses to these attacks have varied, but generally they have centered on the need to professionalize teaching, including the need to raise academic standards for admission to teacher education and to assure better-quality teacher education. Doubts about the value of teacher education have resulted in the creation of alternative routes to initial teacher certification and in efforts to make a case for teaching as a unique intellectual enterprise involving special forms of knowledge and skill. This chapter is concerned with an aspect of the later issue, of making a case for teaching as involving unique forms of knowledge and of the challenge of teacher educators to make the case convincingly to critics. The focus is on pedagogical content knowledge (PCK). The purpose is to locate weaknesses in the case and in the concept as a basis for considering possibilities. A turn toward the much-neglected history of teacher education in the United States is necessary to accomplish this aim.

Pedagogical Content Knowledge 1987: A Response to the Critics

Following the publication of "Knowledge and Teaching: Foundations of the New Reform" (Shulman 1987), it seemed as though a shift was about to take place in how teacher educators thought about the knowledge base of teaching. In the article Shulman argued for the value of pedagogical content knowledge as the foundation of teacher education: "Pedagogical content knowledge is of special interest because it identifies the distinctive bodies of knowledge for teaching. It represents the blending of content and pedagogy into an understanding of how particular topics, problems, or issues are organized, represented, and adapted to the diverse interests and abilities of learners, and presented for

15

instruction. Pedagogical content knowledge is the category most likely to distinguish the understanding of the content specialist from that of the pedagogue" (1987, 8). Pedagogical content knowledge is concerned with how teachers reason pedagogically.

The timing of Shulman's article could not have been better, and quickly pedagogical content knowledge slipped into teacher educator rhetoric. Teacher educators were eager for a more adequate response to the growing criticism of teacher education and for a better means of supporting arguments for teaching as a profession. As Shulman noted, several reports of the period (Holmes Group 1986; Carnegie Forum on Education and the Economy 1986) argued that better schools would follow teacher professionalization. The problem was that the "advocates of professional reform base their arguments on the belief that there exists a 'knowledge base for teaching'—a codifiable aggregation of knowledge, skill, understanding, and technology, of ethics and disposition, of collective responsibility—as well as a means for representing and communicating it. . . . The rhetoric regarding the knowledge base, however, rarely specifies the character of such knowledge. It does not say what teachers should know, do, understand or profess that will render teaching more than a form of individual labor, let alone be considered among the learned professions" (Shulman 1987, 4).

The attack on teachers and teacher educators was intense, scathing, at the time. Starting with *A Nation at Risk*, "The Commission found that not enough of the academically able students are being attracted to teaching; that teacher preparation programs need substantial improvement. . . . Too many teachers are being drawn from the bottom quarter of graduating high school and college students. The teacher preparation curriculum is weighted heavily with courses in 'educational methods' at the expense of courses in subjects to be taught" (National Commission on Excellence in Education 1983, 22). Release of the report was page A1 news across the United States: "Mediocre education puts the nation at risk" (Deseret News, April 30, 1983, A1). Teachers and teacher educators felt the sting and rebuke. Centering its case on the need to professionalize teaching, the Carnegie Forum on Education and the Economy argued in *A Nation Prepared: Teachers for the 21st Century* that standards needed to be raised: "Teacher education must meet much higher standards. The focus must be on what teachers need to know and be able to do. Raising standards for entry into the profession is likely to give the public confidence that the teachers they hire will be worth the increased salary and worthy of the increased autonomy we advocate. These policies will most certainly fail, however, if the education of teachers is not greatly improved. Otherwise, new teachers may be unable to perform up to the new expectations" (1986, 69).

Teacher educators seemed to respond to the challenge to teacher education in *Tomorrow's Teachers: A Report of the Holmes Group* (1986). The

Holmes Group was no ordinary group of teacher educators: "We write as members of the Holmes Group, a consortium of education deans and chief academic officers from the major research universities in each of the fifty states" (3). Again, the argument was that the solution to the education ills of America was to professionalize teaching. A central component of this effort was to improve the intellectual quality of teacher education. The finger of blame pointed inward: "Unhappily, teaching and teacher education have a long history of mutual impairment. Teacher education long has been intellectually weak; this further eroded the prestige of an already poorly esteemed profession, and it encouraged many inadequately prepared people to enter teaching" (1986, 6). Part of the solution to low status was to do away with all education majors in favor of academic majors and minors for all teachers, elementary educators included. This suggestion was the basis for arguing that a fifth year was necessary for initial teacher licensure. The Holmes Group further argued that methods courses needed to be replaced with subject-specific pedagogical courses: Future teachers need to "study the subjects they will teach with instructors who model fine teaching and who understand the pedagogy of their material" (1986, 16). Thus the stage was set for a reconsideration of the nature of teacher knowledge in the quest for status and security within higher education. Enter PCK. In the broadest outline, this story is an old one of teacher educators responding to perceived threats, as will be discussed in the sections that follow.

Historical Context

During the later half of the nineteenth century and the first quarter of the twentieth, normal schools developed and eventually assumed the major role for educating elementary teachers in the United States. Initially these were narrowly vocational schools, but as demographics changed and expectations for teachers grew, their educational offerings expanded to include greater emphasis on general education and disciplinary knowledge. In many parts of the country, particularly within rural America, normal schools were the only avenue available for education beyond the early grades. At the time colleges and universities had little interest in educating elementary schoolteachers. However, as enrollments in secondary schools exploded shortly after the turn of the century, increasingly university administrators recognized the potential for greater resources and for greater student enrollment if they developed teacher education programs. Reviewing the history of the normal school from a participant's perspective and as one of its champions, Charles Harper of the State Normal University in Normal, Illinois, wrote of the battle that was waged between normal schools and colleges and universities over teacher education:

"The struggle was purely a defensive one. It was a vigorously fought movement to maintain what had been won—that is, the right to serve the public schools by the preparation of any and all kinds of teachers needed by these schools. . . . The struggle on the part of the teachers colleges was to avoid being sidetracked by the growing power of the state universities and other strong colleges and universities" (Harper 1939, 129–30). The "danger," he wrote, was that the "newly recognized teachers colleges [that replaced the normal schools] . . . [would end up] aping the liberal arts colleges and thereby los[e] their distinctive characteristics upon which the state teacher-education institutions were originally founded" (ibid.).

Anticipating the criticism of *A Nation at Risk* and *Tomorrow's Teachers*, the attack on normal schools was based on the view that "normals were merely schools of 'methods' and did not stand for scholarship" (Harper 1939, 131). On the contrary, Harper argued, the normals emphasized "mastery of subject-matter" [*sic*], second only to the "ideal of social service" (ibid.). What Harper did not say, perhaps because he did not realize it, was that the battle was already lost. Seeking to share responsibility for educating secondary teachers brought with it direct comparison with the academic standards of colleges and universities and, just as Harper feared, an embracing of those standards by teacher colleges inevitably followed.

Pedagogical Content Knowledge at the Turn of the Century

Walter Scott Monroe identified 1907 as a turning point in the history of teacher education, "a 'banner year' in the discussion of teacher education" (Monroe 1952, 203). "By 1907 most of the larger institutions and some of the smaller ones had established a 'department of education' and in a few cases a college of education" (ibid., 205). Teacher education had achieved a much-welcomed beachhead in colleges and universities. But, Monroe observed, their foothold was tenuous: "The establishment of such provisions for the professional phase of teacher education does not necessarily reflect general approval of including technical-professional study . . . within the work for the baccalaureate degree" (ibid.). Despite the strong support of electives by the Committee of Ten (1894) of the National Education Association (NEA) and of Charles Eliot, committee chair and president of Harvard University, based on the view that most subject areas had disciplinary or liberal education value, education courses remained suspect. Defending the Committee of Ten report, Eliot wrote: "To master one subject so as to be able to give both elementary and advanced instruction in it is for the teacher himself a deep source of intellectual enthusiasm and growth. Real scholarship becomes possible for him, and also a progressive intellectual expansion through life; for only progressive scholars can maintain for many years the mastery of even a single subject. . . . Toward effecting this great improvement, two important measures are the elevation of normal schools, and the creation, or strengthening, of educational departments in colleges and universities" (Eliot 1898, 331–32). Thus one way of improving the academic preparation of teachers was, according to Eliot, for the nation's colleges and universities to support teacher education and thereby elevate the quality and liberalize the curriculum.

Several speakers at the 1907 conference of the NEA focused attention on the content of teacher education, specifically secondary teacher education, which was the turf both colleges and normal schools hoped to homestead. Perhaps unwittingly, several of the speakers built upon the view of content introduced by S. S. Parr in 1888, then president of the NEA Department of Normal Schools, at that year's national convention. Among the qualifications of an effective teacher, Parr argued, was "the teaching-knowledge which is derived from viewing the various subjects in the order fixed for them by their nature and by that of the mind which acquires them" (Parr 1888, 467–68). Parr stated:

> An analysis of the process of teaching shows that there is a special knowledge in each subject that belongs to instruction. This is quite distinct from academic knowledge. It differs from it in purpose, in its relation to the facts of things, and in the mode by which it is obtained. The ideas of an academic subject are arranged in an order which is determined by their own relations. The order of the same ideas, when they are arranged for teaching, is determined by their relation to the learning mind. The purpose of academic knowledge is acquaintance with series of beings in the order of the necessary dependence. The purpose of teaching-knowledge is acquaintance with the processes of the learning mind in the order of mastery. (1888, 469)

Thus Parr helped plant the seeds of PCK: "There is a special knowledge in each subject that belongs to instruction." When ideas are "arranged for teaching [their order] is determined by their relation to the learning mind." It is John Dewey's conception of this difference between the logical and the psychological organization of subject matter that is best remembered, not Parr's. Despite finding support in Dewey's distinction between the psychological and logical organization of subject matter discussed in *The Child and the Curriculum* (1902), the seeds did not grow. At the time other issues demanded the attention of teacher educators, not the least being the struggle for legitimacy, and the case for legitimacy was to be made in traditional academic terms, not in terms of the uniqueness of the content and task of teacher education. This was no time for a radical idea, one that raised questions about the value of traditional academic studies for teaching.

Several speakers at the 1907 conference addressed the issue of the "professional preparation of high-school teachers." Many noted that college graduates who lacked pedagogical training did not know how to manage classrooms or work with children effectively. In particular, they "fail to get the pupil's point of view. They do not," Straton Brooks, superintendent of schools for Boston, Massachusetts, stated flatly, "see the subject taught as the pupil sees it. A large majority of them give greater attention to the logical development of the subject than to the development of the logical powers of the pupil. This is due to the fact that the training of these teachers has been largely, if not wholly, academic, and that their professional training, if any, has been incidental and superficial. Academic training, as here used, means the study of the subject for the sake of mastering it as a subject in its logical and epistemological relations, while professional training, as here used, means the study of the subject with reference to its adaptability to use as an instrument for developing and training the mind of the pupil. . . . To the extent that academic study of any subject prepares a teacher to use that subject as an instrument of child development it is professional in its result" (1907, 547). Brooks went farther and charged: "Professional training [of this kind] cannot be conducted with any high degree of success under the direct domination and control of the regular college or university faculty. The attitude of the college professor is properly and necessarily academic. His attention both as a student and teacher has been so long turned exclusively to the academic side that the case is rare indeed that he is competent to offer professional instruction of even medium quality, yet he is seldom conscious of this and looks with contempt and suspicion upon the efforts of the department of education to discuss how to teach a subject about which it knows academically so much less than he does; nor does he look with favor upon allowing another department to teach in any way a subject that belongs to his department" (ibid., 551).

The majority of the speakers appear to have agreed with these charges, including George Luckey, professor of education at the University of Nebraska: "Scholarship alone is not sufficient no matter how thoro [*sic*] and extended it may have been." The teacher, Luckey argued, must know the disciplines from the "learner's standpoint" as well as the teacher's (Luckey 1907, 589–90). Most speakers seemed to feel acutely the disdain in which teacher education was held by professors of the arts and sciences, although they noted improvements and gave as evidence the founding of a College of Education that year at Ohio State University and earlier a Department of Education at Harvard University.

Paul Hanus sought a middle position, one consistent with his standing as professor of education at Harvard. Hanus also wanted to professionalize academic content. Following a spirited and detailed argument for scholarly attainment as a basic teaching requirement, including "superior attainments in some one field of human learning" (Hanus 1907, 564), Hanus stated: "My point is, once more, that the teacher is not merely a scholar, important as scholarship is. To be available for teaching purposes, scholarship must have been acquired or at least overhauled from the teacher's point of view. The scholar must possess his scholarship in a new way. He must examine it with a view to attaining a clear conception of the *educational resources* of his specialty and an equally clear recognition of its limitations" (1907, 571, emphasis). Hanus's argument would later be echoed in the first Holmes Group report and would be used to support the view that even elementary education teachers should possess academic majors and minors for teacher certification.

There were dissenters. Frederick Bolton, professor of education at the State University of Iowa and a former normal school faculty member, had no sympathy for the normal school except as a place to train elementary school teachers. Arguing for development of a science of education, Bolton stated:

> The high-school teacher needs, above all, a broad outlook upon life, deep and thoro [*sic*] scholarship, and liberality of attitude which is best promoted by the university atmosphere. The normal school, with its ten-weeks' courses and ceaseless flitting about, its many exercises per day, the constant emphasis upon method rather than content, the excessive attention to the little details such as are largely necessary in training the immature and those who are to deal with details of elementary work, all militate against sound scholarship and liberality of mind. Most normal schools are so organized that students are admitted from the country school. These students are in constant contact with the most advanced. This necessitates leveling down to the plane of the most immature. The only place where the science of education can be adequately taught is in the university or in the few colleges. (Bolton 1907, 611–12)

Bolton looked toward Germany as his model where secondary school teachers were all university trained and where "critical, academic, and professional scholarship are absolute prerequisites to teaching in the secondary schools. No deviations are allowed" (ibid., 615). Certainly there was no "flitting about" in German universities.

Teacher educators were sharply divided. Charles Judd of the University of Chicago saw only danger in allowing normal schools to engage in the education of secondary teachers. Supporting Bolton's position, Judd argued that it was only in a college setting that intending teachers could master the "higher branches" of the disciplines without which they should not be allowed to teach (Judd 1907, 582). Judd's position was clear: "The most essential requirement for the preparation of a high-school teacher is elaborate training in the subject to be taught. This should extend into the higher branches of the subject . . . to a sufficient extent to make the student reasonably independent in his judgement of authorities upon that subject" (ibid., 587). In Judd's view, high schools and colleges had similar academic responsibilities.

All speakers agreed that high school teachers needed a thorough education in the disciplines, but they disagreed about what this meant and about what institution was in the better position to provide it. Judd and Bolton made the case for the colleges and universities. Joseph Hill, of the State Normal School at Emporia, Kansas, perhaps best articulated the case for the normal school and in so doing presented a view of what the normal school must become if it was to find and then maintain a central place in secondary school teacher preparation.

> [The normal school] cannot have a narrow scope or a restricted curriculum. . . . Its work is not primarily the academic preparation of the high-school instructor, tho [*sic*] it can legitimately and must . . . lay an adequate foundation for his pedagogic training. That training it can give in a favorable atmosphere and under conditions that nowhere else exist. The normal school must emphasize thoreness [*sic*] in academic training. The students need a living contact with the subject-matter of instruction. He must acquire the facts, grasp the import of the principles, see clearly the relations, but before he is prepared to teach, he must not only have been thru [*sic*] a subject, but around it, must have looked down upon it from above and looked back upon it from beyond, must have reviewed it, not as a subject but as a process, must have seen it grow again in his own mind as he would have it grow in the minds of others. . . . It must be at once a school of educational experiment and practice. . . . For such a work the model or practice school is the laboratory. . . . In its own field it must be a field of research, [but] not in all lines of science. (Hill 1907, 717–18)

The views of these and other educators of the time can be placed on a continuum moving from courses taught strictly from a mastery of the discipline point of view, through a middle position where content remains the same but is presented in relationship to instructional problems perhaps through a special methods course, to the view argued by Straton Brooks, that the subject must be learned by the intending teacher but from the viewpoint of how a child best learns. The second but most especially the third position is represented by pedagogical content knowledge, as Shulman argued eighty years later.

At first glance these positions seem to represent differences in institutional affiliation and in self-interest, but this conclusion masks as much as it reveals. The middle position was widely supported, and not only by normal school instructors. Like Paul Hanus of Harvard University, Burke Hinsdale, Professor of the Science and Art of Teaching at the University of Michigan, championed this position: "The professor also seeks to represent, or at least to illustrate, the method of teaching the subject in the school, commonly dwelling more or less upon the peculiar difficulties that it presents" (Hinsdale 1910, 394). Among teacher educators who supported the middle position were those who sought to develop a science of education composed of instructional practices grounded in what were thought of as the laws of learning. While representing a significant step in the direction of PCK, and as such movement away from the understanding of the disciplines held by content area specialists, those who held this position did not support a full blending of content and pedagogy. Other issues stood in the way of such a radical redefinition of the right relationship between the disciplines and pedagogy, not the least among them being the low status of teacher education generally and the normal schools specifically.

Debate Continues

Debate continued well past the NEA convention of 1907, and new charges against teacher education were added to old ones. Reflecting a growing progressive spirit, Henry Suzzallo of Teachers College, Columbia University, at the 1913 convention charged that "bookishness" was a problem for educators and teacher educators. Those who held tightly to narrow academic purposes stood in the way of educational progress: "Hence the social world moves on, and the profession remains devoted to old knowledge and old needs preserved by the isolation of the school. When at last the school reacts against our over-conservative [*sic*] traditionalism, the schoolmaster's devotions are likely to be caught by a new social demand more forceful than real. . . . The teacher's chief business is to intermediate between childhood and society. He must get children over into social life successfully else they will be failures. . . . Every teacher must acquire an interest in, and command over, the fundamental problems and purposes of modern social life thru personal contact with, and extensive study of, social affairs" (Suzzallo 1913, 366–67). As Suzzallo argued, new content was required for teachers to perform adequately in addition to what by then was the accepted standard fare: academic courses, history of education, educational psychology or child study, principles of education, special methods, observation, and, increasingly, practice teaching, mostly courses that would gain the begrudging approval of professors in the academic areas.

Despite broad agreement on the general outlines of teacher preparation, the distance between academic and professional courses remained and appears to have widened, as Monroe argued (Monroe 1952, 196). Pedagogical training, while increasingly accepted in colleges and universities, was supplementary, an add-on, to academic preparation. That teacher education was an add-on and had little if any effect on the work of the academic disciplines made it tolerable to professors in those disciplines. The lines separating pedagogical and academic content were drawn boldly and broadly. The belief persisted almost unchallenged that for secondary teaching, specialized academic preparation was the essential quality: "Graduation from college, which was generally regarded as an essential qualification, insured adequate general education and competent special knowledge of the subjects to be taught" (ibid., 201).

Teacher educators did not argue over the value of academic preparation. Their concern primarily was to establish the academic legitimacy and educational value of pedagogical studies. Most apparently accepted the uncomfortable position of teacher education on college and university campuses. There was remarkably little discussion of the aims of teacher education, something desired by Suzzallo; purposes were taken for granted (see Monroe 1952, 210–12). Only a few teacher educators sought to "professionalize" subject matter, as PCK was then known, and these may not have fully recognized the potential threat of their position to arts and science professors and their conception of teacher education had professionalizing of subject matter been taken seriously. But it generally was not.

After 1907 teacher educators continued periodically to discuss the "professionalization of subject matter," but there is little evidence that the concept was put into practice. Teacher educators were busy seeking to gain status within colleges and universities and working to better secure the position of the normal schools within the wider educational system and to gain greater legislative support and funding (ibid., 228). In a hostile educational environment, normal school educators diligently sought to establish their academic respectability. In so doing they increasingly came to mimic their competitors who greeted the pleas to professionalize content with suspicion and doubt, and in this they were supported by growing numbers of students who enrolled in the normal schools and teachers colleges with no intention of ever teaching. Academic departments like those established on college and university campuses became the norm, and gradually normal schools became teachers colleges that awarded degrees, engaged in research, and competed with established colleges and universities for students and faculty talent. In time, teacher education was marginalized even on former normal school campuses.

A Determined Few

Despite the turning tide, a few teacher educators continued to argue for the professionalization of academic subject matter. One was William Chandler Bagley, professor of education at Teachers College, Columbia University, and formerly a vice president and director of teacher training at Montana State

Normal College. Speaking at the 1918 NEA convention, Bagley stated that he was "thoroly convinst [*sic*] that the sooner [educators] abandon the unfortunate distinction between the academic and the professional the better it will be for the welfare and ultimate success of our cause. That a house divided against itself cannot stand is as true of professional education as it is of government" (Bagley 1918, 230). He went on to describe what he thought necessary to reform normal schools, and thereby to reform teacher education:

> The normal school of the future will lay much greater emphasis upon subject-matter courses than it has done in the past and relatively less emphasis upon detacht [*sic*] and formal courses in psychology and educational theory . . . what I have in mind . . . is a rather fundamental reorganization of all our work with the professional end constantly in view. Everything that goes into the teacher-training curriculum should be admitted solely upon the basis of its relation to the equipment of the successful teacher. It must include scholarship of a very high order, but a unique quality of scholarship. Not only must the teacher know his subject, but, as we have said so often in defending the normal school from its critics, he must know how to adapt his subject to the capacities and needs of those whom he is to teach. . . . [Courses] are selected and taught with reference to the light that will throw upon the high-school teacher's problem. . . . Instead of holding a proud aloofness from the elementary- and high-school classes, the subject-matter instructor will be compelled by the very nature of his work to keep in the closest possible contact with the training school. . . . [This] will do away very largely with the need of separate and often quite detacht [*sic*] courses in "special methods." . . . I have said that we should reorganize our professional work so that its general procedure will be from practice to theory, from cases to principles, from the concrete to the abstract, rather than the reverse. . . . [The] teacher must have scholarship of a high grade but of a unique quality. This the professionalized subject-matter courses should furnish. (Bagley 1918, 230–33)

Later, Bagley succinctly restated his position in *The Professional Preparation of Teachers for American Public Schools*, a report written for the Carnegie Foundation for the Advancement of Teaching: "Mastery of method in a given material is after all little more than a clear consciousness of the way in which the material shapes itself most advantageously to the learner" (Learned and Bagley 1920, 231).

By this time, Bagley's was increasingly a lone voice. The National Survey of the Education of Teachers, published in 1933, "did not result in the impression that there was wide acceptance of the theory of professional treatment of subject matter, and an attempt to identify the 'concrete ways' of professionalizing the courses was not successful" (quoted in Monroe 1952, 303).

Normal school presidents had anxiously sought the power to prepare secondary teachers, and they gained it, but at the cost of the uniqueness of their
institutions (see Hall-Quest 1925). Nevertheless, criticism persisted. Doubts
remained about the quality of the academic preparation of teachers, and concern was expressed that even when teachers appeared to have adequate academic preparation there was a tendency among school administrators to place
teachers in subject areas they did not study (Douglas 1935).

Then and Now: What Happened to PCK?

The first attempts to create pedagogical content knowledge as a central
component of teacher education, to professionalize subject matter, as Bagley
characterized the challenge, failed for a variety of reasons, political, sociological, and conceptual. The second attempt may fail as well for similar reasons. Whether housed in a normal school, a teachers college, a liberal arts
college or a university, professors of education felt vulnerable and enjoyed
little status. Then, as now, they struggled to establish the legitimacy of their
interests and the value of their contributions to students. Many institutions
lacked a critical mass of teacher educators sufficient to marshal any sort of
challenge to established views of learning to teach. Then, as now, even
within the community of teacher educators, greatest status accrues to those
who, as Goodlad (1990) has argued, distance themselves from the schools
and from teaching practice. Such persons are historians, psychologists,
anthropologists, and sociologists who happen to have an interest in education or schooling and are housed within education faculties. Sadly, curriculum studies is gradually becoming cultural studies on major research campuses across America, and curriculum issues have been given over to other
concerns, critical pedagogy, for example. Emphatically these professors do
not characterize themselves as teacher educators, who are to be avoided.
Then, as now, the courses of these professors mimic those offered by their
colleagues in the academic departments. The gulf Bagley wanted to bridge
between academic and professional courses largely remains, and teacher
educators are still divided.

The politics of higher education and the internal politics of teacher education doomed the first effort. Political issues remain lively and have become
increasingly complicated as the playing field has shifted toward governor
offices, state legislatures, and federal agencies quite unlike the commissions of
the NEA that were dominated by educators, not businessmen and politicians.
Teacher education remains in ill repute, but growing disillusionment with
public education and the frequency with which teacher educators' interests
now conflict with public educators' as both struggle for adequate funding

makes it no longer possible to take comfort in being allies as when Brooks stood and argued the cause of teacher education at an NEA convention.

There are important differences, however. Teacher education now represents a sizable, if not entirely well-respected, research enterprise. Some 1,300 institutions of higher education educate teachers. While some teacher educators express fear about the future of teacher education, not wholly unlike that common to an earlier era, and threats persist, organizations have been developed since Bagley wrote that are politically skillful and heavily invested in issues important to teachers and teacher educators. These organizations and the teacher education institutions and faculty housed in higher education that support them sustain efforts to develop and extend the knowledge base of teaching which, although underappreciated, has grown dramatically since the publication of *A Nation at Risk*.

The pressures on teacher education are both new and old, and together they created the conditions necessary for a resurrection of the idea of professionalizing content knowledge, of pedagogical content knowledge. Currently the challenge to teacher educators is both to meet standards established by the disciplines and their sponsoring associations, and standards established by powerful political bodies to provide evidence that what we do actually makes a difference for teachers and for student learning. These pressures also are internal to teacher education. The claim that teacher education makes a difference was a claim that at least teacher educators at the turn of the century generally could take for granted. They were certain what they did made for better teachers. But no such confidence now exists, and a convincing case has become increasingly more difficult to make, even as it has become more urgent. Evidence of improved teacher performance is required, and arguing for program quality based upon teacher education inputs will simply not do, thus the question: What is it that teacher educators do that no other group can do? We have almost come full circle.

In substance, Bagley's argument is Shulman's (see Randolph 1924). There is a unique content to teacher education, one that despite persistent claims to the contrary reaches beyond standard academic courses—even when coupled with special methods course add-ons—and touches the very heart of the question of what it means to know a subject so that one can teach it. But what does this assertion mean? What is pedagogical content knowledge? Perhaps the central difficulty facing the effort to professionalize subject matter is not so much political or sociological but conceptual. A few years ago Gary Fenstermacher addressed this point: "Although Shulman and his colleagues clearly focus on the topic of teacher knowledge in ways that have deepened our understanding of the interconnections between content knowledge and pedagogical knowledge, their epistemological framing is difficult to isolate and analyze" (Fenstermacher 1994, 16). He asks, just what kind of knowledge is PCK? He concludes that it has both practical and formal elements, each requiring testing and justification (ibid., 32, 38); the practical challenge is to provide "good reasons" for acting and in support of claims for knowing (ibid., 44). Unfortunately, he argues, the "exquisite complexities of knowledge claiming and justifying in the domain [of practice has not been] fully appreciated" (ibid., 41). Nevertheless, he suggests, there may well be a "science for the advancement of practical knowledge as there is a science for the advancement of formal knowledge" (ibid., 36).

Having both practical and formal knowledge elements is a source of much mischief and confusion. The formal elements come into teacher education in the form of propositional knowledge, lists of sorts, of common subject area misconceptions held by teacher education students and pupils that need correcting, what Randolph (1924) described as "recurring difficulties" (156), and suggestions of ways to make a particular subject more accessible for learning. In contrast, practical knowledge is highly context dependent. Thus beginning teachers may be taught a set of strategies, stories, and forms of representation for a content area that may or may not resonate with the context within which they will eventually teach. The danger, then, is that the ideas become "inert," as Whitehead (1929/1961, 13) described such knowledge, and courses that presumably focus on pedagogical content knowledge fall victim to the same charges of irrelevancy as courses in the disciplines and traditionally taught special methods courses.

It is likely that it is this conceptual problem and the reliance on propositional forms of knowledge as the basis of claims for the professional legitimacy of the knowledge base of teaching that has relegated PCK to teacher educator rhetoric and limited its influence in practice. One wonders if the second round of interest in PCK will follow the first into oblivion. I hope not. Recognizing the challenges to teacher education that the practical dimension of PCK presents perhaps points to a partial solution. Much of the work to build teacher pedagogical content knowledge must take place in service, within a teaching context. As long as the focus is primarily on preservice teacher education, it is likely that comparatively little can be accomplished. It is within in-service education that Fenstermacher's argument for practical reasoning as a form of teacher education is compelling. Teachers need help to think more complexly about their practice and the reasons behind their actions in light of how particular pupils learn and in relationship to formal, academic knowledge. Preservice teacher education has a place, however. Edgar Stones (1992) has made a compelling case for engaging teacher education students in the study and practice of learning theory. Such knowledge, formal in form, can serve as a basis for reasoning practically and represents the middle position noted earlier.

CHAPTER 2

Teacher Education Reform as a Story of Possibility: Lessons Learned, Lessons Forgotten— The American Council on Education's Commission on Teacher Education (1939–1942) (2000)

Introduction

Teacher educators live in a lively present, the demands of which enable gestures toward a hoped-for future but generally not an embrace of the past. Politically vulnerable both inside and outside of the university, we react to our contexts even as we seek to better control them. Given the context, memory is short. Hunches, feelings, and common sense most often seem to guide program development efforts. One result is that the story usually told of the history of teacher education reform is a sad tale of persistent themes and little progress—status deprivation, neurotic arts, and science mimicry—and of flight from the dirty work of schooling. Like teachers, teacher educators work within swirling cycles of policy-maker reform talk, talk that is outside of and disconnected from practice (Tyack and Cuban 1995). Disappointment abounds; nothing ever seems to change. Yet it does.

A similar situation frequently obtains in schools. Lessons learned from improvement efforts of the past are seldom shared, especially when the effort was judged a failure, and when they are shared they often are embedded in stories of change that honor the unique features of an educational context but underplay the potential of principles and generalizations to sharpen understanding, orient action, and illuminate even the most diverse of educational settings. In response, a few teachers, not unlike many teacher educators, develop the kind of comfortable cynicism about reform as Horace Smith, described in *Horace's Compromise* (Sizer 1984).

A closer look at this history is required, however. What emerges is a remarkable difference between what counts as reform for policy makers and what counts as reform for practitioners, including teacher educators. The disappointment that flows from the grandiose visions of policy makers for massive, systemic, permanent, and quick change blinds them and those who write about reform from their perspective to the modest kinds of successes that concern and please practitioners. Within the sad and so-often-told tale of educational reform reside other frequently overlooked stories, ones of possibility and hope rather than impossibility and despair.

It is with concern for the past and in the desire to locate stories of possibility in teacher education reform that I turn to a discussion and analysis of one of the forgotten but extraordinarily provocative large-scale reform efforts in teacher education, that sponsored by the commission on Teacher Education of the American Council on Education (1939–1942). The eight volumes published by the Commission represent a remarkable repository of insights into educational practice and reform that lends support to much of the recent research on change, especially the growing and promising emphasis over the past decade on teacher development as the centerpiece of renewal (Bullough and Baughman 1997; Darling-Hammond 1997; Holmes Group 1986). As Clifford and Guthrie state, "Eventually . . . almost no matter how tortured the logic, one is led to the need to upgrade teachers and teaching" (1988, 37). In addition, the commission reports raise oft-neglected questions about the direction of reform and the means for encouraging it and grapple with issues that have long perplexed teacher educators. Remarkably, one sees in the reports the seeds of current partnership efforts that seek simultaneous renewal of the schools and of teacher education (Patterson et al. 1999). But more than anything, one sees examples of successful tinkering, changes that were highly valued by those who produced them, even if the changes did not institutionally long endure. Indeed, endurance may not be the sin qua non of successful reform.

Background of the Study

Commission's Point of View

Recognizing the economic and educational crisis of the time, the Committee on Problems and Plans of the American Council on Education turned its attention to the education of teachers and in January 1936 began an inquiry to determine whether or not to launch a national study of teacher education. In February 1938 a report was issued entitled *Major Issues in Teacher Education* (American Council on Education 1938). The report called for "more experimentation, demonstration, and evaluation, on the basis of hypotheses in which there is reason to have confidence because of previous careful study. . . . The new task confronting teacher education is, in part, the breaking down of the control of tradition and outworn practices and, in part, the building up of

new concepts of education and a creative approach to the problems of teaching" (quoted in Commission on Teacher Education 1944, ix). With support of
the Rockefeller Foundation-funded General Education Board, the Commission on Teacher Education was established with sixteen members representing all parts of the country and diverse educational interests. The board chose
to support the American Council's proposed work in teacher education rather
than that of the Progressive Education Association (PEA), which was a
source of disappointment for PEA leadership (Graham 1967, 92). The commission included many of the most—or soon to be most—influential leaders
in American education: Ralph Tyler, Harold Benjamin, E. S. Evenden, W.
Carson Ryan, and George F. Zook, among others.

During its first year of operation, the commission created a five-year
plan, which was announced in February 1939.

> The program was built upon the principles laid down in *Major Issues* and
> reflected the growing faith, in educational circles, in the virtues of decentral-
> ized studies involving widespread participation of a cooperative nature.
> (Commission on Teacher Education 1944, x)

The point of view of the commission was grounded in two concerns: "(1)
Ways in which higher institutions and school systems could work on their
own to improve their own situations through shared planning and experimenting; and (2) how to make the results of this experimenting available to
other institutions and school systems" (Ryan 1944, 11). An experimental attitude and a commitment to democratic practices—"respect for personality,
acceptance of social responsibility, and reliance upon reason" (Commission on
Teacher Education 1946, 10)—underpinned all of the commission's work and
gave it a unique flavor and direction:

> [The commission] emphasized the idea that improvement in teacher educa-
> tion is always possible, requiring continuous planning, continuous experi-
> mentation, and continuous evaluation. It suggested the very great impor-
> tance of the processes employed in group endeavor—of sensitivity to human
> relations, of the selection of ways of working together that are democratic in
> character and effective in result. In consequence of [the commission's] point
> of view the groups associated with [it] were encouraged to play their part in
> certain ways. They were asked to make participation as widespread as possi-
> ble, to pay particular attention to the cooperative process, and to plan
> together in long-range terms. At the same time they were pressed to focus
> attention on problems felt to be given special importance by the situations in
> which they currently found themselves. (Commission on Teacher Education
> 1944, xii–xiii)

Underpinning the work of the commission was a profound belief in the importance and value of teachers and the dignity of teaching:

> In all civilized communities the task of teaching is chiefly entrusted to a company of experts. In the United States that company numbers approximately 1,000,000; and some 285,000 young men and women are preparing to enter the profession. It makes a difference who and what these teachers are. Social well-being and social advance depend in marked measure on their excellence. But who these teachers are, and what they are, turns directly upon the effectiveness of the arrangements that we make for their education. To improve teacher education is to improve teaching; to improve teaching is to improve the schools; to improve the schools is to strengthen the next generation; to strengthen the next generation is a social duty of the first magnitude. (Commission on Teacher Education 1944, 24)

Accordingly, "Teacher education never ends" (ibid., 164).

Organization of the Study

Beginning with a two-week planning conference in August 1939 at Bennington College, attended by over 100 future participants in the study, a series of conferences was organized to which representatives from teacher colleges and universities, state departments of education, and a sample of school systems were invited to discuss teacher education and its problems and to begin the hard work of improvement. The cooperative study itself lasted three years and ultimately involved seven state teachers colleges; seven liberal arts colleges; a technical college; seven universities; two Negro colleges; three of the five largest city school systems in the United States; four systems in medium-size cities (more than 100,000 but less than 1,000,000 residents); twelve small school systems; six county or other nonurban systems; and one private school. In total, twenty-three states were represented. Participation was voluntary, and no system or institution was accepted into the study without assurances of a serious commitment to the improvement of teacher education and full participation, which included willingness to provide an institutional coordinator for the study. On its part, the commission "undertook to provide central and field staff to facilitate the efforts of the local institution or school system, [and] to work as consultants with the coordinators and committees in the various cooperating units. From time to time the commission brought the coordinators, other institutional representatives, and members of the central and field staff together in working conferences to consider the progress made and discuss further steps" (Ryan 1944, 11). Working conferences were common. A clearinghouse service was created to enable the systematic exchange of information about the study, and a widely circulated monthly newsletter was established to provide a means for regular communication. A diverse range of other publications was supported. A center for child study was established at the University of Chicago, where institutional representatives could study research on child development and work for six months or a year. Some funding was made available for travel, so that institutional representatives might gather or visit other institutions to share developing insights and materials. A workshop service was created and a variety of workshop activities supported, including several workshops conducted by school systems for teachers. The range of these activities was broad and grew in part because of a transfer by the PEA of resources and funds for the support workshops once the Eight-Year Study was completed (Kridel and Bullough 2007). Approximately thirty summer workshops lasting five or six weeks were supported, with a total attendance that ran into the thousands. Generally, workshop agendas were set locally with support of the workshop service. Finally, once the cooperative study was underway the commission supported a series of statewide studies in Georgia, Michigan, and New York and smaller-scale activities in Alabama, Colorado, Florida, Kentucky, Mississippi, Ohio, and West Virginia.

Getting Started

At the Bennington Conference five sets of problems were identified that represented the central concerns of the institutional representatives in attendance. These included the still-persistent problems of preservice teacher education: how colleges and universities might develop programs that would help teachers make "subject matter functional"; have a "good attitude toward teaching"; facilitate "child guidance"; and be able to deal with the "practical problems that actual teaching brings." Concern was expressed for the "planning and conduct of student teaching . . . and the problem of improving the coordination of the activities of educationists and subject-matter professors as these related to teacher education" (Commission on Teacher Education 1946, 31–32). Two problems received special attention, ones that remain perplexing today and are central to virtually all current discussions of teacher education reform: The commission's aim was "the development of an integrated program of school-college relationships calculated to promote mutual understanding and mutual aid, and the general improvement of methods of encouraging and facilitating the continuous growth of all educational workers in service" (ibid., 32). Then as now, it was widely believed that school/university relationships badly needed improvement. Arguably, it is in reference to these two issues that most progress has been made toward reform (Osguthorpe et al. 1995; Smith and Fenstermacher 1999; Sirotnik 2001).

Upon their return about a third of the institutional representatives presented the results of the Bennington Conference as a kind of blueprint for beginning reform. This was not the commission's intention, however: "There is a tendency in the public schools, as in other human undertakings, to have relatively too much confidence in blueprints and pronouncements rather than in widespread study among the people to be affected by the contemplated action" (Prall and Cushman 1944, 199). What the commission members hoped was that the wide-ranging discussion of problems at Bennington would "throw light of a general character on the tasks lying ahead both for the Commission and for the associated centers" (Commission on Teacher Education 1946, 33). The results for this third were disappointing: "This did not work out very successfully. The mortality rate of groups so organized was relatively high" (Prall and Cushman 1944, 12). Most representatives, however, did as was intended: "Their first job upon returning home would be to engage their colleagues there in planning what should be set about locally" (Commission on Teacher Education 1946, 34). The expectation was that each institution would establish its own reform agenda based upon "earnest self-study" (ibid., 51), and that the commission would support local efforts and seek to coordinate them and disseminate the results widely.

> The committee urged that the basic considerations in the development of each program should be the needs of the persons to be educated and those whom they were or later would be teaching, and the perpetuation of the values essential to democracy. Procedures should be such that all participants could be simultaneously teachers and learners, leaders and followers; and continuous institutional self-improvement, rather than either instant or ultimate fixed perfection, should be the goal. (Commission on Teacher Education 1946, 34)

Local responsibility, group participation, reliance on experimentation and rational discourse, and careful attention to the life situations and concerns of those to be educated, teachers and students, were the watchwords.

Local Problems

In this section a few of the specific projects undertaken by the participating institutions are described. Recognizing that perhaps most teacher education problems are persistent and enduring, those chosen for discussion are of particular significance to our time.

Subject Matter Preparation

Then as now, relatively little of a preservice student's time was actually spent in courses taught within schools or departments of education. The relationship between schools of education and faculty within the arts and sciences was strained.

> . . . the undergraduate and graduate faculties of arts and science, each with their own centers of attention, were, if not actually unfriendly to teacher education as they saw it, at least likely to feel little responsibility to do more than offer prospective teachers instruction that could seldom be said to have been planned with professional needs much in mind. (Commission on Teacher Education 1944, 61)

Such divisiveness stood in the way of fundamental reform, which the commission sought: "The Commission preferred to concentrate on promoting the integrated attack of whole institutions on their entire programs" (Armstrong et al. 1944, 3).

At the University of Texas this issue burned but was only part of a larger concern with the quality and focus of academic majors that often had little relationship to the content taught in secondary schools. Beginning teachers were ill prepared to teach their subject areas, and graduates of other competing institutions, particularly teachers colleges, increasingly were preferred in hiring decisions by school administrators. Concern grew, and the School of Education began to respond, but with limited success. A solution required involvement of the School of Arts and Sciences. The cooperative study provided an opportunity to attack this problem in new ways.

The president of the university and deans of the two schools formed a planning committee for the cooperative study. After consulting with the faculty, a decision was made to organize working committees to address the subject area needs of secondary teachers in the natural and social sciences. Later, English, foreign languages, and mathematics committees were formed with a similar charge. The deans sat on all five committees, which were composed of subject-matter specialists and included a professor of education.

The committee on natural sciences illustrates what was accomplished. It spent nearly a year becoming familiar with the conditions in the high schools. Enrollment trends, changes in responsibilities of schools, recent developments in instruction, and the challenge of adapting instruction to diverse student populations each demanded and received attention. The committee discovered that nearly half of all teachers taught in small high schools and were responsible for other subject areas, sometimes as many as four of them in addition to science. Courses of study in the high schools were evaluated, as were textbooks. Visits were made to school science departments to discuss the concerns of teachers. With the commission's support, an all-day conference was organized so that the committee could interact with science teachers, supervisors, and administrators. The conclusion reached was that the course work offered to prospective teachers at the university was of relatively little value to a majority of high school students, and that the program of instruction within the disciplines needed overhauling.

At this point the committee turned to the commission for assistance, and two consultants were provided to assist in program revision. A proposal for curricular revision was completed during the second year and emphasized a "greater range and less concentration in the subject-matter requirements than was characteristic of the prevailing pattern of majors and minors" (Armstrong et al. 1944, 113). Graduates would be acquainted with five sciences, fuller knowledge of two, and extensive work in one. Further plans were made for a faculty position that would include responsibility for "bringing university and high school people closer together so that they might come to agree on the essentials of a permanent program for the education of science teachers" (ibid., 117). Perhaps the most remarkable outcome, however, was a change in attitude toward the problems of secondary education: "'For the first time in twenty-five years . . . the College of Arts and Sciences,' the dean reported, 'has been confronted with the problems of the secondary schools'" (ibid.). Moreover, the dean stated, "The two university schools that joined forces in the project . . . 'are irretrievably bound together from now on in the professional problem of training' teachers for the public high schools" (ibid., 118).

The project illustrates the principles of reform embraced by the commission: focus on local problems; maximized participation and interaction among interested parties; data gathering and self-study; commission support for local plans; and forward-looking planning. The commission anticipated Goodlad's advice to the profession: "In the early stages of redesigning settings or creating new ones, it is not wise to go forth seeking models elsewhere" (1994, 100).

This particular project was but part of a larger reform effort, consistent with the commission's desire to attack problems broadly. The larger project included an extensive study of teacher problems and the design and controlled testing of an experimental curriculum in the school of education that included in the junior year a semester of study of the public school as a social institution followed by a second semester studying adolescence. Student teaching followed the senior year and emphasized integration of theory with practice, a theme common to many of the projects. Focusing on student concerns about beginning teaching, students helped plan the curriculum with the faculty, and much of the instruction involved small committees studying, under faculty guidance, the problems identified by the students. Evaluation was continuous and the results of a two-year trial promising. Revisions of the standard program followed, which included a focus on themes for each year as a way of strengthening program continuity, an issue that will be addressed shortly.

General Education

Analyzing the results of the many projects carried out in the participating colleges and universities, Armstrong and his colleagues recognized failure as well as success. They expressed particular disappointment over efforts to revise general education, concluding that changes in this area are perhaps more difficult to achieve than in any other: "Some very worthwhile achievements are to be reported. But there was after the three-year period far less to show for all this effort, in terms of faculty agreement and actual experiment, than turned out to be true of any other subject chosen for study in the Commission's experience" (Armstrong et al. 1944, 61). This remains today a serious issue in part because of genuine and deeply held differences over the nature and content of general education that make agreement on aims difficult (see Troyer and Pace 1944, 130–31).

When reviewing accomplishments in this area Armstrong and his colleagues identified a principle of reform worth stating, and they offered a warning: "The Commission's experience seems to indicate that *where* you begin is not nearly as important as *that* you begin. This is not to say, of course, that careful study and preliminary thought can be omitted. On the contrary . . ." (Armstrong et al. 1944, 94). They warned of twin dangers, of trying to take on too large a problem at the outset, like agreeing on the aims of general education and forming too many committees as a result of "unnaturally" subdividing issues into "specialized fragments" that would inhibit communication and creativity (ibid.). Both dangers were apparent in the work reviewed on general education reform.

General education related to a wide range of issues addressed by study participants, such as the subject area concerns explored at the University of Texas. Armstrong and his colleagues recognized the serious need for teachers who were broadly and deeply educated, but they seem to suggest that the best way to address this need and issue then was by attacking more manageable issues first or by creating "natural" divisions for study. The first strategy appeared necessary as a basis for building the needed understanding and trust that would enable fruitful discussion. Moreover, they recognized that the complexity of the problems related to general education necessitated more time than was allowed by commission funding, so perhaps disappointment might have been expected. This limiting condition was one that needed addressing up front, since it influenced decisions about which of the many serious issues could be tackled and in what order.

Faculty resistance to change grounded in narrow disciplinary specialization and turf protection proved to be a source of difficulty, especially for those who had relatively limited exposure to the study and its purposes. "General conservatism and indifference or even hostility to teacher education played their roles, as did departmental loyalties and unreadiness to agree on reduction of requirements in one's own field. Faith in the virtues of emphatic specialization was an influential element in several situations, as was the related conviction that any needed leeway in the existing pattern could be far more wisely obtained by sacrifices made by the other fellow" (Commission on Teacher Education 1946, 87). Comments like this one echo across the decades (Clifford and Guthrie 1988; Goodlad 1990).

Evaluation of one of the projects produced a set of generalizations of importance to educational reform, and to overcoming faculty resistance: (1) ". . . faculty developed most interest and gained the clearest insight regarding ways of improving the program when they were taking part in the evaluation" (Troyer and Pace 1944, 117); (2) "the activities that were most meaningful to the college were the ones that called for the most participation by the faculty"; and (3) "the data that were most meaningful were the ones that were expressed in the least technical terms" (ibid., 116). These principles may yet prove valuable when tackling reform, general education reform in particular, which is more insistent than ever.

Focus on Children

School faculties studied a wide range of issues: local communities, curricular and instructional problems, articulation of levels of schooling, school-community relations, teacher-pupil relations, and the broad social scene, among others. But perhaps the most far-reaching accomplishments came from the focus on children and child development, which represented about one-third of the activity of the affiliated school systems (Prall and Cushman 1944, 147). This focus, undoubtedly stimulated by work within the PEA, is an impressive feature of the study that stands in stark contrast to current reform efforts dominated by the quest for specific subject area curriculum standards, competency testing, and school-wide assessment and grading. One wonders where in the current debates is there concern for children and the lives of children. In contrast, such concerns were central to the commission's work with schools.

The challenge was to "understand" children. The commission had a clearly articulated view: "Our definition of understanding a child includes contrasting subjective and objective elements. On the one hand, it calls for the subjective acceptance and valuing of individual boys and girls—emotionally and philosophically rooted and serving to reassure and afford security to all children, even when they misbehave. On the other hand, it also implies objectivity in the use of sound procedures and knowledge to interpret the causes of a child's acts, to appraise his adjustment problems and personal needs, and to work out practical ways of helping him master his developmental tasks" (Staff of the Division on Child Development and Teacher Personnel 1945, 12). The commission argued that there were six characteristics of teachers who understand children: (1) They "think of their behavior as being caused"; (2) "accept all children emotionally, that they reject no child as hopeless or unworthy"; (3) "invariably recognize that each [child] is unique"; (4) "believe . . . that the various sciences concerned with human growth and behavior have demonstrated that young people, during the several phases of their development, face a series of common 'developmental tasks'"; (5) "know the more important scientific facts that describe and explain the forces that regulate human growth, development, motivation, learning, and behavior"; and (6) "habitually [use] scientific methods in making judgements about any particular boy or girl" (ibid., 8–11). While the language used to present their views may strike an odd chord, the point made is a significant one: that teachers need to be experts in child development, and that knowledge of children should inform virtually every professional act.

To this end, and supported by commission and the child study center staff, teachers throughout the nation undertook careful observational studies of children in their classrooms, typically one "normal" and one difficult child. First the teachers were taught how to make rich and detailed observations, to gather data void of quick and easy judgments, and then to develop means for understanding this data in ways and in light of a careful study of the research literature on child development that would facilitate instructional and curricular decision making. Implicitly the commission supported an expanded role for teachers, one that recognized that the lives of children were changing, becoming more complicated and less secure, especially in the face of growing tensions in Europe that eventually led to war, and that they needed the help of thoughtful and invested adults as they matured. An expanded role for professors also was encouraged, one that led to intimate involvement with school problems and with teachers in supportive and surprisingly equitable relationships, a role reminiscent of recent calls of the Holmes Group (1995) and the National Network for Educational Renewal (Patterson, Michelli, and Pacheco 1999).

Through workshops, through the guidance of teachers who with the support of the commission studied at the child study center, and especially through teacher-lead study groups, teachers were helped by commission representatives to break "the habit of making snap judgements about children's actions on the basis of personal preoccupations; [to establish] the habit of noticing exactly what a child does; and [to learn] to record clear descriptions of what the child did and of the situation in which he acted" (Staff of the Division on Child Development and Teacher Personnel 1945, 21). The aim was to understand behavior situationally, in relationship to biography and personality. In the teacher study groups that cut across school faculties, teacher-generated data were shared, cases discussed in "conference," research disseminated for later study, and eventually hypotheses formed for testing in practice and discussion.

> A particular teacher presented information about a child whom she was studying intensively. Then other teachers who had taught him in earlier grades or who knew something about him and his family, through work with his brothers and sisters or otherwise, contributed additional facts. General discussion of the child by all teachers present then took place. The aim was to sharpen everyone's skill in organizing and interpreting data to the point where a reasonably valid analysis of the subject's motives, aspirations, and needs could be made. At the close of the discussion, or after the meeting, each member of the group often wrote answers to questions like the following: What meaning do you now see in the child's present behavior? What further information would you like to have about this child before reaching any real decision about him? (ibid., 131–32)

Although time consuming, participation in the group meetings as a form of in-service teacher education had a profound effect on teachers beyond the formation of strong professional relationships. They learned from one another and came to respect differences in understanding and to use those differences as sources of insight; they learned strategies for thinking about children and for using the results of research to test and validate hunches and to temper the tendency to rush to judgement, to succumb to "middle-class folk prejudice"; they gained a deep appreciation of the deleterious influence of poverty on child development and of the place of prior life experience in shaping current classroom performance; they increased their ability to "see . . . through the child's own eyes" (ibid., 424); they became less likely to offer unsupported judgments about children (Perkins 1950, 554) and they came to welcome the assistance of other teachers in determining the most promising ways of helping the child (Staff of the Division on Child Development and Teacher Personnel 1945, 133–35). Preceding a time when special education became an industry that frequently reduces children to labels that make it unnecessary to attend carefully to the child beneath the label, the work of the commission encouraged thoughtful and focused attention on individual children, even as it stimulated creation of generalizations, but generalizations tempered by the experience of having systematically studied individual children for a year or more. The danger of labeling was explicitly recognized by the commission: "When teachers are given a list of patterns of behavior to be checked in studying a child, they tend to look for and at these patterns as separate, independent items of information. As a result they do not gather the necessary facts in constellations related to each other nor describe the child's behavior against its situational context. . . . Checklists . . . permit a teacher to fail to notice unlisted important things that are right under his nose" (ibid., 415). In short, they do not see the child. Further, the teachers confronted bias, especially of "valuing of middle-class children above lower-class children [that] made them too quick to reject and blame children from lower-class homes" (ibid., 378). And, they came to "a more equitable recognition of the children's own standards and customs" (ibid.).

The impact of child study on children in some instances was profound, and not only because their relationships with teachers deepened and improved. The child study program resulted in some school faculties rejecting long-established patterns of tracking, what then was called "grade-level accomplishment" (ibid., 385). New opportunities for education were opened that formerly had been closed to certain children. Punishment, particularly driven by the desire for retribution, became less frequent (ibid., 387). Adjustments were made in classroom procedure and in the curriculum to better facilitate a child's development (ibid., 389). Above all of these outcomes, there was one nearly unanimous conclusion: Classroom teachers, principals, and supervisors nearly "all reported either that they themselves were happier in their work because they understood the children better, or they reported that the children were visibly happier in their classrooms than they had been before the study began" (ibid., 390). These results followed simply because of a program to systematically study children and share the results of the study.

The importance of workshops and the child study center as training grounds for local leadership in child study and as a source of materials, information, and support cannot be underestimated. Like all work sponsored by the commission, participation within the workshops and at the center was voluntary. Commission members did not believe that change could be forced and be successful. Nor did the commission believe that successful programs could be carefully laid out in advance, a conclusion reaffirmed at the study's end: "On the whole the more elaborate, systematic, and 'logical' approaches [to improvement] proved less rewarding than those that simply enabled many teachers to get to work on specific jobs where study could fairly promptly lead to action respecting the educational program. [Furthermore, efforts] to begin by formulating an educational philosophy for the system or by deciding just what kind of school should be worked toward tended to bog down in verbal dispute, at least when concrete implications were not carefully developed" (Commission on Teacher Education 1946, 127). Successful planning was evolutionary, and ends not fully predictable. Indeed, the commission concluded that "Anything that looks like an effort toward standardization imposed from without, like an encroachment upon basic institutional freedom, will provoke resistance and delay, hence become self-defeating" (ibid., 203). Similarly, clarity in aims was a product of teachers struggling to make sense of and improve their practice. An understanding of the last two points might prevent a good deal of grief and disappointment for would-be reformers who continue to put their faith in systems, as one well-intentioned reform program after another has been carried into the schools often only to flounder and sometimes cause a good deal of harm.

Through its work with the schools the commission confronted a particularly complex problem given its commitment to democratic methods of change, one that is of current significance: balancing "centralization" and "decentralization." In the words of the commission: "The desire to manifest faith in individuals and small groups, to provide them with the greatest possible opportunity to exercise their own judgements and to take responsibility for consequent action, required guarding against tight controls at the center. But such a policy was seen to involve the risk that developments at various points within the system might be inconsistent, if not conflicting. This would inevitably lead to a swing back toward stricter controls. Such an outcome could be avoided, it was thought, only by emphasizing common concerns and developing instrumentalities representative of the entire system that would so operate to preserve and promote what was essential to the maintenance of the right kind of unity" (ibid., 135). The commission's role, in effect, was to make certain that all participants kept talking, and that opportunities to participate remained open.

In-service Teacher Education

Child study was but one of the many forms of in-service teacher education that the commission supported. The program developed by the Des Moines school system was especially ambitious and risky.

> The effort to identify important problems in need of study was begun in a general meeting of all the teachers of the school system. After a brief presentation of the cooperative study and its possibilities, the teachers met in small groups for free discussion. The comments and suggestions that were made in these meetings were recorded and became the basis for a more detailed inquiry. A subcommittee of the planning committee constructed from these statements a list of forty-two specific items. These were presented to the teachers for individual ratings as to timeliness and importance. (Prall and Cushman 1944, 78–79)

Six problem clusters identified as most "acute" were initially accepted for study and action, including home-school relations, understanding children, and teacher welfare. Over time the focus of the various study groups, and the attitudes of teachers toward the topics, changed, as one might expect. A conference was organized prior to the beginning of the 1940 school year to further expand teacher involvement in the study. Beginning in the fall of 1940, faculty began meeting Thursday evenings, and eventually every other Thursday. Sessions ran from 4:15 to 6 p.m. and from 7:30 to 9 p.m., with a dinner and social hour intervening. The project quickly caught on, and during the first year, on average, more than a third of the total school staff attended each meeting. A workshop, a six-week "problems laboratory," was conducted at Drake University during the summer of 1941, which was attended by 124 teachers from the Des Moines schools, among other participants, who were organized into thirty-one study groups around "down-to-earth" individual purposes and objectives (ibid., 214). Opportunities were provided for teachers to engage in arts and crafts activities as part of the study and as a means for opening them up to new experiences.

When evaluating the Des Moines project, Prall and Cushman saw much evidence of teacher growth but had difficulty attributing it directly to the project. The project, they concluded, "as a whole was uneven" (ibid., 90). The large scale of the Des Moines project was a source of persistent difficulty and led to several seemingly inevitable problems: groups working at cross-purposes, for instance. Too little effort was made by the steering committee to coordinate group work and to facilitate communication, they concluded: "... the committee could have made plans for the interaction and mutual cross fertilization of these groups" (ibid., 90–91). A source of serious difficulty was the initial decision made to allow only teachers on the steering committee which, given their heavy workload and the nature of their work, limited the scope and influence of the committee. Under this arrangement, it simply was not possible for steering committee members to be knowledgeable about what the various study groups were doing. Moreover, members were "keyed into building constituencies," which limited their vision (ibid., 91).

Despite the extensive time demands on teachers, remarkably there was little complaining. "Indeed, as teachers took over new responsibilities connected with the study, there were numerous instances of their disregard of time pressure. The load, as measured in working hours, was often heavy, but not much was said about it; satisfactions were more than compensating" (ibid., 92). Much of the satisfaction seems to have originated in the value of working with colleagues on issues that mattered personally. Recognizing this, the conclusion reached from the Des Moines and other projects was that "teachers *should* have a major role in planning the program for in-service improvement," otherwise it will likely fail (ibid., 92). Successful programs "must begin with tasks which seem [to participants] as practical and immediate" (ibid., 93), and include periodic "appraisal of effort, reinterpretation of function and working method" by a central planning committee (ibid., 94). Aims changed; so sometimes did methods. Evaluators concluded that every effort needed to be made to assure effective communication among and across groups. For planning and coordinating groups the challenge was less a matter of taking action than of facilitating the desired action of others (ibid., 96).

Standing back and reviewing the results of the various in-service programs supported by the commission, and recognizing successes and failures, it was concluded that "a thoroughgoing attempt to broaden the basis of . . . participation by classroom teachers [in reform] must ultimately lead to the elimination of traditional conceptions of school organization," which prevent success (ibid., 100). The problem was, then as now, a deep one of significance to both preservice and in-service teacher education: "The ablest young people cannot be recruited to teaching—or if they are persuaded to prepare for the profession, will not enter and remain in it—unless the conditions surrounding their work are satisfying." Serious effort to address this only came in the 1980s. "Moreover," the report went on to state, unless teaching becomes more satisfying "teachers on the job will not be able or encouraged to make the most of their powers, or likely to behave in such fashion as steadily to increase their competence" (Commission on Teacher Education 1946, 263). The tenets of democracy supported by the commission, which insisted on wide participation, could not be fully realized under established patterns of schooling and the accepted definitions of the teacher's role and work. The structure of schooling required reform. Increasingly it was recognized that the school, rather than an entire school system like Des Moines, was the appropriate unit of change (ibid., 107).

A word should be said about the value of workshops. There was concern that workshops would lose their value, as there was a tendency to plan them *for* rather than *with* teachers. Under commission sponsorship, and following on experience gained in the Eight-Year Study (Aikin 1942), workshops were long, intense, and sharply focused on the concerns of teachers (Kridel and Bullough 2007). Their particular value was tied to two "closely related purposes—preparation for change and security while breaking with tradition." A warning was given: "If they are not used properly for such purposes, the time will soon come when they may not be used at all" (ibid., 240). One expectation of the commission that was generally realized was that workshops would provide a means for bringing colleges and schools into closer relationship.

Problems of Discontinuity

Prior to the organization of the commission and to the present era complaints have been frequent about lack of continuity in teacher education programs. Beyond the difficulty of blending arts and science courses with education courses are fractures separating the schools from colleges of education and within teacher education itself where methods courses, foundations courses, and work in the field often lack coordination and shared focus.

The common response then to problems of integration was to state that it was within student experience that integration took place (see Hopkins 1937). While true, this response proved less than satisfactory to many participants in the study, including faculty at Ohio State University. One feature of many projects that sought to address lack of continuity "was movement away from numerous short, specialized, and distinct courses" (Stiles 1947, 142), a curse that continues today. Such a move was part of the program developed by faculty in the College of Education at Ohio State, but only part. In addition, the entire program was reorganized around "laboratory experiences" as a means for developing "experimental attitudes." Laboratory experiences were "designed to give the student opportunity to deal at firsthand with reality, to enjoy the adventure of discovery, and to assume responsibility for his own activity" (Klein 1941, 4–5). Anticipating action research and design studies, the "term *experimental attitude* [was] used to mean the ingrained tendency to employ the method of intelligence in attacking a problem; that is, to assemble pertinent data, to formulate a tentative conclusion or hypothesis on the basis of the evidence, to test the hypothesis by further experimentation, and to revise the hypothesis in the light of new findings" (ibid., 6). The aim, then, was to encourage habits of reflection. These themes were strengthened by being grounded in a conception of democracy as an educational means and aim consistent with the commission's viewpoint, which is not surprising since Ohio State housed the Eight-Year Study, and the commission built on the work of that study.

What made the Ohio State program unique was the focus on the kind and quality of relationships teacher education students were to have with one another and with faculty. Continuity would follow not only from program focus but from continuity of relationships, a belief undergirding the spread of cohorts in teacher education over the past decade. Special attention was given to the first stages of professional education, beginning with an orientation course largely devoted to educational planning. The focus in modern parlance was on self-exploration in community contexts: "What are my goals? What do I need to be and do if I am to attain these goals? Which of the qualities necessary for attaining my purpose do I now have? How may I proceed from where I am to where I want to go?" (Klein 1941, 67). To assist students to answer these questions, they were organized into "conference sections" that met throughout the entire year with college faculty advisors who received special training for this work and who were given a large amount of information on each student prior to the beginning of and throughout the school year. In addition, they participated in one of two large "lecture-laboratory sections" twice weekly. An assistant dean coordinated the program.

The conference sections varied greatly. Student planning committees were formed that worked with the advisor to determine program activities: field trips to schools and social agencies, community study projects which deepened during the sophomore year (ibid., 104), and the like preceded and were followed by discussion. Social functions were held to build and strengthen relationships. Students from previous years met with enrolled students to help them in their planning and to give advice. A good deal of diagnostic testing was done to help the student, with the assistance of the faculty advisor, to think more productively about and plan for the future. A student council was organized from among conference members to disseminate information, to link the groups, and to give feedback to faculty on the program: "As the [faculty] Executive Committee plans for [the future], every proposal is laid before the Council" (ibid., 84).

Evaluation of the program was ongoing, intense, and sharply focused. Revision was data driven. Results were promising, indicating that the program provided the beginnings of what Lortie (1975) would later label a "shared ordeal," a lively sense of belonging to a professional group and of suffering together for a worthy cause. Consistent with commission and Ohio State faculty commitments, a large portion of the success came because of efforts made to involve students throughout in planning and evaluating the curriculum over which they came to have a large measure of ownership, and the emphasis on individual and group study of problems of genuine concern.

Conclusion

The principles that grounded the work of the Commission on Teacher Education originated in a particular, and shared, conception of democracy. These principles, although taken for granted initially, were tested and proven: "[The Commission] emerges from its experience with its basic convictions corrected in detail and further clarified, yet fundamentally confirmed" (Commission on Teacher Education 1944, 262). Evidence generated from the study supports the value of these principles as a basis for the reform of education generally and of teacher education specifically. They proved themselves then, and they have value now. Consider the following commission conclusions: (1) Successful reform efforts were organized around genuine local problems. The standards that proved effective for identifying such problems were relatively straightforward: "(a) The problem or situation to be met should have more than temporary importance; it should be one that is likely to have long-time educational significance. (b) The problem or situation should have a local orbit as well as existence upon a regional or national basis. It should be capable of much local illumination" (Prall and Cushman 1944, 481). (2) Successful reform efforts maximized participation of stakeholders and approached problem solution from positions of respect and equality. The spirit of equality was evident in many of the projects, especially in the workshops, where university and school faculty worked side by side and often shared planning responsibilities. It was evident in other ways as well. For instance, in work undertaken at Ohio State, literally hundreds of teachers were intimately involved in creating an instrument to enable better-quality feedback on teaching. The instrument and the follow-up interview were designed to be "used *with* [not on] teachers and student teachers" (Troyer and Pace 1944, 187). (3) Successful efforts had built into them ongoing evaluation, and the results of evaluation were widely discussed. Moreover, the most powerful evaluation programs, those that most encouraged improvement, involved data gathering by those potentially most influenced by the outcomes. (4) Self- and small-group study were not only effective forms of in-service teacher education but also practical means for school improvement. (5) Although there were better and worse points of departure evident in the studies—some problems or issues were too large for small-group study or too small—the important point was to begin. Projects evolved in response not only to changing social conditions but also to changes in teacher skill and understanding; flexibility proved to be an important feature of the more successful programs. Thus outcomes were unpredictable. Indeed, the most "logical" and most "elaborate" of plans often proved least rewarding to teachers. (6) Resistance to change originated in poor communication; conversely, successful programs emphasized means for widely disseminating information, even to those on the fringes of the study. Initial involvement often deepened over time. (7) A sharp focus on the study of children and the systematic sharing of the results of the studies had transformative power in part because it spoke directly and powerfully to the deepest commitments and most powerful motivations of the teachers. (8) Successful programs were dependent on teacher learning, but the teachers needed outside help to increase their knowledge and expertise and to realize their leadership potential. This assistance took many forms and involved many different groups of people, including other teachers. (9) In the more successful programs, clarity of aims and of guiding philosophy generally came after the fact, after the program got under way, and after the initial results of study groups began to be discussed and evaluated. Discussion clarified aims. (10) Effective programs demonstrated a balance, often a dynamic and shifting balance, between centralization and decentralization, between "bottom-up" (Prall and Cushman 1944, 493) and top-down reform. (11) Successful programs engaged teachers and engendered commitment. (12) Ultimately, it was recognized that if reform was to be driven by the principle of maximal involvement, then school structures needed changing. Structural change was most likely in higher education institutions, such as Ohio State, and least likely in the public schools; structural impediments to change proved to be a source of frustration. (13) Successful reform efforts in university-based teacher education programs supported the value of maximum participation of interested parties, including students, and required changes that enhanced the kind and quality of interactions students had with teachers, professors, and the communities within which they lived and worked.

These are some of the lessons learned by participants of the study, lessons obscured by the cold war politics of post-World War II America and the problems of building and staffing the nation's schools. The results were impressive and the reforms powerful and apparently their educational value long-lasting for those who generated them. The results may not have met policy-maker standards for reform—and in this respect they might be dismissed as nothing more than a bit of additional content consistent with the story of impossibility—but they certainly met practitioner standards. Most of the results, but not all, have recently been rediscovered. And in this respect the commission's work illustrates the value of reconsidering the history of teacher education but from a vantage point outside the received and all-too-disappointing tradition of failed reform. As commission representatives feared, the potential of workshops for inviting teacher change is probably rarely realized, in part because teachers generally have little involvement in agenda setting, and the typical workshop is now of relatively short duration and narrow in focus. As a form of in-service and perhaps of preservice teacher education, one suspects there is still great potential residing in the careful study of children and of the communities within which they live. Undoubtedly the current emphasis on teacher action research opens up rich possibilities for studies of this kind. Nevertheless, it is stunning to realize how little attention is given to child development and the lives of children in current reform debates and in teacher education despite the rising interest in constructivism. Moreover, surprisingly little attention is given to teacher learning and development, the essence of reform as the commission understood it. The study presents compelling evidence that teachers can and will invest heavily in reform when the problems they confront are recognized as legitimate and the outcomes promised or hoped for will make a positive difference in the quality of the educational experience had by children and will enhance teachers' learning. This remains true and is cause for optimism. However, the commission reports also remind us that changed practice requires administrative and structural support, a point not well understood until the late 1980s. Finally, in an age enamored with marketplace metaphors, of fragmented publics caught in shrinking and increasingly walled spaces, and where all social institutions are suspect, the commission reminds us that schools have a unique place in building social democracies, and that democracy brings with it a point of view on reform that is both demanding but also forgiving. Sadly, this insight is now widely forgotten.

PART 2

Studies of Becoming and Being a Teacher Educator

The Quest for Identity in Teaching and Teacher Education: An Episodic Personal History (2005)

Introduction

Certainly since Decartes famously asserted *Cogito ergo sum*, questions of identity have been at the center of the Western quest for meaning. What and who is the "I" that thinks and therefore is? (see Ricoeur 1992). While in college in the late 1960s, the stream of the Western tradition continued to flow as my generation sought to discover and then express our true selves, an original grounding that echoed a Platonic ideal. By breaking one's chains, chains of illusion, then turning and facing the light emanating from outside the mouth of the cave, a true self could be found. But how does one know that the self found is the "true" self? Does rebellion against parents and other bearers of "the establishment" necessarily result in self-discovery? I recall participating in protests that were publicly principled but privately just good excuses to party. Yet phoniness was high treason, an affront to the self and to the sincerity of others' quests for authenticity (see Taylor 1991). True to Enlightenment traditions, and despite a growing presence of Eastern thought via the likes of Alan Watts and other cultural translators, the myth of self-creation first so powerfully portrayed by Henry David Thoreau in *Walden* endured. One could not only find oneself, but, in an act of autogenesis, like Jay Gatsby, actually create oneself.

One wonders, as John Murphy queried, "is this search for an identity proof that a self exists?" (Murphy 1989, 116). Does a generation seeking authentic expressions of the self mean there is a self to seek? No, Murphy argues: The self is a fragile fiction. Identity is merely linguistic, an expression of using a first-person singular pronoun, a habit of speech and of behavior, a performance that ultimately cannot be sustained. Indeed, he suggests, we are inevitably multiple selves depending on the range and variety of contexts we inhabit, each of which calls forth a different self. For some (Gergen 1991), the discovery of multiplicity is cause for celebration. For others, at its extreme, it is a source of crisis, of severe disorientation and confusion (see Glass 1993).

What is to be made of this situation? And why are questions of identity and selfhood of such consequence to teachers and to teacher educators?

From a Student's Position: A Step Backward

To begin to answer these questions it is first necessary to step out of the teacher and teacher educator position and into the student position where we confront full-faced the glare of our moral responsibilities as educators. When asked why they decided to teach and to be a teacher (a statement about identity), teachers give a range of responses. Typically they recall their own experience as students and speak of their teachers. For those teachers I have spoken with or interviewed, content area backgrounds are not often mentioned. Rather, mention is made of the teacher as a person who, for good or ill, deeply touched their students' lives. Qualities, both positive and sometimes negative, are listed: caring, interested, passionate, curious, engaged, involved, humorous or, alternatively, disorganized, mean-spirited, disengaged. From my own schooling experience I can put human faces to these qualities and in doing so my judgement says something profound about my teachers as persons, about how I interacted with their self-presentation and they with mine, and how together we engaged in and struggled with a process of mutual self-definition (Goffman 1959).

To my great benefit, some of my teachers were *fully present* to me in the classroom—no dividedness there. But each and every one of my teachers' lives presented an argument for a way of being with and in the world and for others, a testimony. Some of these ways of being influenced my conception of who I was, how I should and could live, and what I might become. The passion for history of a teacher, Michael Arvanitas, encouraged me to imagine myself as a historian. A life is an argument whether one is a first-grade public school teacher or professor in a distinguished research university. Parker Palmer extends and deepens the point: "Teaching, like any truly human activity, emerges from one's inwardness, for better or worse. As I teach, I project the condition of my soul onto my students, my subject, and our way of being together. The entanglements I experience in the classroom are often no more or less than the convolutions of my inner life. Viewed from this angle, teaching holds a mirror to the soul [or the condition of one's inner self]" (Palmer 1998, 2). Parents certainly are wise to ask of their children's teachers, "What sort of person is she?"

Stepping back into the teacher educator position, questions of identity have profound importance for the kind and quality of professional communities that are formed as well as the programs developed. It is for this reason that Loughran (2006) argues that more studies of the "transition from teacher to teacher educator" are needed (13). As will be discussed shortly, the subject positions opened by institutions and the duties performed within them shape the kind of lives lived, and in turn the kind of lives lived shapes the institutions served. Thus program decisions not only have to do with what students learn and do but how they live and whether or not they and we are able to live undividedly and fully purposefully. In turn, the lives teachers live and the subject positions they occupy and play out serve as models of professional being and provide conditions of community membership. If beginning teachers are to belong, they must find acceptable and recognized subject positions that may require that they conceal conflicting aspirations. Having long histories, subject positions appear natural, but they are not. They are changing human creations sustained in multiple and often unrecognized ways through various forms of institutional labor, including simply going about daily business. And so a genuine concern with teacher educator identity and identity formation necessarily leads to both self and institutional criticism and perhaps toward change and renewal.

Meaning, Self, and Identity

Already I have used two very slippery terms, *self* and *identity*, which require definition and grounding if I am to say anything of value about teacher education and the quest for identity. As a point of departure I draw on the work of Harre and van Langenhove, who helpfully distinguish between two senses of self: "There is the self of personal identity, which is experienced as the continuity of one's point of view in the world of objects in space and time. This is usually coupled with one's sense of personal agency, in that one takes oneself as acting from that very same point. Then there are selves that are publicly presented in the episodes of interpersonal interaction in the everyday world, the coherent clusters of traits we sometimes call 'personas.' . . . One's personal identity persists 'behind' the publicly presented repertoire of one's persona" (1999, 7). Often these two senses of self are confused. In my own work I have found it helpful to distinguish between "core" and "situational" selves (Bullough, Knowles, and Crow 1991). The result of this view is that under "normal circumstances each human being is the seat of just one person, but of many personas. The same individual can manifest any one of their repertoire of personas in clusters of behaviour displayed in the appropriate social context. Taken over a period of time it becomes clear that each person has many personas, any one of which can be dominant in one's mode of self-presentation in a particular context" (Harre and van Langenhove 1999, 7). This said, the extent of any one individual's repertoire will vary, sometimes dramatically.

It is within interaction that personas reveal themselves, are or are not recognized by others, and are judged as fitting—contextually appropriate or inappropriate to the established rules and duties and to the trajectory of an established, living story line. Thus through interaction speakers constitute and reconstitute one another in a kind of moving and often competitive symbolic dance with contextually set rules and established but ever-shifting boundaries. For instance, teachers and students position one another, often oppositionally. To be a good or a poor student is to act and speak in certain ways that are recognized and confirmed or disconfirmed by teachers and other students. When a young person judged to be a good student fails to act in accordance with expectations and challenges a teacher's authority, the teacher responds in a way very different from when the disruptive student is known to be a troublemaker. But in both instances, the teacher asserts the rules and duties that bind teachers to students and that make their interactions congruent. Students may resist, but resistance comes at a cost. Conversely, if a teacher fails to act teacherly or breaks "set" (Loughran and Northfield 1996, 32), then the established routines, students, and other teachers will subtly press the teacher to a return to the *proper* teacher position, to the teacher subject position made available by the specific cultural and institutional context of schooling (Goffman 1959).

The Quest

Whether identity is real or imagined, the quest for it is experienced as real (Erikson 1968). We recognize the quest as simultaneously constructive and destructive, both personally and socially, and that it takes inclusive and exclusive forms: "I am this sort of person but not this sort." On their part, institutions favor and support some forms of identity and some personas over others, and sometimes to the detriment of the individual. One cannot, then, simply choose oneself—we are all caught, trapped by the limitations and possibilities of the human networks within which and through which we live, the "Das Man" self, as Heidegger characterized it, but we are not wholly determined by our location within those networks. We are tugged in multiple directions and are sites of clashing possibilities and conflicting impulses and social demands. As Thoreau argued, there is always the possibility of disobedience, of imagining things not as they are, not as given. This said, social networks and institutions both limit and enable identity formation, and in the limiting and enabling there is the possibility of severe and serious personal and social dislocation as well as self-discovery and even rebirth.

Locating the self of personal identity as the experience of continuity of a point of view and as a source of agency and embracing self-as-multiplicity-of-personas, quasi-role enactments, and self-presentations bring two very distinct but related sets of problems. Problems of origin, content, and form come with the first. Problems of consistency and congruence come with the second. Both sets of questions point toward the need to explore biography and moral position, the history of interaction and of the contexts within which interaction takes place and by which rules are and have been set, and the rules and skills of interaction located in episodes, "structures of social encounters" (Harre and van Langenhove 1999, 5) or sequences of "happenings in which human beings engage which have some principle of unity" (ibid., 4). Episodes, William Wordsworth's "spots in time," "include thoughts, feelings, intentions, plans . . . of those who participate. As such, episodes are defined by their participants, but at the same time they also shape what participants do and say" (ibid., 5).

The stories we tell of ourselves are spoken to specific persons, to an audience and for a purpose, and shifts in audience and of context result in changed stories each of which might be recognized as true and as belonging to a single, whole, embodied life—stories that speak of identity not merely of one's passing persona (Day, Stobart, Sammons, and Kington 2006). When written, however, the narrative is frozen and becomes a thing, reified and resistant to change. Textual coherence reduces multiplicity and "conflates the self as perceiver with the self as perceived" (Harre and van Langenhove 1999, 69). In effect, the order imposed by writing a story of self, a linear unfolding, stands in for the self itself. This is important for how I will compose the body of this chapter. To avoid the reification that comes with the written story form, narratives that have beginnings, middles, and endings, in what follows I will present and reflect upon several episodes that illuminate the challenges of teacher and teacher educator self-formation and point toward the importance of attending to identity formation and context when thinking about teaching and learning to teach and of being with children. On the surface, the episodes will seem to be distinct, but what binds them together is their place in what has become a story line of becoming a teacher educator. Drawing on C. Wright Mills's (1959) insight, I will seek to join biography and history.

Episodes, Identity, and Persona

This section presents seven episodes, organized under three headings that represent different, but closely related, aspects of identity formation, social processes that shape who and what we are. I should mention up front that there are other fruitful ways of telling a story and of parsing the quest for identity (see the Arizona Group 1997). I have settled on these because they resonate with my experience, seem to be shared, and are rooted in a substantial body of research. They certainly are not comprehensive, although I think they have value. The headings are: (1) Identification and Membership; (2) Subject Location: Rules and Duties; and (3) Self-Expression and Enactment. Each of these points toward questions for thinking about one's own identity and for considering how one might assist another to better understand what he or she has become or is becoming and why. Identification and Membership leads to these sorts of questions: With whom and with what do I identify? To what do I belong? Who or what claims me as a member? Subject Location: Rules and Duties points toward these questions: Where do I fit, and what institutional spaces are open to me? What rules do I follow and duties do I perform, and how is my performance connected to and recognized by others? Self-Expression and Enactment raises questions related to authenticity, to how I feel when I play my part and whether or not the part I play is found to be life affirming and enabling of a sense of self-coherence, as well as to whether or not I possess the skills needed for self-enactment. Before proceeding, I must mention that I will have little to say here about temperament—dominating moods—which nevertheless has an important place in identity formation. Institutions favor some temperaments over others, and temperament has a dramatic influence on recognition and membership. It also has a great deal to do with our ability to tolerate ambiguity and manage contradiction and incoherence, a point nicely illustrated by the lives of philosopher David Hume and of Benjamin Franklin, for example. While this is an extremely important topic, I can only touch upon it briefly.

While the seven episodes presented overlap in various and multiple ways across the three processes, they are intended to emphasize one or another point about the teacher and teacher educator quest for identity. The quest itself will be explored in a reflection section following each episode.

1. Identification and Membership

We know who we are in part by who and with what we identify and to whom and to what we belong. Through identification with other teachers and with teaching we take on teacher-like qualities and speak in teacher-like voices and with teacher-like authority when with children and sometimes with parents, particularly less well educated parents. When we see a teacher, we simultaneously see ourselves. We recognize one another as belonging. Formally, teacher education is charged with facilitating the process of identification through socialization (Zeichner and Gore 1990), particularly through field experience. But not all intending teachers need help seeing themselves as teachers. Some, particularly young women who "played" school when small, already think of themselves as teachers; they are "called" to teach. A calling is a "form of public service to others that at the same time provides the individual a sense of identity and personal fulfillment" (Hansen 1995, 2; see also Bellah, Madsen, Sullivan, Swidler, and Tipton 1985; Serow 1994; Stokes 1997; Yee 1990). For these persons, teaching is the avenue through which they find the fullest, deepest, and richest expression of their identities. They literally *are* teachers, they are not playing at teaching, even though they never have taught.

I was not called to teach. In some respects, I stumbled into teaching and then teacher education as a response to the political and socioeconomic period within which I was born and matured. As a young person, I never imagined myself teaching, and I had great difficulty identifying with "regular" teachers and with the institutionalized practice of teaching. When I started teaching, I taught in an alternative program, and what I did with my classes probably would not have been recognized widely by others as teaching. My "students" and I developed a recycle center and studied the court system. We organized an anti-Olympic protest. We made movies. We wrote lousy poetry. Made pots. Played football. Grew a garden. Visited the state penitentiary. And we argued over issues under a widely spread parachute that draped over the classroom and produced a sense of intimacy and encouraged feelings of belonging. For me, teaching came to be a form of social action, which was central to my identity formation, of finding my own place and way of being with others. Because I worked with young people who would not have attended school without the existence of the program, and the program more than paid for itself, since student attendance was the basis for funding, I was given remarkable leeway by school administrators to experiment and explore and build a shared world.

Episode 1: During the fall term of my first year of teaching, a faculty dinner was held. I attended, knowing that some members of the East High School faculty doubted that an alternative program should exist within what historically had been an elite, but, because of shifting demographics, a rapidly changing school. At the dinner, others were polite, but only the special education teacher, Fern Register, spoke openly and was warmly friendly toward me. She recognized and responded to me as a fellow teacher. Fern's program and mine occupied the same floor of the school building along with the ROTC, gym, lunchroom, and auditorium. The serious academic programs occupied the top floor, far removed from us and our students. Auto mechanics occupied the basement. I sensed my place: I was and would continue to be on the fringes of the faculty, which I thought was all right. I was an outsider, one whose position was determined by the limited value placed on my students by other faculty members (but not, I should mention, by the principal or especially the vice principal). I found freedom on the fringes. That I taught students who were of so little concern to so many faculty members produced a liberating benign neglect. That established, institutional teacher-subject positions were not fitting or did not exist for me proved exhilarating. That I was outside of the boundaries and was seen as not belonging meant that I was often criticized, but because of the protection offered by the two building administrators, the net effect of the criticism was only to increase the distance separating me from other teachers and to remove even the faintest possibility that I would identify with them as teachers. Instead, I affiliated myself with other alternative educators who saw themselves as counter-cultural, and I looked toward the university and toward my students' well-being for confirmation of myself and of my teaching persona, such as it was. That university faculty members were intimately involved in the program and in the school made identification with them relatively easy. Naively, I dismissed other teachers as "traditional" as my teaching persona formed in opposition to the institutionally preferred patterns.

Reflection: Stepping into a rapidly changing and dynamic teaching situation profoundly influenced my development as a teacher (or non-teacher). I recall only an occasional tension between my deeper, biographical sense of self, my identity, and the school persona I developed. I came to appreciate being seen by others in the building as odd, as belonging elsewhere. That many (not all) of the faculty did not seem to value what I did confirmed the worth of the work; had they embraced me, had they recognized me as one of them, I suspect I would have had to reject their association in order to have maintained my identity. In opposition, I found self-confirmation and strength. Yet paradoxically, by defining myself and being defined as "not-teacher" the institutionalized position of "teacher" defined me. I played a counter-melody to the melody of schooling, and counter-melodies exist only in relationship to melodies.

Patterns of identification and affiliation reveal a great deal about who we are, at base. We do not seek out others whose lives call forth from us an uncomfortable persona or whose expressions of self shake our own, at least not frequently. Yet we do not only seek confirmation of our identities and the personas we have assumed, we also are animated by other motives, the desire to understand and be understood, for example, as Habermas (1979) has argued in his discussion of the conditions for communication. In desiring to understand others, including our students, we may discover ourselves to be a location of distorted meanings. We might even find that we are oppressors, that our identities and the personas we project have been constructed in such a way that to confirm our worth requires the negation of someone else's sense of worth. In any case, if we attend carefully to those whose call we hear and to which we resonate, we learn a great deal about who we are and about the moral space we occupy. Later I will have something to say about the seduction of teacher educators by the siren song of the arts and sciences and about the educational and personal cost of this identification.

Episode 2: A few months ago, a colleague who needed to speak with me left his card tacked to my office door. It read, "Professor so and so, Professor of Children's Literature." It did not read, "Professor so and so, Professor of Teacher Education."

Reflection: I understand the desire to distance oneself from teacher education, which remains low in status, even in schools of education, labor intensive, and unappreciated. Identifying with work and with others judged second-rate comes at a cost to self. What sort of person wants membership of this kind? Teacher education is not judged serious intellectual work: "The preeminence of scholarly work and the faculty perquisites that go with it are pronounced on the campuses of the major public and private universities. It does not take long even for the previously uninitiated to pick up on some of the subtleties of prestige differentiating fields of study, kinds of publications, awards, and the like. And it does not take much probing to find that gaining campus wide recognition as a scholar is exceedingly difficult if one is connected with a school, college, or department of education" (Goodlad 1990, 192). I recognized the status system even as a graduate student and felt these pressures; I too distanced myself from teacher education, although I knew that if I was to find employment in higher education it would be in a teacher education faculty, as noted in the Introduction. I thought of myself as a foundations and curriculum person and not a teacher educator.

Episode 3: Human Interests in the Curriculum (Bullough, Goldstein, and Holt 1984) was published at the end of 1983, the result of an ongoing study of critical theory with Stan Goldstein and Ladd Holt and of a fellowship spent sitting in on foundations courses with Walter Feinberg, Paul Violas, and Harry Broudy at the University of Illinois. In the book we critically analyzed a range of school programs and did so with a sledgehammer. For a short time following the book's publication, I felt very good about my work and my place in the department. My position in foundations and my persona as a foundations person seemed to solidify somewhat. But then one afternoon, a faculty member, Flo Krall, stopped me in the hallway near my office to talk. In her straightforward manner, she said that she found the book "disappointing" and then remarked, as I recall her words, "there isn't any 'you' in it." I was shaken. I could not help but think carefully about what she had said and why she might have said it. She knew me and my history. Gradually I came to realize that she was right. In many ways the critic's role well suits me, but what she sensed was that I was hiding in the role and behind a borrowed ideology. Criticism was a form of disengagement, in this case a form of disassociation from parts of myself that she knew. Recalling my past, she invited me to engage in an act of self-recovery. I was in bad faith, as Sarte would way. One cannot simply escape history by denying it.

Reflection: Life as a teacher educator in a university requires a double identification and membership, one with teachers and schools and one with the academy. Teacher educators stand between two "communities of practice" (Wenger 1999). To describe this divide as merely a matter of an inevitable tension between theory and practice, as is so commonly done, is to miss the real point. The struggle is over membership and identity—indeed, "formation of a community of practice is also the negotiation of identities" (ibid., 149).

Sometimes schizophrenia results—in asserting oneself, one denies oneself. One lives incoherently. Various attempts have been made to create institutional contexts within which resolution is more rather than less likely. The Holmes Group (1995), for example, championed professional development schools as a way of "forming a tighter bond between scholarship and practice" (60). The promise was that stable, satisfying, and consistently principled professional personas could be formed, and that better teachers and schools would result once the divided loyalties of teacher educators were resolved. New loyalties and, by inference, new identities, members of the Holmes Group seemed to have realized, required new institutional commitments. But the divide continues. As the attack on teachers and teacher education grows increasingly shrill and irrational, the temptation to withdrawal and to fabrication grows apace. "Plasticity" has replaced authenticity (Ball 2003, 225).

Affiliation with teachers assures low status within the academy. Strong identification with the academy and with the arts and sciences produces a crisis of authority with schoolteachers who often and not wholly inaccurately see academics as foreign invaders. In the teacher education classroom, strong identification with teachers, seeing oneself first and foremost as a teacher, and being recognized by teachers as part of their world leads to telling stories about teachers and teaching from one's own experience as a way of establishing authority claims. In contrast, identification with the academy leads to lists of disembodied and decontextualized generalizations and principles and inevitably to charges from teacher education students of irrelevance. Charges of irrelevance may prove hurtful, but identification with the academy and with the work of the academy is the only road to tenure. It is deeply ironic that even as teacher educators mimic the arts and sciences and seek a strong identification with the academy, the academy consistently refuses to recognize teacher educators as legitimate members. Still, we seek membership and to get it many of us distance ourselves from students and teaching. It is little wonder, as Robert Boice (1991, 1996) has noted, that resentment of the demands of teaching is common among beginning professors across university campuses, even as one's greatest professional pleasure may come from teaching.

Episode 4: In the spring of 1984 I found myself sitting in the Trustee Room of Teachers College, Columbia University, surrounded by a collection of deans that comprised the Holmes Group writing committee. In the first Holmes Group Report, *Tomorrow's Teachers* (1986), I am listed as a "participant in the development of the reform agenda" (79). I was to present my view of the state of teacher education and teacher education research in America. Across from me sat Dean Judy Lanier, the force behind the Holmes Group, and above me hung beautifully framed portraits of T. C. notables of the past. With interest I read the nameplates. As I spoke that day, I pulled no punches. What I said reflected my view, an admittedly conflicted non-member's view, of the state of the field. Had a young, intending teacher educator been present, I suspect he or she would have wondered, "Why would anyone want to affiliate with this field?"

Reflection: At the time this question was also my question. As previously noted, it was only while doing the research that resulted in *First-Year Teacher: A Case Study* (1989) that I came publicly to refer to myself as a teacher educator and began to understand the complexity and richness of teacher education as a field of inquiry. I decided to conduct the research for *First-Year Teacher* while driving to West Yellowstone for a brief family vacation. Back home I told a respected senior faculty member my plans. Surprised, he queried, "Why would anyone be interested in a book about an individual teacher?" He could see no possible value in the project, yet I persisted with it. I had come to realize that I could no longer continue to work in teacher education courses and with teacher education students and not embrace teacher education; I needed to become a teacher educator. This meant seeking membership in a new community. To be sure, my foundations and curriculum work had lead to tenure, to institutional survival, and tenure opened up the possibility of risking myself and seeking new memberships and new forms of recognition.

2. Subject Location: Rules and Duties

What if institutional membership brings with it rules and duties that are destructive to self and not just contrary to it?

Episode 5: Before leaving for Columbus, Ohio, in the fall of 1973 for graduate study, I received a phone call informing me that I should plan on attending a meeting once I arrived that would signal the beginning of an effort to redesign the undergraduate teacher education program around specific competencies. I knew something about the competency movement in teacher education and did not like it. Especially I did not like its underpinnings in behavioral psychology, its ontology or its simplistic epistemology. Then, as now, I take comfort in the tendency of humans to foul up every and all systems of control, even the most elegantly designed. I had accepted a teaching assistantship, and my duties included working in the undergraduate program. So I left for Columbus feeling disheartened and in some ways trapped by the commitment I had made and duties I had accepted. Thus began my work with a well-known professor of teacher education. One afternoon in our weekly seminar, this professor and I had a disagreement. Over time, we often disagreed. Foreshadowing the future, he made a point that there was a need to measure outcomes in teacher education. Drawing on words he attributed to Edward Thorndike, he said, "Whatever exists at all, exists in some amount and can be measured." Immediately, without stopping to weigh my words, I corrected him. "No, it was William McCall (1922) who added the phrase 'can be measured' to Thorndike's statement." Then, to trump him, smugly I added, drawing on John Dewey's Kappa Delta Pi lecture of 1929, *The Sources of a Science of Education*, that what is important in education cannot be measured. Fortunately, my insubordination was ignored; after all, I was merely a graduate student.

Reflection: Peter Taubman (1992) writes of the subject positions open within teacher discourse, the dominant being what he characterizes as the position of the "master" (229). What if a teacher does not want and is not well suited to be a master or, in my case as a graduate student, a teacher trainer? What if the positions available do violence to one's identity? If the subject positions of a context are few and highly constrained by the distribution of rewards and punishments and one does not and cannot find place but cannot move on, what does one do? Clearly, as a graduate student, I was highly vulnerable. A sensible strategic move would have been for me to have kept quiet, done my duty, obeyed the rules, and engaged in "strategic compliance" (Lacey 1977) until graduation. Through strategic compliance, I might have been recognized by more of my professors as belonging to them, as having a legitimate claim on them. I might have muttered to my fellow graduate students from a student persona even while presenting to my professors another, more compliant persona, that of the eager and willing junior colleague. Or I could have closed my classroom door and out of sight enacted a subject position more to my liking, more consistent with how I understood and presented myself. Each of these responses was then possible. I had genuine choices before me.

Now it is much more difficult to hide behind a closed classroom door than it used to be. The greater emphasis on teacher accountability generally and high stakes testing specifically has opened wide the classroom door and severely reduced the range of available teacher subject positions as well as tightened work rules. Under a "regime of performativity" (Ball 2003, 223), it becomes increasingly difficult for teachers to engage in role play and not be caught and judged deviant. Similar efforts are afoot in higher education, of which more will be said momentarily. When outcomes are externally imposed and consistently enforced, when aims and means are kept separate and rules and duties carefully prescribed, it is very difficult to express oneself fully in teaching, to be passionate about one's work. For many educators the distance between professional persona and identity likely widens as a result, and professional identity increasingly is experienced as ethically empty. I suspect it is for this reason that teaching is losing much of its appeal, even to those initially called to teach. As a technology, teaching requires little investment of self compared to teaching as an expressive art form and moral relationship. Narrowly prescribed outcomes stand between teachers and students and sunder many teachers' sense of coherence as their practice contradicts their commitments and identities, as they become trainers and managers rather than educators.

Episode 6: Shortly after *First-Year Teacher* was published it happened that David Berliner visited campus and met with my department chair. During the meeting, Professor Berliner, a former president of the American Educational Research Association and a quantitative researcher with sparkling credentials, mentioned that he had read and much admired the book. My chair, whose own scholarly tradition had led him to conclude that it was a soft study, not research at all, was amazed, so surprised that he could not help but mention the meeting to me.

Reflection: This chance event proved to have an important influence on how my chair subsequently viewed my work, place, and status in the department. He reassessed me (he reassessed my work and therefore reassessed me), recognized me as a scholar who simply played by a different set of rules than his own, and, because of David Berliner's recognition, reassigned me to a higher status subject position. Suddenly my institutional life was transformed, and not because of any action of my own.

This episode followed on the heels of what has sometimes been called the "quantitative/qualitative wars" that came somewhat late to my institution but came with vengeance. The central question was: What counts as research? The subtext was far from subtle, which was the question of academic cachet and of what sort of work, or, put differently, what sort of persons and identities would be rewarded within the university and judged authoritative. Part of finding place within a field is finding place within the established modes of inquiry and then following the rules of scholarship and doing one's duty as a scholar. As William James so well understood, questions of temperament are very important here. There is a close connection between temperament, identity, and scholarship—we study what strikes us, which is part of the "inner drama" of research, the "giving of one's self into the research undertaking" (Mooney 1957, 155). We study best when we use methods that get at the full complexity of the questions that grab us. It was the failure of quantitative methods to do this, to get at the complexity of experience and to allow expression of the temperament of large numbers of educators who wished to better understand the nature of educational experience and not merely of human behavior, that led to the rise to prominence of qualitative methodologies. With the broadening acceptance of qualitative methods came new forms of recognition and new ways of being a professor. As an aside, it is this same uneasiness and lack of place that has led to the growing interest in "self study" in teacher education (see Loughran and Northfield 1996; Samaras 2002; Loughran, Hamilton, LaBoskey, and Russell 2004).

For a time beginning in the late 1980s, there was a dramatic expansion of the research subject positions of teacher education, a sea change. But there are now signs of a vigorous and growing backlash, some would assert a much-needed "correction." Among the signs is the remarkably narrow definition of "scientific research" championed by the National Reading Panel and supported by the American president and his education policy makers (Darling-Hammond and Youngs 2002). In policy debates—now increasingly more like friendly insider chats than debates—constricted definitions of what counts as "data" are winning the day (Shavelson and Towne 2002). Rules are tightening. Other signs of constriction include the aggressive shift of the National Council for the Accreditation of Teacher Education (NCATE) toward performance outcomes as the basis for making accreditation decisions despite a lack of evidence supporting the value of the change (Bullough, Clark, and Patterson 2003; Johnson, Johnson, Farenga, and Ness 2005). Seemingly unaware of the failures of the earlier competency movement that I first encountered at Ohio State, the Association of Teacher Educators has established standards for "master teacher educators," complete with an assessment model that includes portfolios, "Assessment Center Exercises," including written examinations and simulations, and interviews (see http://www.ate1.org). One result of these developments, each grounded in an abiding distrust of teachers and teacher educators and deep doubt about the value of our work and therefore of us, will be growing pressure from a variety of sources internal (such as the NCATE) and external to teacher education to constrict the range of available subject positions and to reorder the status of those positions that remain.

The implications of these developments for identity formation are far reaching. It appears that the institutional subject positions encouraged by these developments will have little if any connection whatsoever to the well-being of intending teachers or children and much to do with generating an inflationary political currency tied to standardized test scores. Finding place in the positions that remain will take teacher educators away from their central moral responsibility and source of their deepest professional pleasure, to better serve children and young people. As Ball (2003) starkly states: When a professional life is dominated by judgemental relations, there is "no room for caring" (224). But we have choices about how we respond, and much is at stake for the well-being of the young and of those who work most closely with them in how we choose to respond (Bullough 2001). Courageous responses can only come from strength of identity and clarity of commitment. Too many of us are, using a phrase C. S. Lewis used to criticize intellectuals, "men without chests" (1944/1996, 36). Such persons take established institutional practices as given, almost natural, not as historical and changing human creations, and they comply.

3. Self-Expression and Enactment

Years ago I conducted a study of a beginning teacher who was uncertain about what sort of teacher she wanted to be and responded in chameleon-like fashion to the institutional demands of teaching, allowing the context to fully dictate her actions (Bullough 1992). Since teaching is fraught with contradictions and paradox is the stuff of a teacher's life, she found herself facing the consequences of inconsistency. When grading, for example, teachers weigh quality of work against quantity and effort. What does one do when a high-achieving student puts forth little effort but produces an outstanding product? Conversely, what does one do when a less-able student works diligently and invests extraordinary amounts of energy and time in a product that is good but not great? For this teacher, as I recall, what might be considered the ordinary paradoxes of teaching were debilitating. She spoke with many voices and stood for nothing. Many of her students, who expected consistency of thought and action from their teachers, were frustrated by her actions. A strong sense of self, an established but not wholly rigid identity, is the basis for moral action. Lacking stable identity, a strong persona may produce what appears to be moral action, but to call such action "moral" requires that it be more than a result of a person playing a temporary role—to be moral, action must be committed. As I sat in this beginning teacher's classroom, she lacked classroom presence, seemed timid, insecure and insincere, and uncertain. She waffled. Within the classroom, she could not enact a teacher persona.

Finding that students did not respond to him as he hoped and encountering serious discipline problems, another beginning teacher (Bullough and Knowles 1990) chose to enact the dominant subject position presented by his school: the "policeman." To do this he had to set aside his sense of himself as a scientist born of years of experience working in a lab. Doing this, he temporarily lost his bearings, just as he lost himself. He was not a very effective policeman and did not enjoy the part at all. Still, he played it and became better in the part over time, because within the school both students and teachers understood and recognized as legitimate this subject position. But the policeman persona was ill fitting, uncomfortable.

The first beginning teacher lacked a clear sense of herself as teacher. The second had a sense of himself as teacher, but it was not one that he could enact in the classroom. In the urban school culture within which he taught, he could not be who he thought he was as teacher. Perhaps more importantly, he did not possess the skills requisite for enactment of his sense of self as teacher. For each, teacher education failed to address questions of self-as-teacher. A programmatic emphasis on teaching skills had not prepared them to confront perhaps the most fundamental problem of teaching—finding and making place and expressing self in teaching.

Episode 7: Sitting in a colleague's office chatting, she suddenly realized that class was about to begin. After glancing at her watch, she looked up, smiled, and said, "time to put on my teaching mask." I asked: "You put on a mask?" "Yes, it's like playing a part. I have a teacher's face that I wear when teaching." She left, and I began to ponder what teaching was like for me and what sort of teacher I was.

Reflection: Over years of teaching, my friend had developed a persona that she easily moved in and out of. She knew the teacher's part, and played it well, sometimes brilliantly. She also knew the other players. When occupying the role of teacher, she had a teacher's voice and a teacher's look. Having observed her teach on numerous occasions, I noticed the difference between when she was "on" and when she was "off" stage. Comfortable in the teacher's mask, within the classroom she employed a wide range of instructional strategies. With ease, she would tell stories, have students engage in group work and projects, read research, and arrange then process field trips. As teacher, I realized she played many parts, each well recognized and accepted by those she taught. As I came to know and appreciate her, I realized that her teaching persona reflected a committed point of view. Each persona that I knew was an expression of the underlying unity of self, a life's trajectory and moral force. She knew who she was and how she wanted to be with others when teaching, which was a source of power and influence. Others responded to her as she wished them to; and they recognized the correctness of her role-play. She had developed a variety of skills to support her effort to be. She was one person, but she had multiple personas into which she invested herself fully.

As I have thought about my colleague and friend and compared my experience with my understanding of her experience, I have realized that it is mostly when I am uncomfortable and uncertain that I grab hold of a mask and then my self-expression is stilted and my humor strained. The quality of a laugh often is the best witness of the authenticity of an expression. Perhaps because I am older than she, and time and age matter (Nias 1989), I seem to have fewer personas, fewer available parts to play. After years of professing, mostly I am what I do. Enactment comes rather easily, habitually. Perhaps my habit of self is stiffer and less pliable than her habit, less open to surprise and less likely to change. One result is that I am quite resistant to institutional demands that feel snug, ethically tight-fitting. For good or ill, having a point of view and a sense of agency, an identity, makes resistance possible, and it is for this reason that teacher commitments and beliefs matter a great deal when teaching or designing programs of study. But it also presents the danger of fundamentalism, of becoming too comfortable and closed to contrary experience, unable to grasp opportunities to unlearn the world and be surprised by it.

Conclusion

Often teacher educators ask beginning teachers to write a personal philosophy. The assignment produces flights of fantasy, but the real task at hand, as I have suggested, is to consider questions of identification and membership, subject location, rules and duties, and forms of self-expression and enactment. This is best done through analyzing narratives, as van Manen (1994) argues: "Personal identity can be brought to self-awareness through narrative self-reflection" (159). One must dig for data into the ground of one's being and consider the life lived, the commitments made, the forms and expressions of personal identification and recognition employed—including the emotions of anger, disappointment, and joy—and the beliefs that animate and give direction to action. One also must consider one's desired way of being in the world. For beginning and experienced teachers alike this is a critical but risky practice; still, it ought to be a central concern of both preservice and in-service teacher education and, importantly, of teacher educators. We must not excuse ourselves. Whatever the arena, in teaching and in teacher education the medium is the message (Russell 1997), and the message is the teacher's life and being, how the teacher makes sense of the world and stands within and sometimes against it. Oddly this is one focus for reflection that often has been ignored in the teacher education literature and practice, yet it is the grounding of all that is important within the practice of teacher education. Perhaps this is so because inevitably to ask questions of this kind leads to sacred soil (Mayes 2001a, 2001b). In this chapter I have focused on three aspects of identity formation: *Identification and Membership, Subject Location: Rules and Duties*, and *Self-Expression and Enactment*, and I have reflected on my own quest for identity as a teacher educator. The episodes are mine, as is the meaning I make of them. But I recognize that other meanings also are possible, other conclusions.

A warning is in order, however. Rather than lead to greater moral action and courage of conviction, the habit of turning inward and engaging in self-criticism can, like Jean-Baptiste Clamence in Camus's *The Fall*, leave behind a person frozen in inaction, lost to self and to others. The call is to act on the world, and to act one must stay in touch with oneself and how the world is being experienced. Sometimes to act requires risking oneself for the sake of the self and of the world. Such acts, usually based on only partial information or mere hunches and sometimes only on the judgments embedded in our emotions, point toward the heroic nature of the quest for identity.

A final thought. In some respects, identity might be thought of as a tendency toward the good, a quiet—and sometimes desperate—but insistent desire. In teaching, personal tendencies and longings dress up and masquerade as authorized conceptions of the good, including judgments about the nature of those we teach. Discovering one's tendencies and uncovering one's pretenses is serious and humbling educational work. Freud was right: We are deeply and inevitably contradictory creatures. Humility restrains our reproductive urge, the temptation to try and impose our identities on others, to colonize unto death another's personhood. Teachers know, deep down, that colonization is not even possible, let alone desirable, and inevitably they confront a simple truth: Unlike training, education is always personal and indirect, and its results are unpredictable. But in unpredictability resides hope—the possibility that something impossibly wonderful might happen, the miracle of learning, of a student accepting our invitation to engagement and becoming over time more interesting, more centered, better grounded, and more able than are we. There also is opportunity: New subject positions can be created, ones that invite communion inside of the academy and ever-fuller, richer, and authentic expressions of human engagement. Facing my limitations draws me further inward to a deep desire, a longing widely shared by teachers—to enable for others what I seek most for myself: to discover and fully express what the ancient Greeks described as arête, one's particular and peculiar form of virtue or excellence, to be one's own best, that so concerned Socrates. But to discover the virtue of self we need to witness virtue in others and in its many and various expressions. This is the teacher's argument and testimony. Through such encounters we come to see that arête is possible, that there is a point to the quest for meaning, even as there may not be a fully satisfying conclusion—a fully stable identity. Through identification with questing others, through being allowed—or insisting that we be allowed (and allowing our students)—to occupy subject positions that sustain the quest, and through courageously expressing, investing in, and testing our sense of ourselves, we achieve ourselves for ourselves and for others. The challenge is to remain teachable, open, but not too open, to contrary data, and to stay in touch with the world, and to stay in touch requires staying deeply invested in those we teach and with those with whom we live and work. This is the essence of caring (Noddings 1984).

CHAPTER **4**

Becoming a Mentor:
School-Based Teacher Educators
and Teacher Educator Identity (2005)

Introduction

Acknowledged or not, questions of character and identity and not only technical skill have always been center stage in teacher education.

> Students rightfully expect instructional and content competence from their teachers, but they also expect to be greeted by a whole person, a caring person, one who knows who and what he is, who has moral standing, and who can be counted on to continue standing, face to face, with students. (Bullough and Baughman 1997, 24)

What is true for public school teachers is also true for teacher educators. By the very nature of the pedagogical relationship, teacher identity is easily called into question (van Manen 1994), and it is for this reason that teaching is often experienced as a "daily exercise in vulnerability" (Palmer 1998, 17), a persistent challenge to one's sense of self. Self-knowledge is thus central to being and becoming a teacher and teacher educator, and the issue is much greater than the challenges associated with induction, of assuming a teacher's or teacher educator's professional persona, but also of determining how one will be for and with others. Such matters are morally weighty and deserve careful consideration, for the results open or close opportunities for those one teaches to be and to become (Beijaard, Meijer, and Verloop 2004).

This chapter explores issues related to the identity formation of one class of often-ignored teacher educators, school-based mentors. My intention is to locate opportunities for building a sense of belonging and commitment, the basis for forming a community of teacher educator practice (Wenger 1999).

Field-Based Teacher Educators

Increasing responsibility for teacher education is falling on public school teachers (Cope and Stephen 2001), but even as this shift in responsibilities is taking place and commitment to public school/university partnership is growing (see Goodlad 1994) it appears that the school and the university remain "two largely separate worlds [that] exist side by side" (Beck and Kosnik 2002, 7), often characterized by distrust and misunderstanding (Bullough, Hobbs, Kauchak, Crow, and Stokes 1997; Bullough, Draper, Smith, and Birrell 2004).

In the hope of bridging this gap and improving communication, various new teacher educator roles have been created for what Sandholtz and Finan (1998) call "boundary spanners" (24), individuals who have one foot in the schools and the other in the university. But simply declaring teachers to be teacher educators or mentors, as is so often done, and occasionally meeting with them on campus to discuss problems and programs does very little to improve the situation. As Feiman-Nemser (2001) has suggested, good teachers are not necessarily good teacher educators. Indeed, good teachers may know remarkably little about beginning teacher development and may even "withhold assistance due to the enduring belief that teaching is a highly personalized practice of finding one's own style" (1033). The result is that the "primacy of practice" (Tillema 2000) is assured, and reflection about good teaching, which is central to teacher improvement, is rare (Korthagen 2004). It would appear that as long as boundary spanners' primary and perhaps sole identification is with teachers and schoolchildren, not university-based teacher educators and beginning teachers, it is highly likely that teacher education will remain little more than a weak exercise in vocational socialization. In part, the problem arises from inattention to identity formation.

Context and Data Set

The study reported in this chapter draws on data from a mentor and two interns who were part of a larger study involving nine mentors and fourteen secondary education interns in mathematics, English, history and social studies, and the biological sciences. The primary focus is on Barbara, a secondary school English teacher in her early forties, as she attempted to make sense of her school experience, to be recognized, and to form an identity as a mentor as well as maintain a teacher identity. Contrary to the agreement reached between the university and the school district, Barbara was only freed from two of six periods of teaching to assume her new responsibility as a mentor, a school-based teacher educator. In effect, by taking this action, and taking advantage of Barbara, the school district got two-thirds of a teacher for free— when two interns are hired in a school at half pay, a regular teacher is freed to mentor. This action also had the effect of dramatically increasing the difficulty of forming an identity as a mentor.

Various kinds of data were gathered from both mentors and protégés across the year. First, six times during the year the mentors met and discussed mentoring issues and published mentoring-related research. Four of these meetings were audiotaped and the tapes transcribed for analysis. Second, each mentor produced a record for each intern, a double-entry log describing intern activities and mentor responses. Third, near the end of the year mentors were paired and asked to tell stories about their year's work with the interns. These conversations, which also were audiotaped and the tapes transcribed, were intended to reveal "well remembered events" (Carter and Gonzalez 1993, 223) and important concerns. Finally, each mentor was individually interviewed to gain additional insight into the mentors' experience of mentoring and how they understood their roles and responsibilities.

Two types of data were gathered from the interns. Each intern responded to a weekly e-mail protocol for which they were paid. The interns were asked to identify both high and low points from the week of teaching and to review their relationship with their mentor. Also, every term they were asked to summarize how they thought they were doing as beginning teachers, to evaluate—grade—the quality of the help given by their mentors, and to express any concerns they had about their relationship. Second, as with the mentors, each intern participated in a paired discussion with another intern, during which they were asked to "tell stories" of their internship year.

The data set for each mentor was rich, interesting, and complex. The data from Barbara and her two interns were selected for presentation here because Barbara was a new mentor (although she had earlier served as a cooperating teacher for student teachers); both of her interns responded faithfully to the e-mail protocols; she was unusually open and forthright in expressing her thoughts and opinions; she took mentoring very seriously, as indicated by the extent and depth of her involvement with the two interns and the quality of her logs; and her interns judged her an exemplary mentor, even though she struggled with the role.

Analytic Lens

James Gee's (2000–2001) conceptualization of identity provides the primary analytic lens. Individually most humans have a sense of continuity and a storied life trajectory that stands as an interpretative backdrop for the flow of daily events, a core self, an "I." What is of interest here, however, is not this enduring, albeit often beleaguered, sense of self but rather the "'kind of person' one is recognized as 'being,' at a given time and place," in a classroom, with children or with beginning teachers (Gee 2000–2001, 99), one's persona (see Chapter 3). William James (1892) made the point nicely: "If from the one point of view I am one self, from another I am quite as truly many" (202). A brief description of each of the four perspectives Gee offers on being recognized as a certain "kind of person," which will be used to organize and present the data, follows. But first it is important to underscore a fundamental general point—that identity formation is not a passive but a dynamic affair, which involves a giving and a withholding that simultaneously alters oneself and one's context, with the result that alternative identities may form. It is, as Zembylas (2003) states, and as described in Chapter 3, a "non-linear, unstable process . . . by which an individual confirms or problematizes who she/he is/becomes" (221).

Gee (2000–2001) describes four interrelated "perspectives," "ways to view identity," or "what it means to be a certain kind of person":

> (1) Nature-Identity (N-Identities or NI), that we are "what we are primarily because of our 'natures'" (101); (2) Institution-Identity (I-Identities or II), that "we are what we are primarily because of the positions we occupy in society" (101); (3), Discourse-Identity (as an individual trait) (D-Identities, or DI), that we "are what we are primarily because of our individual accomplishments as they are interactionally recognized by others" (101) and; (4) Affinity-Identity (A-Identities or AI), that we "are what we are because of the experiences we have had within certain sorts of 'affinity groups.'" (101)

Each "way" is embedded in a set of social valuations and locations that shape the form an identity takes.

To begin with N-Identities, to be tall, obese, white, black, or intellectually bright represents "states" of being that are not chosen. However, how the state is developed depends on how it is recognized, so based on nature a person is assumed to be and treated as being a certain kind of person. At this point, the other "ways" quickly enter as institutions and affinity groups shape Nature-Identities.

Institutional-Identities are "authorized" by institutional authorities. Being a teacher, for example, means that one occupies a position composed of rights, duties and obligations (see Harre and van Langenhove 1999) sustained formally by school boards, parent associations, teacher unions, legislatures, universities, laws, and accrediting agencies. Each of these institutions brings its weight to bear in determining what sort of person is allowed to teach and in defining what sorts of actions count as teaching. To "teach" outside of established definitions and subject positions is to threaten one's standing as teacher. Gee observes that "I-Identities can be put on a continuum in terms of how actively or passively the occupant of a position fills or fulfills his or her role or duties. . . . [One] can see an I-Identity as either a calling or an imposition" (2000–2001, 103). Thus one may joyfully embrace an institutional identity or resist it (such responses point toward the place of one's core identity in shaping institutional life), and in resisting may form an oppositional identity.

Discourse-Identities are more difficult to describe. The central notion is that an identity may be formed around a "trait" that is recognized in interaction as specific to the individual. Others recognize one as happy, clever, witty, charming, helpful, hard-headed, or perhaps nasty, and they respond accordingly: She is a nasty person, avoid her. He is charming, engage him in conversation. Gee (2000–2001) observes that while "institutions have to rely on discursive practices to construct and sustain I-Identities . . . people can construct and sustain identities through discourse and dialogue (D-Identities) without the overt sanction and support of 'official' institutions that come, on some sense, to 'own' those identities" (103). The result is that persons can be recognized differently within the same institution and be viewed as one kind of person by administrators and another kind of person by one's peers. Finally, Gee notes that D-Identities, like I-Identities, "can be placed on a continuum in terms of how active or passive one is in 'recruiting' them, that is, in terms of how much such identities can be viewed as merely ascribed to a person versus an active achievement or accomplishment of that person" (104). A teacher might actively seek to be recognized as one kind of person and not another, a leader, a child advocate, a defender of academic standards, a pal or, for Barbara, a kind nurturer.

The fourth "way" is what Gee calls the "affinity perspective." A person chooses to join in a "set of distinctive practices" (105) and by joining is recognized as a certain kind of person with specific allegiances and as someone who belongs. "A focus on A-Identities is a focus on distinctive social practices that create and sustain group affiliations, rather than on institutions or discourse/dialogue directly" (105). One chooses one's affinity groups and is chosen, although choice may be institutionally manipulated, as, for example, by shrewd administrators who have a new program to implement or, more generally, by marketing interests of advanced capitalism. Often ways to identity interact: for instance, as Barbara affiliated with and participated in discussions with other teachers in the English department, her institutional-, discourse-, and affinity-based identities become inextricably knotted together.

Like Charles Taylor (1989), and as represented in Chapter 3, Gee argues that recognition is foundational to identity formation, regardless of the perspective: "Human beings must see each other in certain ways and not others if there are to be identities of any sort" (Gee 2000–2001, 109). He asserts that "people can accept, contest, and negotiate identities in terms of whether they will be seen primarily . . . as N-, I-, D-, or A-Identities. What is at issue . . . is always how and by whom a particular identity is to be recognized"

(109). Thus as previously argued, one may actively seek one form of recognition and identity over another, just as institutions and affinity groups promote some identities but not others.

Data Analysis

The data set was analyzed to identify episodes involving recognition and including, where possible, Barbara's response to the forms of recognition given. While any and all forms of human interaction involve recognition, usually identity is submerged and taken for granted. My interest, however, was to identify moments when identity issues surfaced. At such times something—one's sense of self, however vaguely felt—is put at risk or pleasantly confirmed. Such moments are emotionally loaded, since identity and emotion are so intimately intertwined, with identity speaking to one's "investments" (Zembylas 2003, 227) and commitments. Episodes are explored in relationship to the kind of person Barbara sought to be or was becoming (her identity quest) and the kind of person she was pressed or invited to become by those whose recognition was given or desired. In the section that follows, for the sake of clarity, I necessarily depart from the order of Identities set by Gee.

Episodes: Recognition and Response

I-Identity

A very strong institutional message was sent to the mentors, Barbara included, about the value of mentoring when the district administrators decided that mentors would be freed from only a small portion of their daily teaching responsibilities in order to assume this new role. Disappointed, Barbara remarked in an early seminar that the district was "filling a spot and didn't want to pay a full-time teacher." Interns were thought of as cheap labor, which Barbara resented. She also had been misled: "I didn't have as much free time as I was supposed to [for mentoring]." But rather than respond to this strong message, as some of the other mentors did, by minimizing her involvement with the interns, Barbara invested heavily in the mentoring role, hoping that if she did so the value of the work would be acknowledged and appreciated. More importantly, her D-Identity as a competent teacher and strong nurturer disallowed disengagement. Barbara is not a person who does anything halfway. Her interns recognized and respected her commitment to them and their development: "She's a cheer advisor, she's in the PTA, she's like in every part of the school, and so she has had to take extra time [to mentor]. I feel like she's gone way beyond what the requirements have been. I know that [another] mentor has exactly met the requirement. She has been fine, you know, [but] she hasn't done anything more than [the minimum]. I don't think that she's really provided the same [quality] experience that Barbara has for us as English interns."

Recognizing that mentoring was not highly valued, Barbara was guarded around administrators, never sharing a concern or doubt about either of the interns: "I'm always guarded [around administrators]. I'm not going to openly say, 'You know, I'm having these big problems.'" No doubt part of her intent was to portray herself as competent to the administrators, but it also was a reflection of her strong belief in the importance and value of mentoring beginning teachers. Hers was a deep professional commitment and concern. She cared deeply about the quality of teachers and wanted to do her part in improving that quality.

Underscoring the relative institutional unimportance of mentoring, expectations given to mentors by the university and by the school district were, Barbara said, "overall general," and the work went unrecognized. Other teachers thought mentoring must be easy, a hiatus from the real work of schools, teaching children. Some, Barbara said, expressed a "bit of jealousy" that she presumably had been given a break from teaching. Interns were not given a clear sense of what to expect of their role or of their mentors either. As Hannah remarked, "Honestly . . . I had no idea what it meant to have a mentor. . . . I thought it would be somebody that could help me answer questions [but] I wasn't sure if she was going to just straight out hand me lesson plans. I didn't think so." In short, there was no institutionally defined mentor role with which Barbara could identify. Instead, for guidance she recalled her own experience learning to teach and remarked that "I know what makes a good mentor, and I want to be that kind of mentor myself." She identified with her own mentor, or at least with the memories of that relationship, as the basis for taking action.

N-Identity

Barbara's nature (NI) expressed itself in one overwhelming characteristic: She was a "mom," her central teaching metaphor. To think of this in terms of Gee's N-Identity requires a slight stretching of the category, but the manner in which Barbara spoke of herself and of the kind of person she was suggests that she thought of mothering as a state to which she was born, like being tall or smart. Had she not given birth, she still would have been a mother. "Mentoring," she remarked in an interview, "is . . . a mom thing . . . I feel like a mom." On their part, the interns often responded to her like children who needed assistance and comfort, and their demands were constant.

The data set is replete with examples of Barbara comforting the interns, seeking to protect and support them emotionally. Mary described in an e-mail a terribly upsetting confrontation she had had with a student that produced an "emotional meltdown." Mary was badly shaken, tearful. Recognizing the situation, Barbara sat Mary down for a long mother-daughter-like chat that helped Mary "put [the situation] into perspective" and gave her comfort and courage to go on. Afterward, Barbara observed several of Mary's classes, lingered after school so they could talk more, gave her materials to help her prepare for an upcoming lesson, "offered invaluable moral support . . . and allowed [her] to observe in her class." Thinking back on this and other roughly similar situations, Barbara concluded that she had to "deal with that emotional problem before [dealing] with the academic teaching problem. If [the interns] are emotionally shot, it doesn't matter how good their teaching is." Barbara's first responsibility was to love, protect, and support the interns, as she would her own children.

Mary, reflecting in the paired interview on Barbara's success as a mentor, noted that she thought it was because of her "personal qualities . . . the ability to nurture." From Mary's and Hannah's viewpoints, this was Barbara's nature, the kind of person she was. At this point, Barbara's N-Identity blends into her D-Identity.

D-Identity

Being recognized by both Mary and Hannah as a nurturer confirmed Barbara's sense of herself as a person and as a teacher. She actively sought to be recognized in this way—as supportive, nonjudgmental, responsive, generous, "nice" (her word), and kind, and the more she sought recognition of this kind, the more the interns responded to her as just this sort of person. On one particularly busy Friday, Hannah dropped by Barbara's classroom for advice on how to solve a sticky problem with a student. In seminar, Barbara described how she responded to Hannah's request:

> She told me she didn't want to worry me [and then described the situation]. I thought, "Oh, it's good that she doesn't realize . . . how hard [mentoring] is, that it's Friday, [late], and I had to get home. It's good that she doesn't know all of these things, because it would cause more concern on her part. She already was very concerned . . . [Interns] already have enough to worry about. I told her, 'that's all right, that's what I'm supposed to do. This is my job and it's all right that you are here.'"

Barbara actively pursued opportunities to be helpful, believing that it was her responsibility to give assistance, even if the interns were hesitant to ask for it.

"I try," she said in an early seminar, "to do a little more than they ask for because they are afraid to ask . . . I give help that is not asked for all the time. I think I do that probably everywhere." When the interns sought her help, she gave it, never withholding her advice, time, or materials.

Seeking to be recognized in this way brought with it a cost, although Barbara did not complain. From the initial uncertainty over roles and responsibilities, along with hesitation to request assistance, the interns became increasingly demanding, but still Barbara set no boundaries. Writing in an e-mail in late November:

> [Barbara] worked with me in the library as a co-teacher while the students worked for days on research. She was so awesome! I have thirty-two rambunctious students in that period, and I literally would *not* have made it without her. . . . Sometimes one teacher isn't enough. She knew this and sacrificed an hour and twenty minutes every other day last week to help me get through the library workdays for research. That's a huge sacrifice. A fourth of her day! Yet she offered it willingly. I didn't even have to ask.

Mostly the interns appreciated Barbara's efforts, although occasionally they complained in their e-mails (not to Barbara) that she was not doing enough: "There are lots of times when before school where I need like scissors or something or just a last-minute thing, or even after school . . . I often feel like I have no help to do it. . . . [But it's really my] fault."

Within the school, Barbara had a long established D-Identity as an exceptional teacher, probably, as Mary remarked, "the most popular English teacher [in the school]. She's really cool." Barbara strove to maintain that identity and be seen as competent, but she sometimes struggled with feelings of inadequacy. For example, in late January she invited one of the interns to observe her teaching. "I was nervous. I thought, this is stupid. Why are you nervous? You know this girl. You talk to her every day, and there's nothing to be scared about." Still, she worried about the intern's judgment, even as she knew the intern thought her to be an extraordinary teacher. Similarly, she worried how other faculty members in the school viewed her and her work as a mentor. She wanted to be recognized as competent within this role and emerging identity as well. Standing at the copy machine, waiting to make copies, a colleague remarked that she must be enjoying the break from teaching. This comment upset her: "I wanted to smack him," she said.

> I just feel like there sometimes [is an] attitude of teachers that being a mentor is easy. I get the feeling that people think you're getting time off. I just wish that [they would] respect [me]. I do a good job . . . I hope that the feeling in our building has been that those two English interns did a good job this year.

She fretted over what other teachers were thinking and saying about her and her interns. The success of the interns became crucial to her sense of self as competent. If they failed, she said in seminar, "It would be, 'Wow, Barbara must not know what she is doing.' I was concerned that people would think I wasn't doing my job and I wanted to be doing my job, you know." Recognition of the intern's competence doubled as recognition of Barbara's ability, as validation of her D-Identity as competent and nurturing.

A-Identity

Barbara sought affiliation with other teachers, the university supervisors, other mentors, and the interns. Episodes related to each will be considered in turn.

Other teachers. It is in part because teaching and being a teacher is so central to the kind of person Barbara is and seeks to be that she found the remarks made at the copy machine so disturbing. The comments suggest not only that her colleague knew little about the demands of mentoring but, more importantly, that he thought of Barbara as having moved in some respects outside of the group of teachers. She was recognized as different, and this disturbed Barbara, who was and remained first and foremost a teacher. In frustration, Barbara remarked in an early mentor seminar meeting, "I don't think there is anybody [in the school] who really knows or understands what I am trying to do or what is taking place. I really think that's true." She felt outside of her primary affinity group, even as she thought of herself as still belonging.

Affiliations and identifications may clash. The teacher and mentor roles sometimes tugged at Barbara from opposite directions, indicating conflicting memberships (Gee 1996), and she had to make a choice. For example, Mary came to her one afternoon and explained that she was a little behind in finishing the research unit. She wondered if she could move the due date for the final project back a week. "At first," Barbara wrote in her intern log, "I did not think this change was okay. We had gone over a time frame and schedule for teaching research. All juniors [are on the same schedule]. My concern was more that the department would be upset with Mary not sticking with the schedule. And yes, that would reflect [negatively] on the [interns] and [on] me. Then I stepped back for a moment and realized that my concern should be about students not appearances. For students, learning the process and having time to complete a rough draft and final draft was more important than appearances. So together we went over [Mary's] time frame again and decided that her papers would be due the week after the end of the term." Barbara was right, other teachers were unhappy with the decision. The approval of her teacher affiliation group had been sacrificed to her teacher educator responsibilities.

University supervisors. Early in the school year Barbara e-mailed both of her interns' supervisors, asking, "Will you contact me the next time you come [to school] and we can talk?" Three weeks later, one of the supervisors responded and told Barbara when she would be visiting the school and observing the intern. Barbara suggested that they observe a class together, then meet to talk. "It was wonderful. Good discussion. She thought the same things [about the lesson]. . . . We had a three-way conversation that was very good. I felt like we were sharing ideas." Afterward, Barbara felt confirmed ("It was confirming"), that what she was doing as a school-based teacher educator was appropriate and valued by the university-based teacher educators. She then commented that she wished she had "contacted [the supervisors] from the very beginning. I wish I would have known to do that quickly. But I was afraid. . . . What if we're having problems that I don't know [about, and the supervisors] are trying some things different from [what I do with the interns]?"

Following this initial meeting, Barbara desired additional interaction with the supervisors, thinking that they could work most effectively with the interns as a team of teacher educators. Based on the initial meeting, she was optimistic: "Our philosophies matched very well, and the things that I was concerned with were the same things for the university supervisor. We were almost right on." Despite her request, no additional meetings took place, although several e-mails were exchanged within which they discussed each intern's development. By late January, Barbara concluded that her work as a mentor, as well as the work of the supervisors, was different, and she accepted that they would not be working closely together:

> The world of the supervisor is to evaluate. I realize that that's not the job description but that's the feeling I've gotten. . . . Their job is to evaluate. I feel like my job as a mentor is to help them, support them, be their advocate, help them with whatever they need. I don't think they feel the pressure when I'm there because I have made it very clear that I am only there to help them. . . . Yeah, I'm going to write them an evaluation, but that's not [my central] role.

She was pleased that she was not a supervisor, even though she was disappointed that she would not be part of an ongoing conversation about teaching and learning to teach with the supervisors. The affiliation she desired had been rebuffed, though she was able to reconcile the situation.

Other mentors. There was one other intern mentor in the school, Sally, a math teacher. Barbara and Sally did not know one another well, but their practice as mentors brought them together. For Barbara, this connection was extremely important, as she commented in seminar: "Having [another mentor in the building helps]. I needed emotional support, and it's nice to have her [nearby]. I have come to her a lot: 'What's going on with you?' 'What's happening?' 'What should I do?' It's been nice to have emotional support [from] someone else who is mentoring." The seminar provided a means for Barbara, Sally, and the other mentors to meet and chat about their work. Each mentor valued the seminar, and although friendships formed or were strengthened, it met too infrequently to become an affinity group. Of this, more will be said shortly. Most of the mentors, Barbara included, felt they were on their own as mentors.

Interns. A tight bond formed between Barbara, Mary, and Hannah. They belonged to each other, but in very different ways, and how they experienced their relationship differed radically. As noted, for Barbara the interns often seemed like children. She loved them, identified deeply with their successes and failures, and took how they responded to her as constitutive of the kind of person she was. Their success was also hers. Similarly, the interns saw themselves in Barbara's eyes and in her actions. Each looked to the other for recognition. Thus Barbara was uneasy about having Mary observe her teaching, as mentioned earlier. But the interns did not think of themselves as children. In an interview, Hannah remarked, "I felt from the beginning comfortable with Barbara, that she was a colleague. I didn't feel like that with my university supervisor." In an e-mail, she characterized their relationship in more intimate terms: "I really love my mentor. We have become friends, and I feel like I can go to her for help, that she will help me in a practical and kind way." In the paired interview, Hannah said that "Barbara makes me feel like I'm a good teacher and an equal. I never feel like, well, you know, 'you're only an intern.'" Mary did not feel quite so close to Barbara, which troubled Barbara. "I just feel Hannah got a better end of the deal because [we had more time together]. With Mary, we never had a shared prep period." Although scheduling difficulties prevented development of the kind of relationship with Mary that formed with Hannah, Mary was nevertheless thrilled with their relationship: "It exceeded my expectations. . . . What [Barbara] did was great!"

That Hannah could think of herself as a friend, colleague, and equal to Barbara is quite remarkable. If they were friends, it was a decidedly one-sided friendship: Barbara giving, Hannah mostly taking. They were colleagues only in a very loose sense of the term, although being recognized by one another as teachers was of great importance to Barbara and to the interns and central to their Affiliation-Identities and sense of belonging. However, in no strong sense were they equals, as Mary noted when she troubled over the realization that had Barbara been teaching her classes, the students likely would have performed better. Barbara helped the interns feel valued, cared for, and competent. Their views of Barbara appear distorted but turned just as Barbara wanted them to be: "[Interns] have no idea what [mentors] do for them, they don't know what you are doing." As noted earlier—and acting like a parent—she did not want nor need them to know how difficult it is to mentor. Protecting them from this knowledge was important to Barbara, part of her identity; protecting them from it did not prevent them from recognizing her as she wanted to be recognized, as a competent nurturer. For that they did not need to know what transpired backstage.

Protecting the interns in this way produced some surprising consequences. For one, Barbara struggled mightily with how to give feedback and what sort of feedback to give, fearing that if she was critical of some aspect of their performance her relationship with the interns would deteriorate: "I don't want to offend them, [make it] so they won't come to me. But I want to make them better teachers. Relationships are [so] important, way too important [to risk]." In saying this, she echoes a view widely held by teachers: Teaching is all about relationships (Oberski, Ford, Higgins, and Fisher 1999). Had the interns stopped seeking her assistance, she would have lost recognition, and her quest for a mentoring identity would have been badly sidetracked. Yet sometimes Barbara concluded she had to be critical of the interns because, as she said, "I have to protect the students. They deserve good teachers." Once again we see how affiliations and identities can pull against one another: Barbara the protective and nurturing mentor and Barbara the teacher. As a mentor, Barbara's greatest joy came when the interns phoned to share a positive event or outcome, like her own children would do. "They say, 'This kid is finally doing his homework. Remember, the one that I've been having so much trouble with.'" Then they would celebrate together, having been confirmed as the sorts of people they wanted to be: the interns by their students and Barbara by the interns.

Making Sense of the Data

Barbara wanted to be recognized not only as a competent teacher—a view supported by her selection by the university and the school administrations as a mentor—but also as a competent mentor and educator of beginning teachers. The recognition she sought was not limited to competence, however. Barbara wanted to be recognized as the kind of teacher and mentor who is nurturing and caring. Recognition of this professional identity came from the interns and from Sally, her mathematics colleague who also was serving as a mentor. Emphatically, she did not recognize herself in the comments made by her colleague at the copy machine—as a teacher who took breaks from teaching and shirked her duty. She wanted recognition by the university supervisors as a fellow teacher educator, but she had been turned away after an initial confirming glance. From the university supervisors, Barbara wanted to know if her work with the interns was satisfactory; apparently it was, since nothing was said to the contrary, so she continued as before. She was open to and desirous of learning more about teacher education and mentoring from the supervisors, but she was not invited into such a conversation. As a mentor, Barbara did not feel competent, but, consistent with her D-Identity as a teacher, she wanted to be: "As far as I'm concerned, I'm not competent, or not as much as I would like to be." In seminar, she further stated:

> I don't know about the rest of you, but I can promise you that every day something goes far beyond my reach. Every day [the interns] bring something to me that's interesting and [that] I've never seen before. I have a lot of experience to share, [but] I can't share expertise I don't have.

Her attempts at engagement were simply ignored, but surely not for any malicious reason on the part of the supervisors, who were very busy people and who likely did not include working with mentors as part of their responsibilities, I-Identity or D-Identity, a point noted by Koster, Korthagen, and Wubbels (1998) as a serious failure of university-based teacher educators. Barbara's role was to be strictly limited to working with the interns, alone, even though formally she represented the interests of teacher education and the university within the school. Given this situation, Barbara found recognition where she could and hoped that the quality of her service as a mentor would at some point be understood and appreciated.

That mentoring was little valued in Barbara's school is not unusual. Often it is not highly valued by the university either (Zeichner 2002). Being mostly abandoned by the university and given no guidance from building administrators, she was left alone to develop a mentoring relationship with the interns. Given her N- and D-Identities, it is not surprising that the relationship represented, as Darling (2001) describes, the values and commitments of a "community of compassion" and not of inquiry. "A community may support individual flourishing 'at least in the sense of offering protection,' but it is not the agent of, or catalyst for, growth. At best, community is the backdrop that makes it possible for students (read interns) to pursue learning; although learning goes on alongside the community, it is not generated by it. The purpose of the community is defined by its role as a support group, not by the learning that is taking place" (12). In contrast, a "community of inquiry" involves individuals learning to respectfully disagree, "argue their positions with conviction, and make judgements about the worth and truth of others' claims," just the sorts of actions that Barbara feared would jeopardize her relationship with the interns. An individual's duty in a community of inquirers, in contrast to a benevolent community of compassion, "is to the inquirers, but also to the inquiry and to uphold the standards of inquiry" (16). It is, in short, to be thoughtfully and helpfully critical and to model inquiry (Day 1999).

Barbara's N- and D-Identities as teacher shaped the role she would perform as mentor: to create a community of compassion as befitting a nurturer—a mother. An alternative vision and identity could only have emerged had she been given access to and desired membership in affinity groups based on a different set of practices, such as inquiry, or if there had been clearly established and contrary institutional expectations for mentoring and for the interns, which there were not. Lacking these may be one reason that, as Martin (1997) has argued, mentor practices frequently resemble teaching practices: Teachers do what they know and mentor as they teach. In effect, mentor identities are subsumed under teacher identities (Jones and Straker 2006; Young, Bullough, Draper, Smith, and Erickson 2005).

Potentially the mentor seminar could have developed into an affinity group, organized around the practice of mentoring, a group that would have supported formation of a strong professional persona separate from teaching and teaching affinity groups and closely related to teacher education and other teacher educators. It did not. Largely because of the district's decision to minimize the time set aside for mentoring, meetings were too infrequent. But more importantly, as a seminar leader I did not see grappling with questions of identity formation and recognition as a mentor to be seminar tasks, yet they could and should have been. Only later did this issue emerge as important, only when data analysis was well underway.

To achieve identity as a mentor and school-based teacher educator requires what Williams, Prestage, and Bedward (2001) call "structural collaboration" (260), arrangements that support sustained interaction about teaching and that have the potential to produce, over time, collegial collaboration and subject positions supportive of collaboration. To this end, Barbara and the other mentors needed to be joined in seminar by the university supervisors where they could together develop a discourse and set of relationships, including both the practice of teacher education and the assignment of facilitating beginning teacher development, distinct from other practices, duties, and obligations. That Barbara longed for such interaction and affiliation is evident not only in her disappointment with not working more closely with the supervisors but also in her expression of appreciation for Sally's support and advice.

Frequently one reads of programs that aim at "training" mentors, which, no doubt, have a valuable place in teacher induction and education. But a more important purpose of mentoring programs, at least for mentors like Barbara, as Korthagen (2004) suggests, is educational. It is also relational, about belonging: not just a matter of developing specific skills but of helping those who work in schools with beginning teachers to (re)conceive of themselves as mentors and of mentoring as distinct from teaching. This is an important task

for university-based teacher educators to embrace (Koster et al. 1998). Ultimately the challenge, as Zeichner (2002) states, is to "[integrate] clinical faculty and staff into the mainstream of programs" (63) and, in this way, to
develop new forms of affiliation and identity that will better serve beginning
teachers and offer opportunities for those who mentor to expand and enrich
their senses of self as teacher educators. How to do this requires the careful
and systematic attention of university-based teacher educators for whom
questions of identity formation are necessarily of growing importance.

CHAPTER 5

Life on the Borderlands:
Action Research and Clinical Teacher
Education Faculty (2004)

with Roni Jo Draper,
Leigh K. Smith, and Janet R. Young

Introduction

Shifting from classroom teaching to teacher education new clinical faculty move from one culture to another with very different status and symbol systems. Uncertainty follows as they seek to find place in and bridge two institutions while not fully meeting "the traditional expectations" of either (Cornbleth and Ellsworth 1994, 61). As "boundary spanners" (Sandholtz and Finan 1998, 24), they often feel they do not fully belong to either world. Many tenure-track faculty fear the "clinicalization of teacher education," even as program dependence on clinical faculty grows (Bullough, Hobbs, Kauchak, Crow, and Stokes 1997). Recognizing these tensions but believing clinical faculty are crucial players essential to improving teacher education, Sandholtz and Finan (1998) make the now-oft-heard plea: Clinical faculty must be moved from the "borderlands" and into "a new institutional coalition where the boundaries between the practitioners and the professors are blurred, where equal partners are working together in a mutually beneficial relationship, and where their collaborative work is recognized and rewarded" (24–25).

The Study

Following analysis of a series of interviews conducted with clinical faculty and tenure-line faculty, each of these issues emerged as serious considerations for the teacher education program at Brigham Young University. This chapter reports on an action research seminar that was organized in the hope of strengthening the sense of belonging of clinical faculty members, softening the boundaries separating them from tenure-track faculty, increasing clinical faculty members' understanding of research, and expanding their conception of themselves, their identities, as teacher educators. There is, of course, a two-way challenge. For these aims to be achieved, tenure-line faculty also would need to change: "Academics must acknowledge teachers as theorists and interact with them as such if they are to have significant influence in the field" (Beck and Kosnik 2001, 226).

The decision to offer an action research seminar that would involve both clinical and tenure-track faculty was based upon a number of considerations. Action research has been shown to be a means for fostering "collaboration and professional development" and for "changing views of research" (Burbank and Kauchak 2003, 511–12). There is a good deal of research supporting the conclusion that collaboration among teacher researchers in learning communities that build knowledge can change "relationships which, in turn, affect teaching practice and educational change" (Christiansen, Goulet, Krentz, and Maeers 1997, xvi). For over a decade, collaborative research has been suggested as perhaps the most promising means for encouraging crossing the boundaries separating school and university. However, this aim has proven to be extremely difficult to realize, in part because the interests of university researchers in programmatic research and the problems that energize and capture the imagination of practitioners so seldom seem to converge (Winitzky, Stoddart, and O'Keefe 1992). On their part, "Teachers often see little relevance in studies that answer questions they do not ask and reports that use terminology they do not understand. As a result, the gap between research and practice widens" (Knight, Wiseman, and Cooner 2000, 27). There are parallel and equally troubling tensions within university faculties between clinical and tenure-line faculty members. In both situations, lack of trust looms large. It is these tensions that concern us and that we hoped a seminar would help meliorate.

Background

Since 1984, the College of Education (now the McKay School of Education) has been involved in a partnership with five school districts. An original member of the National Network for Educational Renewal (Goodlad 1994), the school and the districts share "governance, resources, and responsibilities" (Osguthorpe, Harris, Harris, and Black 1995, 283) for teacher education as they seek "simultaneous renewal" (Goodlad 1994). As the partnership has evolved and as new responsibilities have been accepted, traditional roles have necessarily changed. A variety of clinical faculty roles has been developed: (1) Given the large size and complexity of the program, a liaison position has been created. Liaisons are employed by the university from among the outstanding teachers in a district to coordinate teacher education efforts within that district. Liaisons teach courses, work intimately in program and course design, and participate on various university and district committees. Working closely with departmental leadership, they help oversee the program; (2) Clinical faculty associates (CFAs), of which there are thirteen, work closely with the liaisons. The CFAs are outstanding teachers who are hired by the university with the support of the school districts for two- or three-year appointments. During this time, the CFAs may pursue graduate education if they wish. They work in district teams and are responsible for student teacher supervision, some teaching, and coordinating with cooperating teachers. They participate in a variety of seminars designed to help them understand and successfully perform in their varied responsibilities; (3) Partnership facilitators mentor interns (see Chapter 4). Interns complete all but the student teaching portion of the preservice teacher education program and, receiving half salary and full benefits, take the place of an in-service teacher. In this way, the assignment of two interns to a school frees a teacher, a partnership facilitator, who then mentors the interns and participates in a variety of professional activities typically not available to teachers.

The three clusters of clinical faculty differ dramatically in how they relate to the university and connect with one another. The liaisons meet frequently and identify with one another and with department and district leadership and have considerable power, influence, and autonomy. The partnership facilitators generally maintain close affiliation with the school faculty. Their responsibilities are reasonably clear and set. In contrast, the CFAs are torn between multiple masters. Unlike when they taught in the public schools, CFAs are not masters of their own workplaces. Like university supervisors, generally they face the difficulty of negotiating the "student teaching triad" from an outsider's position, as one who faces a "strong coalition between [cooperating teachers] and [student teachers]" (Veal and Rikard 1998, 113). They are visitors to the schools, and since their appointment is for two or three years, in some respects they are just passing through the university as well. While they meet frequently with the district liaison to whom they directly report, they also meet monthly with a second liaison who is responsible for coordinating all CFA work. In addition, they meet with individual tenure-track faculty who have responsibility for specific course offerings.

Action Research Seminar

The seminar was organized in this way: In the CFA orientation meeting held during the late spring of the year prior to the beginning of the study, the liaison responsible for coordinating CFA work outlined the plan for the next year, that an opportunity would be provided to participate in an action research seminar and to work with a few tenure-line faculty members. Several weeks before the first seminar meeting, two reviews of recent developments in teacher education that support the value of teachers studying their practice were distributed to the CFAs, along with a statement of seminar purpose and a request that participants come ready to discuss the readings at the first meeting, September 13. At the opening seminar, an overview of action research was presented, and additional readings on action research, including data gathering, were distributed for discussion in the second meeting. The readings were chosen to represent a range of views of action research, including both practical and emancipatory action research. The specific model of action research chosen to guide the work of the seminar was drawn from *The Action Research Planner* (Kemmis and McTaggert 1988) and included emphasis on the "action research spiral": plan, reflect, act, observe, revise.

Based upon prior conversations with the department chair, who explained that part of the CFA role definition was participation in program evaluation and improvement efforts, I understood that all CFAs would participate in the seminar. This understanding proved to be a source of serious confusion. Four tenure-track university teacher education faculty members were invited to participate in the seminar and to study it. These were faculty members who I thought would be supportive of the project and valuable resources for the CFAs as they conducted their studies. The expectation was that the tenure-line faculty would support the CFA projects and not lead or direct them.

Data Gathering and Analysis: The Plan

Seminar meetings were scheduled monthly, except at the beginning of the year, when it was necessary to meet more often. During the seminar, the tenure-line faculty planned to take notes of what transpired. The intention was to record impressions and describe important events. After each seminar the tenure-line faculty and I would meet to discuss what transpired. Based upon these conversations, plans would be made for subsequent seminars and adjustments made. Once the CFAs had a basic knowledge of action research, the intention was for time in the early seminars to be spent identifying possible topics of interest around which, eventually, research teams would form. Topics would be discussed and then refined. Through conferences with individual teams and via e-mail, adjustments would be made until each team had a clear, although an evolving, sense of direction. Additional team conferences would follow, sometimes on campus, sometimes at schools. While I would meet most frequently with the teams, the other participating tenure-track faculty members also would meet with them outside of the seminar and as invited. Each would be available to lend assistance. Once teams began their studies, the monthly seminars would become opportunities for reporting progress and exploring problems and making adjustments. After the first seminar, other sessions would be tape-recorded and the tapes transcribed. At the end of the year and following the same protocol, each CFA would be interviewed by one of the participating tenure-track faculty members about the seminar, but not by me. The notes and transcribed interviews would be analyzed in two ways, first to get the story of the seminar and then to identify themes, or what Egon Guba (1978) called "recurring regularities" (53). The story that follows highlights the tensions and issues that arose once we began.

Seminar Story

September 13 was the first seminar meeting. Regularly scheduled CFA meetings were held every second Thursday. The decision was made that the time would be divided and the second half of the meeting, about an hour and a half, would become the action research seminar. I sat in on most of the first half of the first meeting to learn the CFAs' names. When the second half of the meeting began, I reviewed the names and introductions followed. A brief revisit of the CFA role and responsibilities followed, including consideration of the possible ways in which CFAs might pursue research. A brief overview was presented of the nature of theory in teacher education and teacher education research was presented. Then the idea and practice of action research was introduced. Finally, an invitation was extended to become involved in action research with the support of the tenure-track faculty members in attendance. A few articles on action research were passed out. The CFAs were told to read them prior to the next meeting to gain a better sense of what sort of studies might be conducted and to underscore the value of working together on topics of mutual interest. These articles would be the point of departure for the next meeting.

At the conclusion of the seminar, I was left puzzled by the muted reaction of most of the CFAs. Some seemed surprised by the expectation that they study their work or in other ways participate in research. Others were obviously distrustful. The job description of the CFAs included two statements that lent institutional legitimacy to the decision to conduct an action research seminar: "Develop a program for personal professional development" and "Assist the District Liaison in conducting inquiry and research projects" (Role Description, Clinical Faculty Associates, n.d.). Based upon this job description and assurances of the department chair, I naively assumed that the CFAs already expected to participate in research of some kind and, in this belief, anticipated uncertainty about but not resistance to the idea of conducting action research. There was much unanticipated confusion, even when discussing the CFA role. Later this issue became very important to two of the CFA action research projects.

Recognizing the confusion and sensing significant resistance to the idea of conducting research on their own practice—a difficulty anticipated in the work of Goodson (1994)—prior to the second meeting plans were made to present an alternative project that would focus on the study of a program issue and be directed more like a traditional research project. Thus during the second seminar meeting, CFAs would have a choice of either engaging in an action research project or participating in some fashion with me and other participating tenure-track faculty in a planned study.

The October 11 seminar began with a recap of the previous meeting. The option of participating in an alternative study was presented, and discussion began. The group was tense. Heads hung low, but nothing was said. Thinking that a discussion of the articles would clarify confusion about what was involved in conducting an action research project, I invited questions or comments about the readings. Soon it became apparent that half of the group had not done the reading. Complaints were expressed about being and feeling "overwhelmed." "I thought participation in the seminar was optional," one said, "and so I didn't do the reading. Perhaps I misunderstood." To this comment I responded, but "[I understood that] your role includes participation in some sort of research." We turn to one set of observation notes:

> [The CFAs said] their heavy schedules and . . . their responsibilities in supervision and teaching were simply overwhelming. There was an openly belligerent tone to K's challenge to Bob and to the idea that research should be included in the set of expectations of the CFAs. Others from [the same school district] were sympathetic. D was vocal about how extensively she felt she needed to support the interns and student teachers she supervises, and what a time-intensive job being a CFA was. She seemed to feel it was her job to "save" the struggling interns in her district—sometimes spending the whole day with one in order to model best practice and to plan with the intern to solve management or other problems. K talked about how he was willing to do what needed to be done, but that his last years had exacted such a toll on his family life that he would need to let go of something else if this new role were to be added to his load. . . . J seemed to be the only one who had much of a sense of what it would be like to do action research, and she seemed willing and maybe even eager to engage in it.

I tried to turn the discussion to ways in which action research and working in teams might actually help improve the situation. K, who had not done the reading, would have none of it, and he continued to press his complaint that he was overworked and underappreciated. The claims were undoubtedly legitimate, but in themselves represented a deep misunderstanding of the role of the CFAs as conceived by the department leadership who wrote the job description. In the hands of these CFAs the role had expanded beyond what was intended or perhaps humanly possible. Sensing a crisis, I turned the discussion away from K and toward others I thought might have a different view or understanding. Two of those who had done the reading, including J, remarked that they were interested in conducting action research projects, even though they were a bit uncertain about how to proceed. They had issues and wanted to study them. At this slight sign of a turn in the discussion, K, sitting red-faced and fuming, exploded (observation notes): "I feel like you are ignoring me," he charged. "You are right, I am, I've heard what you have to say." A sharp exchange followed, which had three effects: K was silenced; I was deeply troubled and puzzled about what to do next; and the remaining CFAs were stunned. I then said, "We need a break," and I excused from the meeting those who really did not want to or felt they could not be part of an action research project. K left, and so did B. It was evident that only two of the CFAs had any knowledge of action research and that the suggestion the CFAs become involved in it was seen as unreasonable, especially since so few had done the reading. After the break, I apologized for getting upset and suggested that the group stand back for a moment, take a deep breath, and consider the benefits that an action research project might have for their work.

The impact of the confrontation with K lingered. As one CFA remarked in an interview at year's end, "It took me a while to warm up again after the K issue. I had felt connected with K, as we all had felt connected with each other, and that incident in the meeting was very disconcerting for me, because I didn't know [Bob] at all. I only knew K." After this meeting, I wondered if the seminar could be salvaged, however, I found hope in the willingness of the group to meet off cycle, October 22, to consider the readings and to determine if, in fact, a project was worth doing. The lesson of the blowup with K was not lost on me, although it came a bit late. Referring to what they call "holistic approaches" to action research, Leitch and Day (2000) argue that "emotions are key . . . due to the recognition that emotions across the range are such powerful determinants of thinking processes . . . and that turbulent emotions, whether past or present, limit thinking . . . and encourage responses based on restrictive patterns of behaving" (179).

Prior to the October 22 meeting, K and I met. K shared that part of his frustration was due to serious and very stressful personal problems in his family. Apologies on both sides followed, and K withdrew from participation. I also met with B, who was told that it was his decision whether or not to participate, and that he would be welcome to rejoin the seminar if he wished. He did so and became a very active participant. Greater sensitivity to the pressures the CFAs felt resulted in more time being made available within the seminars to address concerns and to pacing the work so as not to overwhelm the participants. But the conflict with K points to a set of issues well beyond family problems, issues to which I will shortly turn.

The CFAs (except K) came to the October 22 seminar prepared to discuss each reading. Despite having done the reading, uncertainty was high (from the observation notes): "At the beginning of the meeting (as in previous meetings), the same general feeling of fear or uncertainty about their roles as researchers was strong. They resisted the idea and were both fearful of a process they didn't understand, as well as reluctant to take on more work." It quickly became obvious that I needed to backtrack and address some basic questions. As one of the CFAs remarked, "We have no schema for this [action research]." On the whole, they had difficulty thinking of themselves as researchers and did not think of their own experience as legitimate sources of data. When they thought of research, they thought of number counting and statistics. I asked, "What counts as data? What is data?" Other questions followed: "Who can help us gather data useful for thinking about our practice?" "Once we have some data, what do we do with it, how can we make sense of it?" They were uncertain about what a good question to study might be. They did not think of posing questions of their own practice and of attempting to resolve practical problems as even related to research. In this meeting I tossed out some possible questions for study that I thought might be of interest. (Observation notes): "As the meeting progresses, CFAs begin to add more and more to the conversation—begin to smile and appear to be more enthusiastic about the process of gathering data and of finding questions that they are mutually interested in answering." From a second set of observation notes written by another observer: "The tension in the room began to fade and the CFAs gradually began to contribute to the discussion until at the end of the meeting they expressed feelings of relief—that this was something they could do and that it was something they could do as a group with common concerns and questions. . . . As they broke into small groups, conversations were animated and interested, especially as they established questions [for possible topics of study]." The transformation was amazing. The meeting ended with the CFAs eagerly working in teams and beginning to settle on possible questions for study. Plans were made for the groups to contact me before the next seminar with the questions they thought they would study, which required that the CFAs communicate with one another in between meetings and with tenure-line faculty members. They also were told that they should expect their initial questions to evolve as the studies evolved, which they did.

Prior to the November 8 meeting, teams met and e-mailed draft questions to me. I responded with detailed feedback. The CFAs' tendency was to state a question of such scope that to attack it would take not only significant resources but also time well beyond what was available. The challenge for me was to help reign in the CFAs' ambition while still enabling them to frame an engaging problem. During the November 8 meeting, each team, which initially formed around school district assignments (participants worked in schools within the same school district), shared a preliminary problem statement with the entire group. These included studies of why some teacher education students chose internships in urban schools, of CFA supervision practices, of teacher education expectations of CFAs, of the relationships between CFAs and partnership facilitators, and of the value of student teacher seminars. Each topic was explored by the entire group, possible data sources and potential problems with the study were discussed, and possible benefits were identified. Energy was high. Preliminary data gathering soon began, which included, for some, designing surveys.

The spirit of the December 14 meeting is nicely captured in the observation notes by one event: "B (who had earlier withdrawn from the seminar but returned) made an interesting statement almost at the end. . . . He sort of leaned back in his chair and said that he thought the results of their [preliminary] survey showed that they were just on the surface of some really important things. I took [this] to mean that he had just caught a glimpse of the power of the process of being systematic about data collection and analysis. Perhaps he meant that there were more questions that had been sparked by [the survey], and he was just coming to see how research is a self-extending activity. The group brainstormed new ideas and extensions of what they had already done, and as they recognized that they needed to clarify a new level of questions before they went forward into their next step in data gathering." There was still uncertainty, but there also were signs of growing confidence among each of the CFAs—something good was afoot. Trust was building.

Dramatic changes took place between the December 14 and January 10 meetings. These changes were evidenced in a shift of the communication pattern within the seminar. Formerly, most talk had gone through me, but not at this or subsequent meetings. The CFAs spoke directly to one another. By the January meeting, five action research teams were established and functioning well. Study topics were relatively firm, although, in the words of one CFA, some "tweaking" took place, and data gathering was underway. Two teams developed surveys that were piloted. At the January meeting, the team studying the quality of communication between CFAs and partnership facilitators reported the initial results of their survey, which proved to be a source of growing confidence as well as a means for beginning to rethink one aspect of the program, the intern and student teacher seminar. This team discovered that in the eyes of the facilitators, they were doing some very good work, which was a welcome discovery, particularly for the two new CFAs on the team who were uncertain they were performing adequately in their roles. The team studying why some beginning teachers opted for urban internships reported data from an instrument designed to identify individuals "called" to teaching. What they discovered was that nearly all of the urban interns felt called to teach, but they wondered if this finding was unique, and they began to make plans to gather similar data from individuals who chose nonurban internships. Results from posing this question would lead to a fundamental shift in the project.

I began the February 14 seminar, which was tape-recorded, with a question: "It's really time for us to take stock. . . . You've been doing something that we call action research. What distinguishes what you have been doing from traditional research?" Several CFAs spoke: "We are looking at ourselves, our own practices as opposed to watching someone else's." "We change as we go—like if we see that, 'Oh, this isn't really working out,' maybe my question [needs] tweaking." "You are supporting us. It's not, 'We are helping you with your research,' you're helping us with ours." A second question followed, one designed to broaden the CFAs' perspectives about action research and the value of other more traditional forms of research: "Is there a place in action research [for] other literature . . . research literature?" A lively discussion followed. With my help, the team that focused on urban education was reading studies related to teacher calling and urban schools, which influenced the team's thinking. I commented, "It seems to me that some of you are at the point where getting into the [wider] literature makes a lot of sense, and I want to encourage that movement and connection. When you look at traditional research, typically what [you find] is that there will be a body of literature, and you [as researcher] stand in the middle of it. The question [that drives your study] actually comes out of the body of literature, because you kind of live it and you have some questions that [perplex you]. . . . I suggest that that's where several of you are. You have a question, you have a problem, you have worked it through, you have gathered some data, and I urge you to think about situating that question now in a wider conversation."

The discussion that followed indicates that I had pushed the CFAs to the edge of their comfort zones. Tensions rose as I suggested that they consider sharing the results of their studies with the wider faculty. Several suggested that no one on the faculty would be interested: "Sometimes I have felt like, and I will put it just like I [feel], like the illegitimate child [here]." Others disagreed: "I feel that the professors that I work for view me as a credible person." All were hesitant to share: "If our project developed into something we feel proud to present, then maybe we will step forward and say, 'Yep, I'll want to share this.' But [right now], it's like (laughing), I want to do this?!" I suggested that we would return to this question in the near future. Team reports followed, during which time I encouraged each team to consider additional data sources and alternative interpretations of the data presented.

This proved to be a pivotal meeting. Gradually, the CFAs were beginning to come to terms with a wider purpose for the group, yet tensions remained. The fear of sharing persisted. Darling (2001) sheds some light on what transpired in this particular seminar session. She describes how a "reform initiative explicitly founded on the concept of a community of inquiry for teacher education" collided with the conception of community embraced by preservice teachers (7). For the beginning teachers in Darling's study, the "purpose of the community [was] defined by its role as a support group, not by the learning that is taking place" (12). Darling suggests that these represent two different types of communities and call forth different virtues. "Inquiry . . . requires the virtues of conscientiousness, including such virtues as honesty and truthfulness. In a community of inquiry, people must learn to disagree . . . argue their own positions with conviction, and make judgements about the worth of the truth of others' claims. Their duty is to the inquirers, but also to the inquiry and to upholding the standards of inquiry. . . . Teacher educators have a responsibility to model the virtues necessary for inquiry and to do our best to persuade students of their value" (16). In contrast, a "community of compassion" calls for "the virtues of benevolence, and the virtues of conscientiousness" (15).

I pushed the values of inquiry and while attempting to be supportive pressed for deeper understanding, which included, as I articulated in the seminar, the need to connect the projects to a wider research literature and to share the results of the studies, to open them to discussion and possible criticism. At this point in the evolution of the seminar, these aims were threatening, although the evidence suggests that confidence in me and in the four participating tenure-track faculty was growing. On the whole, the CFAs sought and gave support but resisted challenging or questioning one another. The expectation of support as the main function of the seminar may help explain a portion of the deep negative reaction to my confrontation of K. At times, the "virtues of conscientiousness . . . need to take precedence over virtues of benevolence" (Darling 2001, 16).

Between this meeting and the next, I met with and corresponded through e-mail with each of the teams attempting to facilitate the studies. I responded to requests but did not initiate them. Teams also met with the other tenure-track faculty to discuss their projects and obtain assistance as needed. With some encouragement, eventually three of the five teams requested help locating published research related to their studies. A fourth group conducted its own literature review. Only one group chose not to delve into what others had to say about its topic.

Four of the projects were presented during the April 18 meeting. Two made PowerPoint presentations of the data gathered and orally shared interpretations of the data. A third created a handbook designed for use by future CFAs in the hope of assisting them to better understand the nature of their role and responsibilities. A fourth, the urban teacher education team, spoke from a rough draft of an article it planned to submit for review when completed. A fifth, a study of CFA supervision practices, would be presented in the May meeting but had completed data gathering. With each presentation, I urged the groups to theorize, to push their interpretations, and to consider the meaning of the findings for different groups, student teachers, mentor teachers, future CFAs, teacher education admissions committees, and their own practice. In addition, I took the opportunity to remind the CFAs of the way in which action research cycles, so that new questions emerge for exploration along the way, and I suggested new questions for consideration. Once again, I urged them to consider "going public" with their findings. Members of one group said they had already made arrangements to share the results of their study of CFA, mentor, and intern relationships in an upcoming orientation meeting for new CFAs. Members from another group agreed to share their study in the opening fall faculty retreat, and on the spot the presentation was scheduled. These teams seemed eager to share their studies.

Interview Themes

Views of Research

Eleven CFAs were interviewed following a set protocol. The first questions focused on the CFAs' understanding of research. Two CFAs had previous experience with action research. Nearly all the CFAs thought of action research, and the "action research spiral" that they had been taught in seminar, as an extension of what teachers normally do when reflecting on a problem or issue, yet with a subtle, though an important, difference: "It's something that I've done all along . . . but it's . . . more formalized." McMahon (1999) captures the nature of this difference when he asserts that while reflective practice may set the stage for action research, unlike action research it does not necessarily involve "strategic action." The CFAs held a similar view, echoing the assumptions of practical action research: "[Action research] is studying my own practice, trying to see if what I am doing is working for the children, for myself, for my associates . . . and then trying out some new ideas." "The action part is what you do after you look at [your practice], after you reflect on your practices, after you look at data, then you would go back and change [your] behavior in some way." The place and importance of systematically gathering and then carefully considering data in order to take increasingly effective action were central to the CFAs' views of action research. More importantly, nearly all said that in the future they would pay greater attention to the value of data in decision making: "[My action research project] has given me a new appreciation [for] actually collecting data and writing it down and analyzing it . . . for future events. . . . There's lots of things I wonder about." Noting a contradiction in her practice, another CFA remarked: "Here I am trying to teach my students that when they assess they need to document—and when I assess my children I document—but I've not documented [my own practice]. Now I can see the value of [gathering data], having it on paper, [and not merely taking] mental notation."

The CFAs were asked to compare action research to other forms of research. Responses to this question revealed some surprising results. "As teachers, we're so afraid of the word 'research,' are afraid of the word 'publish,' [but now] I'm not as afraid anymore." Another CFA spent the first few seminar meetings confused, as she recalled: "I actually had a misconception. I thought we were going to be engaging in a research project for the university, and that we would be the gofers. I didn't see, as a CFA, that we would actually be doing inquiry on our own work, our own practice. That was a little bit shocking at first." With two exceptions, those who had some prior experience with action research, the CFAs thought of research as something others do, not teachers, not CFAs, but professors. Lines between practitioners and researchers were drawn broadly and firmly, and CFAs stood on the side of the practitioners. Perhaps it is for this reason that early in the seminar the CFAs resisted engagement with journal articles. "Action research is different [from other types of research]. I think it is more fluid. I have more options with it. It can change as it goes along, where as I see [with] other kinds of research you are stuck with an initial question. . . . [With both types of research] you are studying a problem. You come up with an initial problem and then you study that problem, pull together different data sources. [Traditional research] is more tight." Because action research is "more fluid," may not involve a "hypothesis," "control groups," or "statistics," or aim at publication, initially it appears that several of the CFAs did not think of it as research at all and had to stretch to imagine themselves as researchers. This view, they said, changed.

The Value of Research Literature

The change in views was encouraged once several of the CFAs began to grapple with their topics and wonder if others might not have insights worthy of consideration. As noted in the earlier seminar story, when I believed it would be helpful for a team to engage in the wider literature, I offered assistance. Despite initial resistance, three of the five groups eventually accepted the assistance, and one team worked on its own, with very positive results. "The more I read, the clearer my understanding was regarding the importance of preparing preservice teachers to teach in diverse environments. However, it left me with many more questions about how we ought to do this not only on the university level but in relation to teacher induction programs . . . I began to see the bigger picture." "[Bob] gave us some literature that we could review. We separated it out between the three of us . . . and jigsawed it. Then when we met to go over the pieces, it was like little lights turning on. 'We could do this, we could try this,' and we came up with a couple of different ideas than we originally thought would be the direction we would be going. The literature review . . . really [got us] quite excited." Seeing their work in relationship to others' enhanced confidence that what was being done was worthwhile as well as broadened views of research and encouraged exploration of new directions.

Uncertainty: Changing Conceptions of the CFA Role

As noted in the story of the seminar, a great deal of uncertainty accompanied the first several meetings. All of the CFAs, but most especially those new to the role, felt terrific pressures on their time: "I was very apprehensive just because of the time restraints that we were under." Time pressures and "the rigors of the immediate demands of practice" are oft-given reasons for teachers' limited involvement in critical reflection (Cope and Stephen 2001, 922) and in action research (Burbank and Kauchak 2003). Early in the seminar, for all but two of the participants, the term *action research* had no particular meaning, which added to their uncertainty and feelings of being overwhelmed. Looking back on the beginning of the seminar, the general criticism raised was that I did not tell the participants exactly what to do: "I was a little confused about what we were expected to do. We were given readings, but we were never given a syllabus that said, 'Here is what you should do.' (laughter) I was kind of confused about what we were supposed to do, and I had a little trouble focusing on something here that I was interested in [to study]. . . . [But] as I started getting involved in a project, started seeing some applications for the work I was doing, it started getting more interesting, and I started realizing that we really [were] expected to do some research here. Finally [I realized], we're really even expected to share it. . . . It just sort of gradually fit together."

Finding a topic and thinking through how to attack it proved to be very difficult for some. Indeed, finding a topic may be not only difficult but very stressful (see Leitch and Day 2000). One CFA gave up and joined a group, even though the "project that we ended up working on wasn't one that I was passionate about." He felt he was wasting time. To this person, the aim was to "fit in," as he said, and get a project finished. Yet ironically at year's end he felt very strongly that action research had value, although he was not certain he could conduct a study on his own: "I'm not sure that I'd be comfortable doing something by myself." Despite warnings to the contrary, for much of the year, being very task-oriented, half the group felt rushed and needed constant reminding and encouragement to slow down, to gather data, and to reconsider topics and direction. "One of the things that changed was [that at the first] we were trying to proceed too quickly. We needed to step back and actually do a survey and see what our mentors thought about the problem we were posing. At that point, it relaxed. It changed. I really enjoyed doing the mentor survey and having them come back with information [that we could] compare." As busy, and very practical, people, the CFAs were used to grabbing hold of an assignment and finishing it as quickly as possible and then moving on. Feeling constant time pressures, the rush to judgment was an ever-present danger. Indeed, until near year's end, talk in the seminar of action research cycles made little sense.

The Value of Action Research

When asked, all of the interviewed CFAs reported that they expected to engage in action research in the future, even as they recognized that pressures on time would persist. "I will [do action research], especially when I go back into the classroom. I'm really interested in being a bit more brave, [I'd like to] publish a bit, and [continue] studying things to become more clear." B, who initially wanted to withdraw from the seminar, dramatically changed his views: "Absolutely! [I'll do action research]. As I've gone through my own course work, I think action research ought to be a big thing, a big part of any teacher's practice or school's practice. You know, what's the sense of doing something if you're not going to evaluate it and see how you can improve it?" The CFAs especially enjoyed working in teams and said they'd prefer to work with others in the future rather than conduct individual studies. "There is such great value in collaboration, and that is really what I see [we have done]." Importantly, it appears that the virtues associated with building communities of inquiry gained in prominence. For example, with the exception of one team, the same team that failed to delve into the wider research literature, the CFAs became more openly critical of their projects—indicative of the virtues of honesty and truthfulness—and increasingly anxious to improve their studies to better answer their guiding questions. One CFA who shortly thereafter assumed a position as a principal had very strong opinions about the value of action research: "I think it is going to be very, very important for me to observe my practice. To really be able to see how I am conducting faculty meetings, how I am interacting with teachers, parents, students, and to really sit back and reflect on, 'Is this effective practice?' . . . [The seminar and study have] given me a kind of parameter on how I might go about moving into my new job." She continued: "[Action research] has given me some empowerment; [I feel] I am able to try some things."

Hesitancy Remained

Despite growing confidence and a desire to continue to participate in action research, the majority of the CFAs at year's end were still hesitant to share their studies with any but carefully selected tenure-track faculty and others closely linked to the schools, people they assumed were allies. While the distance between the CFAs and the participating tenure-track faculty members lessened, there is no indication of a transfer to the wider faculty, no dramatic move of clinical faculty from the borderlands. "I still don't see our role as being really valuable. . . . We can study our own practices, but the effects of our research pretty much are limited to what we do within the confines of our [small group]." While desirous to be further involved in action research, about half of the CFAs expressed hesitancy about working alone. This conclusion was grounded in two very different sources. On the one hand, all of the CFAs, with one exception, greatly valued working with other CFAs on their projects and wished to continue in similar sorts of relationships. On the other hand, a few thought they lacked the knowledge about the process of action research needed to successfully bring a study to conclusion. They wanted additional experience, practice with the process. In some ways, research remained mysterious.

Making Sense and Looking Ahead

Wenger's (1999) concept of "boundary crossing" between "communities of practice" is helpful for making sense of what transpired in the seminar and of what the CFAs said in interview. Generally speaking, a community of practice is a group of people sharing a social context bound together by a set of problems and a shared pursuit for solutions to those problems, which involves developing a body of knowledge held in common and shared expertise. Participation in a community of practice brings with it a sense of belonging and commitment to others within the community and identification with the expertise that forms the basis of the shared practice and its improvement. Thus while communities of practice are everywhere, and everyone belongs to multiple communities, there are boundaries that set off one community from another, even when the communities are to some degree overlapping and problems are shared. The conflicts encountered in the seminar point toward the difficulty of boundary crossing between communities of practice.

Wenger writes:

> Crossing boundaries between practices exposes our experience to different forms of engagement, different enterprises with different definitions of what

matters, and different repertoires. . . . By creating a tension between experience and competence, crossing boundaries is a process by which learning is
potentially enhanced, and potentially impaired. (1999, 140)

My conflict with K was jarring. Uncertainty increased, because as several of the CFAs reported, I did not give specific directions on what was to be
done nor outline specific expectations. Then there were the lingering doubts
that tenure-track faculty, outside of those they worked with in the seminar,
would care at all about what the CFAs did or about what they accomplished
with their action research projects, even as the CFAs saw genuine value in
their work. And there was self-doubt about their ability to study practice on
their own. Each of these points to the challenges and difficulties of boundary
crossing, of moving between established communities.

The CFAs came to the university as members of their respective teaching communities of practice. Their identities were and are deeply embedded
in those communities, and participation within them brought ways of making
sense of teaching and of being a teacher that helped form the boundaries of
practice and the terms of membership. As noted, the CFAs were chosen to
work with the university precisely because within their respective communities they were powerful and successful people, skilled teachers of children.
Within these teaching communities, also as noted earlier, research did not
enjoy a particularly prominent place. For the CFAs articulating problems for
study and systematic data gathering were foreign actions. Moreover, distrust
of university faculty was and is endemic to these communities. When the
seminar began, the new CFAs were in the process of engaging a new community of practice, an evolving community with a history beginning with the
appointment of the first CFAs in 1996. Moving from one to another community of practice often is a source of considerable difficulty, in part because
what is required is a renegotiation of action, meaning, and ultimately of identity. Uncertainty abounds (Utley, Basile, and Rhodes 2003). This can be
frightening; it most certainly is unsettling, even as it may be exciting and ener-
gizing. Similarly, the implicit invitation, some thought requirement, of the
action research seminar was for all of the CFAs to connect in some fashion to
yet another community of practice, one inhabited and born by the tenure-
track faculty. What followed is what Wenger (1999) calls a "boundary
encounter" (113), made difficult by the perception of the CFAs that they were
generally not welcome into this, the university community. No doubt their
perceptions were not wholly inaccurate.

While university-based teacher educators acknowledge the value of
clinical faculty to teacher education, they are deeply ambivalent toward
them (Cornbleth and Ellsworth 1994). The CFAs felt they were unwelcome
outsiders; at best they would be allowed to participate on the fringes of the

university community of practice. To me and to the other participating tenure-track faculty members, the invitation to engage in action research with support seemed like a "productive enterprise around which . . . diverging meaning and perspectives" could be negotiated (Wenger 1999, 114). This view was not shared by the CFAs who, based upon their prior experience, initially and implicitly sensed a kind of colonization was about to take place. That it did not was a source of surprise and relief, which should open up possibilities for learning in future seminars well beyond what was possible in the one reported here. But their hesitancy raises questions about the very nature and differences of these two communities, which require direct exploration in their own right by members of both communities.

While the CFAs came to think of themselves in some ways as researchers, and research came to be accepted as a legitimate part of the role, they continued to think of their interests and the tenure-track faculty's interests as related but fundamentally different, a point underscored by Winitzky and her colleagues (1992). In their uneasiness, perhaps they were right: While they were invited to come in from the borderlands, they were not invited to settle in the university community of practice. Serious mistakes were made in the way in which the seminar was initiated, where a formal statement of CFA responsibilities was used to justify the seminar. That the tenure-track faculty members kept to a supporting role also was probably a mistake, one that confirmed their superiority to the CFAs. In retrospect, the message sent to the CFAs was that the tenure-track faculty members were in charge. To fully welcome the CFAs into the university community would require, as some within the tenure-track faculty sense and fear, fundamental changes in that community's practice. On the other hand, university tenure-track faculty members have little interest in attempting to join teacher communities of practice and perhaps little reason to believe they would be welcomed. Both communities are "guarded" (Wenger 1999, 120). Maybe the solution is not so much a matter of bringing clinical faculty in from the borderlands as it is to create a shared and new community of practice, one standing between and overlapping the other two but not replacing them. We believe that such a community can be formed perhaps supported by a center of pedagogy (Patterson, Michelli, and Pacheco 1999). But it is far from clear just what such a community would entail, although we suspect action research would be central to its practice.

PART 3

Studies of Becoming
and Being a Teacher

CHAPTER 6

Learning to Teach as an Intern: Teaching and the Emotions (2002)

with Janet R. Young

Introduction

A Conception of Emotion

In *The Praise of Folly* that most remarkable of humanists, Erasmus, wrote of the relationship of "Passion" and "Reason":

> Wisdom is nothing else than to be govern'd by reason; and on the contrary Folly, to be giv'n up to the will of our Passions; that the life of man might not be altogether disconsolate and hard to away with, of how much more Passion than Reason has Jupiter compos'd us? Putting in, as one would say, "scarce half an ounce to a pound." Besides, he has confin'd Reason to a narrow corner of the brain, and left all the rest of the body to our Passions. (1942, 117–18)

Remarkably, despite being creatures of passion, as Erasmus suggests, it is only within the past very few years that attention has been directed toward the emotional lives of teachers, in particular, the place of the emotions in learning to teach (Nias 1996; Day and Leitch 2001; Hargreaves 2001; Sutton and Wheatley 2003; Zembylas 2002). Hargreaves makes the point directly: "Educational policy and administration, and most of the educational research community, pay little or no attention to the emotions" (2000, 812).

The description offered by Kelchtermans and Ballet (2002) of what is at issue during the induction phase of learning to teach underscores the importance of attending to emotions:

> Being a teacher and in particular being a "beginning" teacher implies far more than a merely technical set of tasks that can be reduced to effectively applying curriculum knowledge and didactical skills. The person of the teacher is inevitably also at stake in these professional actions. . . . When

105

one's identity as a teacher, one's professional self-esteem, or one's task perception [is] threatened by the professional context, then self-interests
emerge. They always concern the protection of one's professional integrity
and identity as a teacher. (110)

Even when the first year of teaching is judged successful, it is a trying time,
one that tests the beginning teacher's competence, commitment to teach, and
conceptions of self. As Kelchtermans (1996) has written elsewhere: "Teachers
talk about their work immediately reveals that emotions are at the heart of
teaching" (307).

The philosopher, Robert Solomon (1993), offers an analysis of emotions
that grounds this study. His position stands common sense on its head, clearly
separating emotions from feelings, and in so doing he provides the means for
gaining helpful insights into the development and challenges of beginning
teachers.

An emotion is a (set of) judgement(s) which constitute our world, our sur-
reality, and its "intentional objects." An emotion is a basic judgement about
our Selves and our place in our world, the projection of values and ideals,
structures and mythologies, according to which we live and through which
we experience our lives. (125–26)

The assertion that emotions are judgments, "predisposition[s] to react in certain ways . . . before-the-fact" (ibid., 139), is crucially important to Solomon's
position. He goes on to state: "My embarrassment *is* my judgement to the
effect that I am in an exceedingly awkward situation. My shame *is* my judgement to the effect that I am responsible for an untoward situation or incident.
My sadness, my sorrow, and my grief *are* judgements of various severity to the
effect that I have suffered a loss. An emotion is an evaluative (or a 'normative')
judgement, a judgement about my situation and about myself and/or about all
other people" (ibid., 126).

As judgments, as "evaluative frameworks," emotions have intentionality,
in the sense that they are always about something, some object, and are strategic. They are not reactions to the world but interpretations of it and forms of
action upon it. As such, emotions are embedded in narratives or stories.
Therefore, to "understand an emotion . . . it is necessary to understand its
'object,'" what it is about (ibid., 112) and what is trying to be done. Thus one
"is not simply afraid, but afraid of something." Here Solomon draws a helpful
distinction between mood and emotion: "There are passions which need not
even begin with a particular incident or object, which need not be *about* anything in particular; these are *moods*" (ibid., 112, emphasis). In a sense, moods
are about the world, one's life situation in general. Thus as we shall see, many

beginning teachers portray a mood of vulnerability, a general orientation or way of being in the classroom and toward others, separate from any specific emotion and its object.

Emotions are logical, Solomon asserts, rooted in history, and purposeful. They include intentions about the future, and embedded in them are our hopes, expectations, and desires. As such, they often have a "moral edge" (ibid., 194) and set responsibility. They are about the self, reflecting one's "personal ideology" (ibid., 153) and the place of the self in the world. They point toward one's character; they "form an organized system of projected rules and standards within which any particular emotion takes its place, borrowing from but also contributing to that system in much the same way that a magistrate both borrows from the law and contributes to a common-law and 'constitutional' legal system" (ibid., 127). Indeed, a person can be and often is *characterized* by this system, which may be seen as a function of inherited temperament, personal tragedy, family background, or perhaps even a result of a childhood brain injury, but as Solomon argues, it also is, importantly, a matter of choosing.

The purpose of "emotional judgements is always our own sense of personal dignity and self-esteem. Whatever its particular object and strategy, whether it is committed to collecting butterflies or to ruling Asia, an emotion is ultimately concerned with personal status, self-respect, and one's place in his or her world" (ibid., 129). It is through them, Solomon argues, that we "constitute ourselves" (ibid., 128) and "constitute and mythologize our world, projecting our values and passing judgements on ourselves and other people, our situations and the various 'intentional objects' in which we have invested our interests" (ibid., 153). There is, then, a close link between emotions and identity.

While emotions are rational, they are not generally reflective. Rather, they are "undeliberated, unarticulated, and unreflective (except on rare occasions: 'Should I be angry or not?' 'Should I allow myself to continue to love her or not?')" (ibid., 131). This said, an emotion can become the object of reflection, which may strengthen or weaken its hold, with the result that beliefs may change and character may form in desired ways, as well as views of self and other. Suddenly, for instance, a beginning teacher discovers that her visceral and negative reaction to a student is based upon a lie; he did not, after all, vandalize her car. She learns something about herself and chooses to react differently next time something goes amiss. Emotions of distrust and perhaps even of hate are set aside.

The Study

During the school year, arrangements were made to have 100 interns respond weekly to a protocol via e-mail as part of a study of beginning teacher development and learning. Four times in the year the interns, who were teaching full time, were asked to stand back and review in writing their development as beginning teachers. In addition, mentor teachers were asked to assess the development of the interns three times.

The e-mails were analyzed in the following manner: E-mails from each respondent were organized chronologically, then each set was analyzed for central themes for each response. We then met and compared interpretations. There were remarkably few differences. Those that did emerge were discussed, and consensus was achieved. The basic question asked of each response was, "What is going on here?" Next an effort was made to make sense of the individual interns' development over time, which necessitated generating a system for coding themes and changes in themes across the year. To this end a matrix was created (Miles and Huberman 1984) that enabled comparison. It was at this point early in our analysis that we realized that the initial purpose of the study needed to change: One theme simply overpowered the others, the emotional aspects of learning to teach. Mentor responses also encouraged the shift in purpose. The mentors wrote of having difficulty giving critical feedback to the interns, fearing how the interns would respond and worrying that their feedback would do more harm than good. Clearly, emotional support of the interns was their foremost concern, not necessarily intern growth. In addition, as the year progressed, nearly all of the mentors gradually withdrew from involvement with the interns, arguing that they (the interns) needed to work on their own, a common practice noted by Feimen-Nemser (2001). The interns reacted in very different ways to mentor withdrawal—some experienced feelings of abandonment and responded with anger, while others reacted with delight, seeing the mentors' disengagement as a sign of trust.

Sixteen sets of responses were analyzed for this study, a random sample of about one fifth of the elementary interns and representing, we thought, a number sufficient to capture the group's experience. Only one intern was male. The number of weekly responses from the individual interns varied considerably, from a low of four to a high of twenty-nine, spread from September to May. For these sixteen interns, the average number of responses was eighteen. When the two lowest and two highest responding interns were dropped, this figure only increased slightly to a fraction above eighteen.

Our intention is to present a partial picture of the emotional life of these interns, one that we believe will be helpful to mentors and to teacher educators who work with beginning teachers and who are concerned with teacher induction. We will consider the play of three sets of emotions in the lives of the interns: love, anger and contempt, and guilt, about which a considerable amount has been written.

It is important to note that in many respects the interns are like other first-year teachers who bear the responsibility for planning and implementing an instructional program for students over an entire academic year. However, unlike most first-year teachers, interns have ongoing involvement with university supervisors and have an assigned mentor who has the time and formal responsibility to be significantly involved in the classroom. In this way interns are similar to student teachers. But unlike first-year teachers and interns, student teachers practice teach for only a term or semester, passing through a school quickly and having rather limited involvement with parents, other teachers, and even with children.

A Roller Coaster and a Trajectory

We begin with a horizontal presentation of the data, sliced to reflect dominant patterns of emotion. But before characterizing the interns "evaluative frameworks" (drawing on Solomon's earlier analysis), we offer a brief description of the general emotional and developmental pattern of the year, which was powerfully portrayed in the lists of adjectives generated each week by the interns to describe their experience. For simplification, we include lists from three interns, representing somewhat different patterns, from three periods of time, the first entry, and the first entry for January and April. (Note: All names are fictitious.)

> *Marge* (Forty-six years old, married with children, middle-income school):
> First entry: busy, exciting, frustrating, noisy, fast, happy, fun, productive
> January: cooperative, compassionate, productive, busy
> April: challenging, insightful, fun, busy
>
> *Jossey* (Twenty-three years old, married, no children, low-income, urban school):
> First entry: rewarding, good, eventful, stressful, interesting, improving
> January: Exciting, rewarding, hard, frustrating, eventful.
> April: rewarding, difficult, beneficial, disappointing, busy
>
> *Cheryl* (Twenty-two years old, single, low-income school):
> First entry: exhilarating, fun, exhausting, challenging
> January: Fun, long, exhausting, nerve-wracking, busy, lucky, exciting
> April: Boring, tiring, nerve-wracking, frustrating

For the most part, the interns began the year on a high and positive emotional note, committed to working hard and sharply focused on student learning. With only three exceptions (including the aforementioned Cheryl), the interns ended the year feeling very good about what they had accomplished and anticipating with considerable enthusiasm their second year of teaching.

Even a quick perusal of the adjective lists of the three teachers indicates something about the emotional volatility of the internship (see Murray-Harvey, Slee, Lawson, Silins, Banfield, and Russell 2000). Teaching, the interns said, is difficult, challenging, often frustrating, ever-exhausting, always busy, and, remarkably, for one, sometimes boring. In the same week, even on the same day, interns would swing from optimism inspired by a single successful lesson or an unexpected thank-you note from a struggling student to self-doubt and discouragement following a student's outburst or a lone activity that fell flat. But these sharp swings must be seen within the overall trajectory of development over the year. Certainly, the year can be accurately characterized by extreme emotional lows, times of profound self-doubt and uncertainty, and remarkable highs, periods of feeling one can do and accomplish almost anything. But generally the emotional trajectory apparent in the data, including the mentor reports, was one of growing confidence, grounded in increasing instructional competence and emotional control, where trial-and-error approaches to problem solving gave way to successful tinkering and testing, and a growing richness and depth of relationship with mentors, students, and other teachers.

Because of its importance to our analysis we should mention one low period within this overall positive trajectory. Prior to Christmas break, for about a fourth of the interns this general trajectory was jolted, more than bumped, by an event, a disturbing and surprising emotional outburst. These outbursts were represented by the interns as a loss of patience. "I need to be more patient." We see them as signs of physically wearing down and as signs of frustration, tied to perceived threats to intern self-concept. Suddenly, feeling threatened and frustrated, anger burst the boundaries of self-control and the experience was soul-shaking and disappointing. To the interns, such moments were disturbing challenges to who they believed they were as people and as teachers. While these outbursts were inevitably tied to specific events by the interns, they were embedded in more general and simmering concerns: "I hate it when I can't seem to motivate my students. I hate beating my head against a brick wall over and over and over again for students who refuse to try." More will be said shortly of anger and of the need to protect one's sense of self as a loving and decent person.

The Emotional Life: Love as a Central Theme

It is a commonplace, almost a standing joke to some, that elementary teachers and student teachers say they "love children." Often this takes the form of a moral claim, as though no one else loves children quite as intensely as do teachers. But the meaning of this phrase, "to love children," and the nature of the emotion are too seldom understood or appreciated. Love takes many

forms and is embedded in mutual respect and an unqualified but not alto-
gether selfless interest in the other's welfare. Love becomes something else
when self-interest overwhelms interest in the other. The object of the emotion
is another person, while its aim or purpose is to simultaneously make oneself
happy, to raise one's self-esteem and feeling of worth. It is, as Solomon (1993)
argues, "an emotion of strength; it requires strength to endure, and it requires
strength for its expression" (279). Love inspires investment in another, sacri-
fice and service. In loving, one hopes to be loved. Strength is needed when
loving leads to rejection, and threatens a diminishing of one's sense of self. To
love is to risk discovering that one is not lovable.

Love was at the center of the interns' emotional lives as teachers. To
teach was to love: "I love my students and my students love me, and that is what
I think the number one important thing in teaching is, to love and respect each
other" (words written by an intern at year's end). At the beginning of the year,
however, the objects of their love, the students, were not well known. Rather,
drawing on their histories as loving people, they assumed that their students
would be like others they had loved. They anticipated love's return. Early in the
year, most of the interns came to question the kind and quality of their relationships with the children, especially those interns working in urban schools.
Challenges to the interns' authority as teachers were experienced not merely as
challenges to their ability to manage a class but to their identities as loving people, many of whom felt called to teach (Serow 1994). Still, midst the challenges
were times of peace: "I love the thrill of helping such sad and lonely children
become happy for a few moments in the hours of the day that they spend in
my room. I feel like a calm sea where troubles outside can't enter in. They are
calming to my soul as well. I simply love them."

Bridget's written comments give insight into the dilemma and challenge
of love and of why Solomon argues that love is an emotion of strength. In September, within a short time of the beginning of the school year, she wrote that
she felt "humbled." The children, she said, seemed not to care about learning:
"I sometimes feel like I'm singing and dancing and doing everything I can to
help them learn and they don't care. . . . [They] had no intention of listening
to me." In response to rejection, she got angry—a form of self-protection—and
students were seen as less lovable. "I tend to spend 90 percent of my time and
energy focused on the three students who are disruptive . . . while the other
twenty-three suffer the consequences. Today I made an effort to remove the
detractors and get open with those who were willing to work. I was much happier, and class went more smoothly." To be happy, she had to get angry, punitive. A few weeks later she reported that she was depressed, still struggling with
a few students but determined to turn the situation around. Gaining control of
the classroom was her aim, a strategic necessity for protecting, then achieving,
her sense of self as teacher. For a time she did not speak of loving the children.

Slowly, she reported, the situation improved, and with a diminishing of her classroom management problem prior to the Christmas break, she reported that her resolve to teach strengthened, and her feelings toward the students were increasingly loving. That Richard, one of the boys who concerned her most, turned in some homework was positively thrilling. Writing effusively: "I love [teaching]! I love the students! I love the curriculum! I can see improvement!" Right after returning from the Christmas break a math lesson went awry and in dismay she lost her temper. Disgusted, she decided the problem was the children, who, she concluded, "have attention problems." Blaming the children was one way in which she could maintain her self-esteem and self-respect: She was a good teacher; the problem was that the children were not good students. Another turnaround followed a short time later, and as her focus shifted more directly toward student learning and away from classroom management concerns, she again proclaimed, "I love my students. I love learning and watching them learn. I love the little successes."

Kelchtermans (1996) uses the concept of the "proper teacher" to help explain one source of vulnerability felt by teachers, that there is a socially recognized conception of what a teacher is and is supposed to be able to do, and that falling short of the ideal undermines one's sense of self. The interns had internalized a view of the proper teacher, which included loving children, what one of them deemed the "perfect teacher." Not loving them is a source of failure that calls for the need to engage in what Hargreaves (2000) calls "emotional labor," work done to maintain, regain, or recreate lost feelings, ones that are seen as essential to the work of teaching and to the character of the teacher. Put differently, the task is to recapture a lost sense of self, as Solomon would suggest, as a loving teacher without which one loses self-respect and moral standing. Part of the challenge is to be upbeat and positive when feeling discouraged, and this *is* hard work. Consistently, several of the interns remarked on their need to avoid being negative. When their sense of self as loving and as competent was recaptured, the result for Bridget and her peers was comforting, and sometimes a source of a profound feeling of well-being that spread outward to the children: "Teaching is for me." At such times, even the children sometimes noticed that the interns were unusually happy: "'Miss C., why are you so happy today?' I just wanted to laugh. Last week was rough for me, and I know I was very short of patience. It was obvious the kids noticed that. I just told her: 'Because I love you all!' She ran to her friend and said: 'Miss C. said she loves us!'"

Facing Children's Lives: Anger and Contempt

The cost of love is investment in the lives of children and the risk of self. To love students requires getting deeply into their lives (Palmer 1998). To fail to get deeply into children's lives is to fail as a loving teacher. For several of the interns, particularly those in urban school settings, the deeper they got into the children's lives, the more complex and volatile their own emotional lives became and the more intense their emotional labor. Lily provides a powerful example. In October she commented on how wonderful the day was because a particular boy was absent. He upset her and helped make some days "nerve-wracking, headachy." Near Halloween she finally had the boy suspended from class. Even as she did so, she was troubled: "If you love someone and that person is struggling to behave or learn and is openly noncompliant, you wish for some kind of productive, possibly life-changing change. . . . Due to my love for this [child], it was very sad and hard to see [him be removed] . . . I cannot help but wonder what could be done differently." In desperation, she wrote: "Surely he will learn proper behavior? Right?" The boy was returned to her class several days later, and even more serious problems followed. Gradually, anger overwhelmed her, and she found herself unable to recapture her loving feelings. In an act of self-preservation, she accused the school administration and counselors of failing to assist the boy by putting him in a special placement. All that was left in her was anger, directed toward the administration. While this struggle continued, she became very concerned about another child in her class who was taken into child custody with state family services because of a "drugged-out parent." "It was very sad. Two state social workers took her and her brother into protective custody last night. She just smiled and went her way . . . I want to know that everything is alright with the family. I talked with the principal again today and he asked me to lock up the room and let no one in. The mom was upset and kept calling the school to find out what happened to her kids. She was on drugs this morning and on her way to school. . . . No child should have to live in hell within their own home." Lily felt powerless, unable to help, and emotionally drained. Yet this was not the only struggling child in her room who troubled her, who forced her to face the limitations of her influence and ability to make children's lives better. Her anger bubbled up as she described the situation. "My newest student came for her first day on Thursday. She cried for two hours wailing that she wanted to go home. She was supposed to be in my class at the first of the year but her mom decided to keep her home and homeschool her. There had been a death of a friend that caused the mom to coddle and baby this daughter. The mother is now a regular client of a local therapist." She then described how she was working to help this child.

The one male intern in the study confronted challenges similar to Lily's but responded quite differently:

I teach a class of about 80 percent ESL [children]. Various other students [are classified] as obstinate-defiant syndrome, obsessive-compulsive disorder, emotionally disturbed, and the usual forms of attention deficit hyperactivity disorders. I have had one mom want me to fill out forms to scam the social security system using her son as a pawn. I have had two students in state custody. I had one try to commit suicide in class. I had another witness his dad put the mother in the hospital before Christmas. Several other parents have been in and out of jail for various offenses during the year. One little boy was grossly abused in a sexual way by an adult male. I have three students at or above grade level for reading, and math isn't much better. I have had more than a 50 percent turnover rate in the class while maintaining the same number of students.

In response, he became increasingly angry, not at the students, but at their parents and at a social system that appeared numb to their needs. His anger seemed reasonable; he found an enemy toward which he could direct his energy and make sense of the situation. To be sure, the fact that he would be judged by how the students scored on the year-end state standardized achievement tests when so few of those who would take the tests would even be with him the entire year was upsetting. But this was a tangential issue. "I love teaching and believe I want to be a teacher," but "not in the public schools." He developed contempt for public education, an emotion ensconced in a sense that he was a better teacher and person than the context allowed him to be, and disgust for many of the parents of the children in his class. He was morally outraged, which confirms and strengthens one's sense of self. His deepest concern remained that the students were not learning as he had hoped: "I am frustrated that it is so hard to hold all students to the same standard because of the terrible situations in each student's life." Unable to bear such emotions or manage them effectively, by year's end he had disengaged and took a kind of moral holiday. Surprisingly, even as he unplugged, his mentor continued to report that he was a very effective teacher. In the classroom he did his job, but emotionally he was elsewhere. Teaching became merely a job. Increasingly the "highs" he described in writing had nothing to do with teaching, such as his thrill at seeing "a bull moose, two cows, and two cow calf pairs" on a weekend outing. Sadly, disengagement is not only an intern survival strategy. Another intern who similarly cared deeply about the children in her classroom and struggled to cope was given this bit of advice by a teacher: become "apathetic toward what children feel."

Married with two children, Lily also became increasingly angry, and in February she wrote in dismay: "I need to go home and be mom!" However, she did not disengage. Her sense of herself as a teacher would not allow this. To do so would have required that she be other than herself. She remained loving, even as other emotions clawed at her identity. The challenge, as many of the interns remarked, was to find balance—connect with the children, but

not too deeply, not to the point where work became overwhelming emotionally and physically and for those with husbands and children harmful to their
families—but, given their strong sense of responsibility, balance proved elusive
for many, and for some, turning inward, guilt, not resentment, followed. "My
heart aches to be at home with [my children] daily. I almost want to cry
because of how much desire and longing I have to really be 'mom.'"

Not Good Enough: Guilt

> In guilt a man is his own judge, typically a more ruthless and less reasonable
> judge than any other he could find. He may blame himself for nothing,
> reproach himself totally. (Solomon 1993, 259)

Guilt brings with it a sense of moral failure, of somehow not quite measuring
up to an internalized standard. In virtually all teachers, this standard lives in
imagination as the specter of former beloved teachers and in interns in images
associated with other, more experienced, and, if not in fact but in belief, more
able teachers like their mentors. Additionally, several of the interns struggled
to meet their internalized standards for being a good parent and spouse. There
is, then, a comparative element to guilt, a comparison of an imagined state of
bliss and righteousness with a state of deeply felt sinfulness. In a religious
sense, one may be guilty before God, but for teachers, there is a more fearsome
and unforgiving judge, a group of fourth graders, a set of parents. Other
judges, a couple of substitute teachers, and perhaps the teacher across the hallway may in their gaze evoke feelings of shame, but probably not of guilt.
Shame, as Solomon (1993) writes, is "more specific than guilt, less vehement
than remorse, limited in its scope and not generally self-demeaning" (301).
Losing one's temper produces feelings of shame, and if the behavior persists,
shame may turn into guilt. Facing such demanding and needy judges, it is easy
not to measure up, to demean oneself, to punish oneself, and then to fail to
forgive.

Despite generally holding feelings of success tied to a sense of improvement, part of the year's trajectory, nearly all of the interns said in one form or
another that they had "a lot to learn." Mostly this comment was a sign of optimism about the future, an imprint of a growing confidence. However, for a
few, the balance was tipped in the other direction, albeit slightly. "Sometimes
I feel like I should be doing so much more than I am. I want to be able to help
the low students and the high students a lot more, but I don't know how and
don't have the time to. I really want to teach them all that I can and so much
more, but right now I can't do that much. I sometimes feel that my students
could be doing so much better with a teacher that has more experience."

While Natalie said she would do better, she remained bothered and disappointed by how slowly she progressed. Although most of the interns eventually mastered management, a few greeted the end of the year as they did the beginning—struggling to keep a few children focused and on task. Failure to be able to manage a class, where management is understood as a necessary condition to learning, brought feelings of failure and for some a measure of guilt, of having let the children down.

Illness, which was remarkably common among the interns, and resulting in having to leave the children to substitute teachers, produced guilt. This guilt was complicated by feelings of longing, of missing and of needing the children. Interns came to school sick, which in the case of one led to a prolonged illness and even deeper feelings of having let the children down. "[I felt] like my students weren't learning anything because they had so many subs." Teaching, when feeling poorly, often went badly, which counterbalanced the need to be present for the children and do what good teachers do.

Year-end competency testing terrified most of the interns, who worried that their students would not do well and that this would reflect poorly on their teaching. But something more serious was at stake: All of the interns began the year dilated on student learning as the aim of teaching. To be sure, they wanted the students to reciprocate their love, and it thrilled them—confirmed their sense of self—to have parents report to them in parent-teacher conference how much their children enjoyed school. But these desires must be understood in relationship to the great—and self-confirming—pleasure the interns took in witnessing student learning and, conversely, how disheartening they found student failure and disengagement from learning. Contrary to the early work of Fuller and Bown (1975), while the interns were concerned about themselves and how students felt about them, they were certainly as concerned, if not more so, about student learning. Given their commitments, the interns feared to the point of dread that their students would not do well on year-end tests and would not be prepared for grade advancement. One intern felt dismay when she discovered that her students were behind those of other teachers in preparing for the tests. One mentor commented on how her interns felt "like failures" for not covering all of the curriculum. Another intern wrote: "I keep thinking that my students haven't learned all that they need to and . . . I'm worried that I haven't done enough, that they will bomb at the end." If they do "bomb" the tests, tremendous guilt will result. Particularly in the urban schools, anticipation of poor test results drove the interns, adding to their stress. Given a less-intense commitment to facilitating student learning and less love, the typical response to the emotion of fear, self-preservation, may have reared its head. We did not see signs of this reaction.

In contrast to shame, guilt is not an emotion that has any apparent benefits. A beginning teacher might be shamed to action, to reconsider how she or he treats a particular child or, following release of poor test results, to a renewed determination to plan the curriculum more carefully next time. In contrast, guilt tends toward disengagement and eventually to discouragement, bitterness, and perhaps burnout. It is not an emotion available to mentor teachers as a source of motivation for intern learning.

A Mood of Vulnerability

As in Kelchtermans's (1996) study, vulnerability is the dominating mood running across our intern data set. Sources of vulnerability are many, both internal and external (Pinnegar 1995). Self-doubts that have a history, limited experience with children, coupled with constant classroom surprises, and unsuspected content area gaps are all sources of difficulty when teaching as well as constant and sometimes jolting reminders that there always is something more to learn and do. Externally the interns were subjected to ongoing evaluation, not only from their mentors, the university supervisors, and occasionally from principals but from the children whose engagement or disengagement or joy or sorrow sent clear and forceful messages to them. Rickie was dismayed when the vice principal dropped by to observe her class and the children misbehaved. All of the interns worried about how their mentors would rank them on the evaluation sheet that would go into their placement file. Comments from parents were sources of elation and deflation. Then, at year's end, facing a serious budget shortfall, the state legislature ordered substantial cuts to education, which shattered the interns who hoped to stay and teach within the state. Jobs would be eliminated. In response to a deteriorating situation, one intern wrote: "I am not in control of my destiny." Holidays, Mondays (when there was uncertainty about how the children would behave), field days, team planning sessions, changes in the curriculum, and mentor illness were reminders that forces outside of the interns' control would shape the quality of their professional lives. At every turn, who and what they were as people and as teachers was challenged; frequently the challenge produced confirmation of self, but not always, and in the interaction of competence and experience came learning (Wenger 1999). In the face of these challenges, like all teachers, interns need to know that they have made and are making a positive difference in the lives of children, but this is not always certain.

On Learning to Teach

An internship, like the first year of teaching, is a confrontation with self and the limitations of self. Who teachers are is displayed in their emotions, as they struggle to make sense of their experience and in making sense preserve an identity that might not be fully stable or secure. This involves hard work of various kinds, including work on the emotions. Induction, then, is not just a story of how someone becomes a teacher, how one moves from being a novice to becoming an expert teacher, but of how a teacher is made and remade and in context. It is to work by, on, and through one's emotions, and it is exhausting work, as was readily apparent in our data.

Thinking about learning to teach in these terms makes the disengagement of so many of the mentors from the interns especially troubling. Most of the mentors thought of their role as having two components: emotional support and coaching. Once they judged that the interns no longer needed their support, were able to control the classroom, and had a modicum of skill, it appears as though they assumed withdrawal was the right action to take. Yet our data suggest that the emotional component of learning to teach never disappears. It may shift, its intensity may diminish for a short time, but it does not go away, because what is at stake is always the teacher's dignity and place in the world, as Solomon argues, and this world is dynamic and ever-changing. The importance of giving interns support for their journey into teaching cannot be underestimated, but support is no substitute for thoughtful criticism nor for ongoing, honest, and abundant conversation about teaching and one's development as a teacher. Mostly the mentors were praised by the interns because of their availability and willingness to be of help, but at least half wanted more and more pointed feedback and concomitantly a more intense, intimate professional and personal relationship with their mentor. It is, we believe, within the realm of the emotions as constitutive of the self and as central to teaching success that lies one of the most important areas of research for teacher educators.

CHAPTER 7

Continuity and Change
in Teacher Development:
First-Year Teacher after Five Years (1993)

with Kerrie Baughman

Introduction

In *First-Year Teacher: A Case Study* (1989), I told Kerrie Baughman's story as she negotiated a satisfying role and struggled to develop teaching skills during her first year and a half as a seventh grade teacher. In the study, I described how Kerrie, then twenty-nine years old and the mother of two children about the same age as her students, came to terms with the common problems of beginning teachers and showed how she dealt with changes in the teaching context during her second year, changes that brought an increased emphasis on teacher accountability and curricular standardization.

The study reported in this chapter resulted from a desire to know what had changed and what had remained the same for Kerrie after five years' teaching experience. I was curious about the path of her development as a teacher. My recognition of the paucity of longitudinal studies of teacher development, of the dramatic increase of interest in such studies and their growing influence in conceptualizing teacher education (see, for example, Hargreaves and Fullan 1992), also prompted the study.

Methodology and Data Gathering

I began gathering data prior to the start of the school year when Kerrie and I met and conducted an initial interview during which she shared what she considered the significant family and professional events that had occurred since *First-Year Teacher* was published. With data from this interview as background, we conducted three other extensive semi-structured interviews during the fall. In preparation for the second interview, we reread *First-Year Teacher*. In this interview she discussed what she thought were the significant changes and constancies in her teaching and thinking about teaching. I transcribed all

119

interviews for later analysis. Interview protocols were written in response to the data I was gathering and reflected my evolving understanding of Kerrie's classroom and her thinking about teaching. In the last interview we compared perceptions. I also conducted ten classroom observations at random times, within which I took extensive notes and sought to identify themes and patterns of action characteristic of her current teaching and to recognize changes from how she had taught during her second year. At random times professionals employed by the university videotaped twelve entire class sessions. I analyzed these tapes, first, to identify and confirm themes and patterns in Kerrie's instruction, and, second, to locate segments capturing the changes I had noted. I also identified interesting or unusual events that I thought would show changes in Kerrie's thinking about teaching and herself as teacher. We viewed these portions of the tapes together, and she thought aloud as an audiotape recorder ran.

Continuity and Change

Kerrie was teaching seventh grade in the same room in Rocky Mountain Junior High School, but she no longer taught social studies. She taught two classes of English and two of reading, linked together so that she has the same group of students for both subjects. Because of being appointed teacher specialist by the principal at the end of her fourth year of teaching, Kerrie taught four of seven class periods. One noninstructional class period was for preparation and two for her duties as teacher specialist, including occasional substitute teaching within the building and conducting teacher evaluations.

The school appeared to have changed little, inside or out. This was a surface appearance, however. While standing in the hallways and watching the students rush by during class breaks, I noted some differences. The school was more crowded, and new student groupings were evident. Most noticeably there was an increase in the number of "cowboys." Cowboys are, as Kerrie put it, "kids who spit on the walls, [and trash] the hallways. We have a huge cowboy element in our school right now. We had to ban cowboy hats."

During Kerrie's first year of teaching she was part of a three-person team. By the end of the second year, the team concept, as she had known it, fractured. Since that time, even though the possibility of teaming remains, Kerrie had gone her own way.

Inside the Classroom

Prior to my first observation, I stood outside of Kerrie's classroom, as I had on previous occasions, and glanced in, expecting to see familiar sights. The classroom was still brightly decorated, but the desks were in a large "U" shape with a stool at the head of the "U" and a table; one wall had been reconstructed so that two four-foot sections jutted into the classroom and divided the wall into thirds, making three large boothlike areas. One large carpeted wall was essentially empty except for a sign that read "Our Publishing Wall." While this was not the classroom to which I had grown accustomed in prior visits, the changes in it were superficial compared to the changes in her teaching.

The pattern of Kerrie's curriculum and instruction for the first four and a half years of her teaching was essentially set during her first year of teaching, with each year bringing an elaboration and a refinement of the previous year's work. Thus as I reported in *First-Year Teacher* (1989, 116–17), Kerrie began every reading class in front of the room reading from a book she had chosen because of high student interest. Sometimes she would pass out a short story illustrating a concept such as plot that was under study. The class would then discuss the story, and Kerrie would give a quiz or a follow-up written assignment. She also gave students free reading time when they finished their more formal work.

English was similarly patterned and routinized. Spelling occupied parts of Monday, Wednesday, and Friday lessons; on Friday she gave a spelling test. Packed around the study of spelling was the formal study of language for which Kerrie relied upon the textbook. She also developed and refined literally dozens of units on her own, drawing upon diverse sources for ideas and materials. For example, she developed a variety of games, such as GRAMO, a bingo game for learning grammar, and "spelling baseball."

She had warned me that I would be surprised by the changes in her program. I was. Little was familiar. In English, a typical day began this way (from observation notes): 7:50 a.m.: All students are in their seats ready to work. 7:58: Announcements from the office end. Kerrie: 'O.K., let's fix these sentences.' Sentence: 'The poem crystal moments describes how dogs catch a fleeing deer don't it [*sic*].' Immediately several hands go up. 8:05: The students finish correcting the sentences, and Kerrie states, 'Now, we need someone to turn off the lights. It's a hard job, but someone must do it.' A boy hits the lights. Kerrie places a transparency from a book on the overhead. 'Where do you think this is from?' '*Charlotte's Web*,' a student volunteers. 'Right. All the punctuation is missing on this page of *Charlotte's Web*. I need your help to punctuate it. Let's do it together.' Hands begin going up. She tells them, 'You need to read it to yourselves, first.' As they finish reading, hands go up and she begins making the suggested changes. She compliments them and (8:15) turns away from the overhead and states: 'You people are doing some lovely writing.' 8:17: 'Everyone needs to get out your stuff and get working—don't wait for me to call your name.' She then quickly goes through the roll. As she calls a student's name, the student tells Kerrie what they are working on, and whether or not they need to conference with her. 8:25: Students are working.

Kerrie is at the front of the room at the table meeting with an individual student and talking about the student's writing. Some students are conferencing
with one another, helping edit work (in one of the three boothlike areas noted
earlier). A few staple "published" works on the carpeted wall (under the sign
"Our Publishing Wall"). 8:42: Kerrie, ending a conference: 'O.K., I need
everyone to get in your seat and put away your material. You're going to hear
the most fantastic story ever written.' At these words a girl, now sitting on
Kerrie's stool in front of the class, and beaming, began to read her story: 'This
story is called Piggywood,' she begins. Buzzer, class ends. 8:55: Reading class
begins. Without a word, Kerrie begins reading from a novel (I recognize this
activity, but little else). What Kerrie calls a mini-lesson on "conflict" in writing follows (9:10). The main points of the lesson are outlined on a large pink
chart that will be hung somewhere in the room. She ties the lesson into the
book.

I wondered why she had discarded virtually her entire program, including emptying file cabinets full of materials. Why so many changes? What
made the changes even more striking was that as I observed Kerrie, I also
could observe the two teachers who shared her "pod," one of whom she had
teamed with during her second year (Kerrie's room is one of three connected
to form a pod). I recognized the patterns used by these teachers as similar to
what Kerrie's had been. Kerrie commented that these teachers still teamed and
traded students about every three weeks. She did not; she chose to work alone
because she disagreed strongly with what they were doing. "I am," she said,
"possessive [of my] students. I want to have them all year long. [These other
teachers] want to [trade] kids. I figure you just don't make any progress with
kids unless you have them for a year." Kerrie had turned her back on the type
of teaching formerly characterizing her work.

Kerrie explained some of the reasons for the change. During her first
year of teaching she compromised her desire to have students write extensively
and rewrite their work. Having compromised a fundamental value, she felt
guilty, but given the heavy workload, she saw no alternative. "I don't have my
kids write much," she said then, "[I can't because I take] so much time correcting it" (Bullough 1989, 85). Describing this period in her development,
she commented, "It is like, well, I [didn't] know what else to do, so I'm going
to continue on and do the best I can and refine the things that I know I'm
doing well."

Early in her fifth year of teaching she attended an International Reading Association conference and obtained a copy of Nancie Atwell's book,
Writing, Reading, and Learning with Adolescents. Lights went on: "I picked up
the book, I read it, and I realized, *this is it*! I've gotten the gospel according to
Nancie Atwell, and I thought, 'fourth quarter I'm going to chuck it all and I'm
going to do this,' [and] I did." Her uneasiness with how she had been work-

ing came out: "It was like I would add a new really neat trick [to my program] but it still didn't do [what I wanted]. It didn't take those kids to where I knew they needed to be." She found a new faith: "It is like discovering a new religion (laughs). [Atwell] was the end of the old." Atwell's book in hand, she was reborn as a teacher.

During the last term of her fifth year of teaching, she implemented as much of Atwell's Writing and Reading Workshop program as possible, changing it even as she did so. Atwell emphasized students writing, then editing and critiquing one another's work, but she asserted that the teacher should do the final editing. Once completed, the original is placed in a portfolio and a Xerox copy is "published" and displayed in a public spot. Kerrie saw no reason for her to do the final editing and articulated several good reasons for the students to do it in conference with her, including her desire to coach them in developing editing skills. During this trial run, she noticed patterns in student errors and organized brief lessons on these and other topics of general importance (e.g., the mini-lesson on conflict noted earlier), and, in order to directly teach some skills, she included sentence correction. She continued to emphasize class novels such as *The Westing Game*, as well as individual student novels, although Atwell stressed that students should be reading their own novels. She followed Atwell's suggestions more closely on how to organize a class for writing, beginning class by having all students quickly report what they were working on, determining if they needed a teacher conference, and grading emphasizing progress and goal setting, a view consistent with her own. Kerrie remade Atwell's program to fit her context, and the results pleased her. Even while experimenting with the program, she observed significant improvement in many students' writing, including grammar and spelling, and in their self-esteem, indicated by the confidence with which they shared their writing. She became convinced that teaching skills out of context was busy work; transfer would come only when she taught skills within the context of their usage—"I didn't think [what I taught] was really absorbed." This too distinguished her thinking and practice from that of her two colleagues.

Kerrie's decision to change was self-initiated. She chose to change her program, recognized within the school and by the principal as exemplary, in the face of considerable pressure to leave it as it was from the other teachers in her pod, a few students, and parents concerned that their children would not learn grammar.

Teacher Development

The literature on teacher development illuminates Kerrie's decision. In *First-Year Teacher* I placed her development within Ryan's (1986) proposed stages of learning to teach. I did not ask Kerrie to characterize her own development but placed her in others' schemes. I may have lost some of the richness of her story as a result.

Kerrie's Phases

Huberman began his study of teacher life cycles by asking teachers "to review their career trajectory and to see whether they could carve it up into phases or stages. For each phase, they were to provide an overarching name or a theme and to note the features constituting that theme" (Huberman 1989, 40). I asked Kerrie to do this and to identify the core problems associated with each phase. Identifying core problems was important, because the development of teaching expertise (see Chapter 8) is essentially "a process of progressive problem solving, in which mental capacity that becomes available when problems are solved at one level is directed toward solving problems at a higher, more complex level" (Scardamalia and Bereiter 1989, 39). From this view, one would expect that over time what Kerrie saw as a central problem would change, and that more complex problems would command her attention. They did.

Kerrie had no difficulty either carving up her experience or identifying themes and problems. The first stage she labeled "follower: I watched A" (her mentor, or "tormentor," as she laughingly called her during her first years of teaching). "I did what [she] said, I modeled things that were modeled for me, pretty much." In contrast to being disappointed in her mentor during her first two years of teaching, she now recognized her as a positive influence and was less judgmental and more forgiving of other teachers. Discipline and curriculum development were the central but certainly not the only problems of this phase: "[I was] very shaky on curriculum and totally shaky on discipline . . . I changed, she said, at the middle of the first year." About this time she began "adapting to the realities of student behavior." Her success confronting some typical problems of learning to teach gave her confidence, and she became less of a follower. I labeled this period in *First-Year Teacher* a transition into the mastery stage of learning to teach, that period during which the novice begins more or less to systematically study practice. Sharply focused on student learning, she began to remake the curriculum and "was beginning to feel more empowered . . . I could start to manipulate things. Also, I was becoming more consistent with discipline." Although discipline remained a problem until year's end, she felt she made good progress in the area.

The next phase she labeled "follower/independent," placing it at the beginning of her second year of teaching. "Independence was growing; it was like, 'okay, I've been through it one time. I'm teaching the same thing [as I did the first year and] I will be able to make some changes, now.' It was," she said, "a new start." Her position as association building representative, which brought opportunities to exercise leadership within the school, was of particular importance to her development. Discipline remained a concern, although it slipped to the back burner, and curriculum was no longer an issue; she knew what she wanted and needed to teach and, for the most part, how she wanted to teach it. Her major concerns were student motivation and how to establish relationships with the students that encouraged engagement. Her mentor left the profession at the end of Kerrie's second year of teaching, thus ending feelings of dependency. She no longer felt someone gazing over her shoulder.

The next phase, occurring during her third year of teaching, Kerrie labeled "independent." She felt powerful, in control of her professional development, and she was enjoying the success of her students. In addition, she was building and enjoying a reputation within the school as an excellent teacher and an influential voice in school matters. Student motivation persisted as Kerrie's central concern: "I want the kids to really be motivated to work."

She thought of her fourth year as a transition year, from independence to teaching mastery (independence/mastery). This label is of particular interest, because it presents and mixes a feeling about Kerrie's relationship to other faculty members—independence—with an acknowledgment of her being in control of the craft of teaching. She felt the "rush of craft pride," which Huberman notes (1992, 136). During her fourth year the principal selected her as teacher specialist. Student motivation remained a concern, but she felt she had made giant strides toward achieving her desired aim for the vast majority of students. How better to engage a few students, the lost sheep, was an issue. "I look over there and see [that the students] are engaged. They feel pleased, they are so happy when they come up and we've conferenced. They are just thrilled with their progress. Now I'm looking to include the lost sheep."

A few weeks after this interaction we discussed her development and the phases she had identified in relationship to the pathways that Huberman indicates a teacher's career may follow. I thought it would shed additional light on her thinking about her own development and the core problems demanding her attention.

Huberman observed that when launching a career teachers generally fall into two rough categories, easy or painful beginnings. Kerrie characterized her beginning as easy. "Easy beginnings involve positive relationships with pupils, manageable pupils, the sense of pedagogical mastery, and enthusiasm" (Huberman 1989, 42). A second phase, associated with teachers with four to eight years of experience, he dubbed "stabilization or stabilizing. The theme invariably contains two features. . . . The first has to do with pedagogical stabilizing: feeling at ease in the classroom, consolidating a basic repertoire, differentiating materials and treatments in light of pupils' reactions or performances. The second feature has to do with commitment to the profession." From stabilization, he observed, teachers commonly move in different directions (six to ten years of experience) toward experimentation, responsibility, or consternation. Experimentation and responsibility are of interest here. Huberman described the experimentation phase this way: "Once a basic level of classroom mastery is achieved, there is a need for refinement and diversity. On the one hand, informants come to see that they can get better results by diversifying their materials and their modes of classroom management. On the other hand, they feel the stale breath of routine for the first time" (Huberman 1989, 43). Responsibility refers to the move into administrative roles and positions of authority, such as teacher specialist.

Kerrie concluded that her independence/mastery phase was in some respects similar to Huberman's experimentation phase, but with some important differences. She had not felt stale, just not fully satisfied by her program. She could see that no amount of refining or diversifying the program would produce the desired results. Until she came across Atwell's work, she saw no alternative course of action; she had accepted that there was little she could do to teach student writing effectively. Having identified an alternative, she believed that much of her program had to go, and she felt confident and powerful enough to discard it. "I'm feeling pretty empowered," she remarked. But without the alternative, she would likely still be refining her former program and feeling frustrated.

Somewhat in contrast to Huberman's phases, Kerrie anticipated that a second stabilization would follow mastery of her version of the Atwell program, and yet further cycles of experimentation/stabilization would follow, each representative of her feelings of independence and of her growing professional and personal power. While it remains to be seen if her assessment is accurate, I believe it significant that she considered her development more cyclical than linear. Additionally, it is noteworthy that Kerrie did not think of experimentation, as Huberman does, as a "somewhat haphazard process of trial and error" (1992, 136). Rather, she thought of experimentation as a relatively systematic testing of ideas based upon an informed sense for what will work: "I have a feeling for what is going to work." She asserted she minimized error by planning with great care: "I . . . [plan things] all out first. . . . I really don't do [trial and error], I don't think I do." This represents a dramatic change.

Professional Identity

Kerrie felt powerful enough to discard the program because she was comfortable and secure about herself as a person and teacher and in her craft knowledge. She could take risks: "I think I used to feel that it was very important for my kids [to like me]. [Now] I'm much more secure with myself as a teacher, and as a person." Knowing who she is as teacher, she trusted her intuition, her tacit knowledge about teaching (see Holly and Walley 1989)—and approached problems confident that she could solve them naturally. "I solve the small problems as I go. You know, reflection comes on the way to and from school, and that has always been the case. I've done a lot of reflecting, but you can't [always pause to think while teaching], that can't happen in the classroom. You are way too busy [for it]; it happens at the quiet times. [Much of my problem solving] is [done] in my subconscious. All of a sudden [an idea] will come to me."

Teachers' conceptions of themselves are, as Nias argues, crucial to their performance in the classroom, in particular to "the way [in which they] construe the nature of their job" (Nias 1989, 155). Initially, Kerrie, like many other mothers who are teachers (see Bullough and Knowles 1991), saw teaching as an extension of mothering: teacher is mother and nurturer (see Chapter 11). She relied heavily upon her experience with her own children to identify and frame problems. She thought of the classroom as a home and of the class as a large family. In many ways this self-understanding made teaching meaningful for her, but in other ways it did not. Gradually, she made adjustments in her self-understanding and formed a comfortable teaching persona or professional identity (see Pajak 1986), an authentic expression of her inner self or identity, one productive for framing and solving increasingly complex problems.

Teaching Principles

Over time, Kerrie developed a seemingly simple but complex cluster of principles that grounded and to a degree replaced the mother teaching metaphor. These principles capture her vision of herself as teacher and represent her matured theory of teaching, a product of her "progressive problem solving" (Scardamalia and Bereiter 1989). Embedded in them are the values and concepts she brings to bear when addressing problems. Echoing the values of mothering, the first principle "is love them along. [A lot of my success comes from] learning how to deal with the students and to treat them the way they need to be treated, positively. I call it 'loving them along,' because that is what works for me. I want to have a loving environment in my classroom where my students can blossom."

A second principle is that a classroom should be a warm, fuzzy place like a family, where students feel loved and cared for, but more than a family—a caring community where students feel connected and responsible for one another. A third is captured in the phrase, I feel "like I am very much a student-centered teacher." Student success and building self-esteem are primary values, evident in curriculum decision making, grading, and discipline and management. The fourth principle is "skills taught out of context are nothing." To learn grammar, students must write and read and use it; to learn spelling, they must use words, not merely memorize them for Friday tests, as before. A fifth is that at the end of seventh grade, "a student ought to look like an eighth grader." By this Kerrie meant that it is her job to help the students mature intellectually and emotionally. Although she could not express in detail what an eighth grader looked like, she obviously knew, and knew what it would take on her part to nudge a student along in this direction.

The combined expressions "I take teaching seriously" and "I see myself as putting all I can into teaching" form a sixth principle. Good teachers are committed to teaching and pay the price needed to enable student performance. In a related vein, good teachers are professional: "I work professionally with other teachers," Kerrie stated matter of factly. During her second year of teaching, Kerrie thought of professionalism essentially as a matter of continuing her education and of being involved with other teachers, particularly through association work. While pursuing additional education she first encountered Atwell's work. Involvement remained important to her definition, but other characteristics were evident. The association became somewhat less important to Kerrie, but working collaboratively with other teachers—despite her rejection of teaming—gained in importance. There were numerous examples: During her fifth year of teaching, and in response to two incidents involving first-year teachers on the verge of tears because of classroom problems, she organized a support group for them (the school had seven first-year teachers out of a faculty of forty) that ran until springtime. Some of these teachers credited Kerrie for their survival. Kerrie also shared her new program with other teachers at workshops and in informal settings.

Each of these principles, products of experience and of thinking and talking about teaching, *worked* for her; tried and true principles, they underpinned much of what Kerrie did in the classroom and her teacher persona. Because Atwell's program resonated with these principles, Kerrie first adopted and then adapted it. Principles in place, coupled with the skill needed to make them workable, Kerrie believed she did not need to engage in trial-and-error approaches to teaching. She knew in a profound, but not always an explicit, way what she was doing and why she was doing it: her actions seemed natural, comfortable, and right to her. Evidence that the principles work came not only from classroom observations but also from the analysis of the videotapes and her discussion of them.

Teaching Expertise

Several of the characteristics of teaching expertise Berliner (1990) identified were readily apparent in the tapes and in Kerrie's discussion of the lesson segments shown to her. Her lessons were purposeful; they flowed easily, seemingly effortlessly to their conclusions. Transitions were nearly automatic, so that lessons appeared almost seamless. Kerrie easily handled unexpected events. For example, when students who had agreed to read their writing to the class backed out at the last moment, she was unflappable. She easily categorized problems and framed solutions. For example, during a think-aloud viewing of a videotape segment when a few students interrupted a conference, Kerrie said: "[They will continue to do this] until everyone has gone through the cycle (writing, peer conferencing, teacher conferencing, publishing) a couple of times. They [will] get it, but it takes a long time. Some kids haven't gone through [the cycle] yet." What seemed like a problem to me was not even a concern for Kerrie, who understood the issue contextually and much more deeply than I did. At the conclusion of our viewing of the tapes I asked Kerrie to critique and then assess her performance. After noting an area or two that she thought needed work, particularly to improve her conferencing skills, she remarked, "It looks good, doesn't it? It looked really good. I look like I know what I'm doing all the time. I can't help but think, I would love me so much [as a teacher] if I were a seventh grader (laughs)." This, too, as Berliner notes, is a sign of expertise: "Experts are more confident about their abilities to succeed at instructional tasks than are novices" (1990, 30).

Conclusion

Kerrie developed greatly as a teacher during the previous four years. When I asked her to graph her development as a teacher, she drew a line moving constantly upward with but a few small drops downward. She viewed her development as continuous and positive; she expected the line to continue to move upward into the future.

When I consider Kerrie's story from the general perspective of teacher development, I see a few points meriting mention. The title of this chapter begins with the terms *continuity* and *change*. Focusing on teacher development brings with it a bias favoring change over continuity. It is easy, as Walsh and his colleagues (Walsh, Baturka, Smith, and Colter 1991) suggest, to be blinded to continuity by the appearance of change. Kerrie's decision to abandon her established program must be understood in relationship to the general constancy of her vision of herself as teacher, her professional persona which, like Nan, in Walsh's study, "is deeply embedded in her identity as a person" (ibid., 83). Thus as Goodson and Walker (1991) and Ball and Goodson (1985) suggest, teacher development is inevitably idiosyncratic and must be viewed in relationship to the unfolding of a life—life history—and in context, points made earlier in the Introduction and in Chapter 3. Kerrie's principles grow out of her life experience generally and her teaching experience specifically. As good as Kerrie and her colleagues thought her program was, she changed it because among other shortcomings it did not encourage student writing, and good teachers, according to her principles, have students write.

Viewing teacher development in relationship to life history and context is crucial for understanding the richness and complexity of teaching expertise. Of this, more will be said in the chapter that follows. During the past decade, some writers (Bullough 1987; Bullough, Goldstein, and Holt 1984) may have overemphasized context. Kerrie's story, particularly her decision to discard much of her program and to resist contextual pressures to conform, nicely illustrates the problematic nature of such orientations. Teachers not only resist pressures to conform (Bullough and Gitlin 1985), they also take advantage of or create opportunities to more fully express their visions of good teaching within schools. Moreover, deeply embedded and valued principles, not personal convenience, often drive their actions. Understanding this is essential if school reform efforts are to succeed.

Still, we ought not underestimate the power of context to both enable and limit teacher development and shape teacher vision. The trick is to find a productive balance: Both context and person matter. When beginning teachers join a faculty, they ought to encounter contexts rich in programmatic and instructional alternatives available for exploration in sensitive and responsible ways. Kerrie's program has broadened the range of possibility for teachers at Rocky Mountain Junior High School; the context has become richer, more educative, and more enabling of teacher development. I doubt that Kerrie would have embraced Atwell's work earlier had she known about it, perhaps as part of her preservice teacher education or been told about it by someone in the school during her first or second year of teaching. Because of the short duration of teacher education we often cram courses with everything thought useful for a teacher to know. In some institutions Atwell's program would be on the list of useful things. However, I believe Kerrie successfully adapted Atwell's work because during her first years of teaching she had mastered a basic repertoire of teaching skills and understandings associated with handling large groups of students. Lacking these skills and understandings and the craft knowledge and confidence that mastery brings, Kerrie might have judged Atwell's approach unworkable or, perhaps, simply unimaginable. Then, too, lacking a mature theory of teaching enabling her to see in the program possibilities for achieving her own aims, Kerrie may have found Atwell uninspiring. These speculative musings raise the general and extraordinarily complicated issue of what we *ought* to teach in preservice and in-service teacher education, and, recognizing developmental limitations, when we ought to introduce topics and activities. It is with respect to these issues that I find the various stage theories useful.

Aware of some researchers' quest for certainty, I must invoke a caution: Stages should be viewed warily. Life is not as neatly segmented as such schemes suggest (Bullough 1997a). Still, such schemes are heuristically useful. They are rough means for making initial sense of some aspects of teacher development and for helping novice teachers think about and perhaps better direct their learning. For more experienced teachers such as Kerrie, linearity gives way to increased complexity and diversity. Within the line Kerrie drew to represent her development are internally and externally driven cycles of experimentation and stabilization defying easy categorization and yet capturing who she is and what she is becoming as a teacher. Lastly, and more generally, stages inevitably introduce distortion, an old criticism of stage theories that ought to be kept in mind. Kerrie reminded me of the seductive power of stages, when description blurs with prescription, in our last interview when she laughingly remarked, while viewing Huberman's charts of teacher life cycles, "Tell me what the next stage is so that I can identify when I [will] move out of it!"

Lastly, as we have renewed our shared study of teaching after a hiatus, we are reminded of the importance to development of ongoing conversation about teaching, views of self-as-teacher, and the context of teaching and of the value of extending that conversation. Clearly, conversation is both a means for establishing conditions conducive to teacher development and a condition in its own right; Kerrie's participation in such a conversation led to Atwell, and her commitment to extending it led to the creation of the first-year teacher support group. And it was because of conversation that Kerrie found participating in the research that resulted in *First-Year Teacher* valuable. Unfortunately, as Huberman (1992) implies, not all teachers, nor probably teacher educators (see Chapter 3), want to be part of the conversation about teaching. Nevertheless, a significant challenge facing teacher educators and others concerned with teacher development is to discover ways of extending the conversation. Perhaps one way is to produce and study cases such as Kerrie's. Certainly teacher educators have a lively interest in the outcome of such efforts for better programs and the more interesting and significant work that will follow.

CHAPTER 8

Changing Contexts and Expertise in Teaching: First-Year Teacher after Seven Years (1995)

with Kerrie Baughman

Introduction

Much of the research on teaching expertise has involved making comparisons of novices with expert teachers and noting differences (see Berliner 1986, 1988). How expert teachers become expert has remained an elusive question, however. Yet this is a crucially important question to teacher educators and others interested in school improvement. My experience resonates with the arguments of Bereiter and Scardamalia (1993), that expertise is more a process than an end state. It is "a venture beyond natural abilities" (ibid., 4), one that involves boundary pushing, as classicist Hugh Nibley suggested several years ago:

> Only if you reach the boundary will the boundary recede before you. And if you don't, if you confine your efforts, the boundary will shrink to accommodate itself to your efforts. And you can only expand your capacities by working to the very limit. (quoted in Gillum 1993, 220)

"The career of the expert is one of progressively advancing on the problems constituting a field of work, whereas the career of the nonexpert is one of gradually constricting the field of work so that it more closely conforms to the routines the nonexpert is prepared to execute" (Bereiter and Scardamalia 1993, 9). When facing problems that exceed capacity, like nonexperts, experts simplify the problems, but they do so "to the minimum that their knowledge and talent will permit" (ibid., 20). Put differently, experts work at the upper edge of their competence; they push boundaries ever outward, as Nibley suggests. Clearly, practice does not make perfect.

When looking for expertise, "we have to find it in the ongoing process in which knowledge is used, transformed, enhanced, and attuned to situations" (ibid., 46). Both formal and tacit, or hidden, knowledge play crucial roles in developing expertise. Informal, impressionistic, and self-regulatory knowledge all come into play in addition to the more obvious declarative and procedural types. Informal knowledge refers to "educated common sense" (ibid., 51); impressionistic knowledge to ones feelings about things; and self-regulatory knowledge to how experts know themselves. It is "knowledge that controls the application of other knowledge" (ibid., 60). The key difference between experts and nonexperts is how this knowledge is applied:

> There is something experts do over and above ordinary learning, which accounts for how they become experts and for how they remain experts, rather than settling into a rut of routine performance. . . . Experts . . . tackle problems that increase their expertise, whereas nonexperts tend to tackle problems for which they do not have to extend themselves. (Bereiter and Scardamalia 1993, 78)

Moreover, once a problem is solved, experts reinvest the energy saved in "progressive problem solving" (ibid., 82).

In this process contextual demands and individual traits, including temperament, matter a great deal. Respecting the former: "It seems that our skills develop up to the level that is required for the environment" (ibid., 91). Respecting the later: "Persistence, industry, and desire for excellence are relevant," as are innate talents (ibid., 43). People reinvest their energy in progressive problem solving for various reasons. One is "flow," where investing in "the process of expertise . . . actually *feels* good" (ibid., 101). A second reason is that the context supports the development of expertise. And a third acknowledges that there is a "heroic element in expertise . . . which is not an explanation of why people put effort into the process of expertise, but rather an acknowledgement that the other explanations do not quite do the whole job" (ibid., 102).

The Current Study

If expertise is a process, then longitudinal case studies of teacher development are an especially promising means for increasing understanding. As part of an ongoing study of teacher development (Bullough 1989, ch. 7), the decision to focus this study on expertise resulted from Kerrie changing schools and teaching assignments, and in recognition that, as Berliner notes, expertise is highly context-dependent: "Knowledge is, for the most part, contextually bound"

(1990, 10). For the first six years Kerrie taught at Rocky Mountain Junior High School and the last two years she taught there, she was recognized as an expert teacher (see Chapter 7). She demonstrated many of the qualities associated with expertise, as Berliner (1988) characterizes them:

> The experts are not consciously choosing what to attend to and what to do. They are acting effortlessly, fluidly, and in a sense this is arational, because it is not easily described as deductive or analytic behavior. . . . Experts do things that usually work, and thus, when things are proceeding without a hitch, experts are not solving problems or making decisions in the usual sense of those terms. They "go with the flow." (1988, 43)

For a variety of reasons—increased salary, proximity to her home, and a desire for new challenges—Kerrie left the security of Rocky Mountain Junior High and assumed a position at Clarke Intermediate School. As will shortly be noted, the schools were dramatically different. I wondered how Kerrie would handle the new problems that would confront her in Clarke, and what, if anything, might be learned about the nature of expertise from how she responded to them. I also wondered what knowledge might transfer from one context to the next, and how this knowledge might enable or limit her professional development.

Data Gathering and Problem Focus

Established case study methods were followed (Yin 1989). Weekly observations of two class periods were conducted and extensive notes taken beginning with the first week and running through the last week of the school year. About every three weeks a semi-structured interview was conducted. These interviews were audiotaped and transcribed for analysis. Interview questions were formed from the analysis of the observation notes and previous interviews. In addition, to gain insight into the work context the principal was interviewed and the tape transcribed. The initial focus of the observations was to understand what was transpiring in Kerrie's classes and to identify characteristic instructional patterns and patterns of interaction. Additionally, I sought to understand how Kerrie's performance was different from and similar to what I observed at Rocky Mountain Junior High School in previous studies, and I sought to identify problems that captured or demanded her attention and energy. As initial interpretations of the data were formed, questions were asked that sought to test their plausibility and to refine them.

Instructional patterns were identified representative of Kerrie's teaching at Clarke Intermediate School. These patterns were compared to those identified in the earlier studies. Differences were explored in interview, which proved to be a means for illuminating the influence of contextual factors on Kerrie's development. Interview transcripts were viewed as potentially factual statements and cultural artifacts (Silverman 1993, 100). As such, comments made in interview were tested against classroom observations. As cultural artifacts, statements were viewed as representing shared ways of making meaning representative of a particular context. This is important, because although there is much that is common to schools—the patterns of action and interaction that distinguish school from other forms of institutional life—contexts differ, and from this difference arise situations and ways of responding to these situations that are unique and potentially challenging, providing new opportunities for teacher development. Thus teaching at Clarke Intermediate School presented new as well as familiar situations to Kerrie to which she responded, and in responding she drew on past experience gained at Rocky Mountain Junior High, as well as resources—ways of framing and responding to problems—made available to her within the new context. Once a draft was written, it was shared with Kerrie "as a way of corroborating the essential facts and evidence" (Yin 1989, 114) and to receive feedback on the interpretations made. She agreed with the interpretations and amplified a few points, especially in the section dealing with mainstreamed students. Her comments strengthened this section.

This chapter focuses on three teaching problems. Following Bereiter and Scardamalia, a problem was defined as existing "whenever there is a goal which we do not already have a known way of achieving" (1993, 82). I focus on multiple problems because problems interact and affect how or even if a teacher will address them. This point emerged early in the study. The first problem, initially identified through classroom observations and confirmed as serious in a subsequent interview, centered on providing an appropriate curriculum for mainstreamed students, part of the general problem of needing to effectively teach students quite different from those Kerrie worked with before at Rocky Mountain Junior High. The principal and many of the faculty in the new school were committed to mainstreaming, to including in the regular classroom students who formerly were taught by specially trained teachers in separate settings. As the principal stated: "It's good in terms of the diversity issue; this world is made up of all different types of people, and they need to all be respected and valued." Here I focus on Kerrie's work with a student born with Down's syndrome. The second problem is a carryover from Rocky Mountain Junior High School and represents Kerrie's career-long effort to create ways to better teach writing, partially reported in the previous chapter. Finally, I focus on planning for the Extended Learning Program (ELP) that Kerrie taught in the afternoon as part of a four-person, interdisciplinary team. I had been observing in Kerrie's classroom for nearly three months before I fully realized how different her planning was in the ELP program compared to her other planning, and that she was expending an extraordinary amount of energy in the effort, energy likely taken from other activities.

As these problems were identified, adjustments in data gathering were called for. Interviews and classroom observations were generally adequate for addressing the first two problems but not the third. Accordingly, arrangements were made to have the ELP planning meetings audiotaped for the purpose of discourse analysis (see Silverman 1993). As with my observation notes and interview transcripts, I sought "recurring regularities" (Guba 1978, 53) in the tapes. I realized that there were dramatic differences not only in the amount of talk generated by each team member but in the roles they played in interaction, and in the types of issues or concerns that demanded their attention. From these initial impressions, and through the process of constant comparison (Glaser and Strauss 1967), I identified a set of categories and created a simple matrix (Miles and Huberman 1984) for analyzing the tapes. Categories were created to get at the purpose or function of a statement. For example, was the intention of an utterance during a planning meeting to set the agenda, defend a point, or present an idea? A statement was assumed to be a complete thought. In addition, tapes were analyzed to identify types of questions asked by participants. These were coded by noting whether the information sought by the questioner was to understand *what* needed to be done, *why* (purpose) it needed to be done, and *how*, *when*, and *by whom* it should be done. Questions were coded that sought *confirmation* or *clarification* of a point or an idea or to *challenge* a point or an idea. With but very rare exception, these categories captured the questions posed during planning meetings. Finally, to get a rough measure of the amount of participant talk, at ten-second intervals the speaker's name was noted and for each speaker a percentage calculated of total tallies. The assumption was that when combined the analyses would provide a reasonably accurate description of the roles played by participants in each planning session and further that by comparing the results of the coded planning sessions, changes in team members' roles and in their understanding of teaching ELP students might be revealed. I wondered if I could track an increase in expertise, and if so whether it would alter team member roles. In part, this is a concern because small group role specification typically increases over time, and groups become more highly organized (see Slater 1965).

School Contexts and Background

During her first years at Rocky Mountain Kerrie taught two groups of seventh grade students reading, social studies, and English in a core. Later, social studies was removed from her teaching load, and she taught English and reading to the same students in two class period blocks. Given this arrangement Kerrie was able to integrate content. At Clarke she was hired to teach social studies—including geography—and English. During her first year there she traveled from room to room, which was disorienting, but during her second year she was assigned her own room. Rocky Mountain Junior High was a suburban and generally middle-class school, with a young rather transient faculty. The surrounding neighborhood was composed of relatively new and modest, but well-kept, homes. In contrast, Clarke was an urban, ethnically and socially diverse school that drew students from among the wealthiest and poorest neighborhoods in the city. Half the student body was bussed to school. In contrast to Rocky Mountain Junior High's faculty, Clarke's was stable and mature. Kerrie asserted that Clarke students, unlike those at Rocky Mountain Junior High, did not mix easily: "They don't mix; that's a big problem, and they snipe at each other during class all the time." To Kerrie, Clarke students seemed more "street smart [and] sexual" than the students at Rocky Mountain Junior, and there was much more gang activity.

Unlike Rocky Mountain, Clarke was committed to a middle school philosophy that included a commitment to integrating content across the disciplines and to mainstreaming students. For Kerrie, this meant during her second year teaching at Clarke that she had nine or ten resource students sprinkled throughout her first four class periods, including Enrique, a blind child from Mexico, and Ashton, a student born with Down's syndrome. Generally speaking, these students were placed in classrooms by counselors without consulting teachers. This situation stood in stark contrast to Rocky Mountain Junior High, where students were tracked and students like Ashton were placed in self-contained classrooms. During her first years of teaching, Kerrie worked with the average- and low-ability classes but eventually began teaching the "advanced core"—reading and English. She enjoyed this work. Clarke had its own version of an advanced core but it was smaller, more exclusive, and tied to the desire of some parents to have a gifted and talented program—an ELP—in the school. In contrast to the advanced core at Rocky Mountain Junior, ELP teachers designed the curriculum from scratch. Just before her second year of teaching at Clarke—the year data were gathered for this study—Kerrie was chosen along with another teacher to join two highly experienced, veteran teachers to be part of the ELP team.

A Biographical Note

Kerrie moved to Clarke during her daughter's junior year in high school. Her son had already graduated from high school and was working. While in some respects her home obligations had lessened from what they were when she taught at Rocky Mountain Junior High, other, and different, personal obligations increased in intensity. These need to be mentioned at this point because the amount of energy a teacher has and how it is invested in teaching should be considered in relationship to life inside and outside of the classroom—after all, a teacher's life is not neatly segmented (see Spencer 1986). Like other teachers, Kerrie was not only a teacher, she was a wife, mother, "housekeeper—I hold things together," primary president (head of a religious organization responsible for instructing and providing activities for children eleven years old and younger), and much more. Balancing the demands of these roles proved at times difficult. Winter, she noted, was an especially trying time at school and personally. Having started a new business, her husband was often away from home long hours and working with people Kerrie did not know. In response, Kerrie found herself worrying about their marriage relationship and seeking ways of strengthening it. Her position as primary president also was demanding:

> One of my problems is that both of my counselors have three or four children and babies—so I have to pick up a lot of their slack. I kind of resent this sometimes.

And to make matters worse, her father began undergoing chemotherapy for cancer, and her mother needed considerable emotional support. Given these demands, like other teachers Kerrie made decisions about how and where she would invest her energy. Since the work of teachers is unbounded and can easily consume all of one's life energy, these decisions are crucial ones and have a direct bearing on the development of teaching expertise. As mentioned, expertise needs to be considered in terms of the interaction between person and place.

The Problems

Diversity and Mainstreaming

As Kerrie reviewed her first year and a half teaching at Clarke she identified her most serious problem as "getting to know the [student] population." Without this knowledge, what Grimmett and MacKinnon (1992) call "pedagogical learner knowledge," she found it difficult to "troubleshoot," to anticipate difficulties within the classroom and prevent them. At Clarke, Kerrie was not an expert teacher, and she knew it. As noted, the Clarke student body was much more diverse than the population at Rocky Mountain Junior High School, and generally more challenging.

I think it was [a] bigger [problem] than I thought it would be. I'm still adjusting to it . . . I'm unsure . . . of where [some students] are coming from. . . . But, I [am] learning how to connect with different groups of people. . . . The kids are less well behaved [than they were at Rocky Mountain]. . . . [Excluding the ELP kids], they don't do homework, they don't buy that this is important.

Kerrie made good progress learning about her students, and during her second year at Clarke she seemed to have no difficulty troubleshooting: "Now I can troubleshoot things that I couldn't troubleshoot [during my first year at Clarke], because I didn't know [the students well enough]." Implicitly she recognized that knowledge of the links between teacher and student actions is essential to effectively evaluating classroom events (see Sabers et al. 1991). Experts possess just such knowledge; they seem to know their new classes even before they meet them (Berliner 1986).

While this was true for most of Kerrie's classes, it was not true for her eighth grade English class, which included Ashton, the boy born with Down's syndrome, along with thirty other students. In other classes she tended to forget which students were labeled "resource" and focused on responding to their needs as she could and as she understood them: "I don't like to keep reminding myself that they are kind of deficit, I like to give help to whoever needs it." Like other teachers showing expertise, she had "learned that every child takes on a different character in every classroom, and educational records . . . cannot be trusted" (Berliner 1990, 8). Kerrie had never taught eighth graders before and had never worked with severely retarded children except, as she stated, when "going to the Special Olympics and being a hugger." Ashton forced Kerrie to confront a limit to her expertise.

A few observation notes follow that give the flavor of the class and of Ashton's behavior within it:

September 1: 11:36 [Students working]. Kerrie circulates and goes and sits next to Ashton. He pulls out a sheet of paper—she questions him, encourages him, with his writing. While working with A she scans the classroom and tells one student who is very loud to quiet down. 11:42: still working with A. She looks him straight in the eye as they talk. 11:43: Kerrie leaves A and begins circulating. A puts away his paper. 11:44: A out of his seat. Kerrie engages him; takes him to the back of the room and shows him a magazine. He is not interested. 11:45: A goes and sits on a chair and begins digging at his shoes. He gets up and wanders, looks at the magazine rack, takes a *Sports Illustrated* with him to his seat, and puts it in his backpack.

November 11: [Students are going to present filmstrips that tell the story of a book they've read]. 11:08: Kerrie finished reading to the class. "Okay, how many of you are ready for the Clarke Filmstrip Festival? Are you ready to do yours, Ashton?" "Yeah." "Okay, Ashton looks like he has a killer filmstrip." Kerrie helps Ashton get set up. K: "Have any of you read this book, it's one of my favorites, *Ralph S. Mouse*." Everyone is silent and attentive. On an audiotape made at home, A haltingly tells the story of Ralph S. Mouse. Kerrie, referring to one of the frames, "There's Ralph, in a pocket." Ashton stands at the projector, there is a noise when he is supposed to change frames, but he's not able to keep the pictures and the story together. As the end approaches, he nervously rocks back and forth. The class sits silently, only able to understand small parts of the tape. A finishes. Kerrie: "What do you say, guys?" Applause. A boy yells out across the room: "Just think, Scooter (his nickname), you're better than 1/2 the kids in the class!" Kerrie: "Who can top that? Who's next?" . . . A asks to go to the bathroom. He's gone ten minutes. . . . 11:36: Students are getting a bit restless. A sits picking his nose and rolling boogers, which he sticks on the bottom of his desk and then roots for more. This goes on for ten minutes without interruption.

Kerrie struggled all year to come up with ways of engaging Ashton in the classroom. Instead of beginning with a separate curriculum for him, she began the year by having him try what she had planned for the other students to see "what he was going to be able to do." She began with what she knew and understood about teaching other students. Then, early in the school year, she participated with other teachers, counselors, and administrators in two four-hour meetings to set learning goals for Ashton. Having threatened a lawsuit, the mother brought a lawyer with her to each meeting. School district lawyers also attended. Kerrie wanted to provide an appropriate curriculum for Ashton, but lacking experience and knowledge, she simply did not know how to work with him: "He was definitely different." Moreover, she received no help from the special educators on faculty. In the meetings she helped set specific learning objectives for Ashton and solicited ideas from his mother, who helped set the goals. One objective was to teach him how "to write a friendly letter or note, a thank-you note." It was agreed that Ashton's work would accumulate in a portfolio and stand as evidence that he was taught.

As Kerrie learned more about Ashton's abilities and limitations, she adjusted the curriculum, seeking ways for him to engage in activities roughly similar to what the other students would be doing. She began writing "real concrete things in [her] plan book every week to do with [Ashton]." She did this, in part, just to "remember to service him." Nothing seemed to engage Ashton, however, and she became increasingly frustrated. For example, Kerrie was told by Ashton's mother that they wanted "him to be able to deal with the media." When thinking how to accomplish this aim, Kerrie asked his mother if he read the funnies. She said he did. Kerrie then made a plan:

> I was trying to get an idea of what interested him. . . . I'm going to take the funnies every week and have him choose one, cut it out, put it on a piece of paper, and write what it's about. A sentence.

This effort also failed: "He really can't do it without you practically placing the words in his mouth." With Ashton, Kerrie was a novice teacher, one who necessarily engaged in trial-and-error approaches to problem solving. Nevertheless, she remained determined to nudge along Ashton's development.

The situation in the class itself, however, conspired to frustrate Kerrie's desire. Ashton was not the only student struggling in fourth-period English. Throughout the year, Kerrie had a steady flow of troubled boys, starting with Jake, who was combative and constantly demanding attention. Kerrie did her best to keep him on task, which consumed a good deal of time and energy. After Jake was transferred into an alternative program, the counselor replaced him with Jerome, a boy who had been in four different junior high schools. Although not aggressive like Jake, Jerome still managed to be seriously disruptive. He spent his days happily chatting with others in the class, seemingly oblivious to their desire to get their work done. Jerome left before Kerrie could get him into the class routines. Without Kerrie's consent, Jerome was replaced by Sweetpea, who terrorized others in the classroom.

Sweetpea teased Ashton and taunted other students. He was a bully: "Everyone is afraid of him," Kerrie remarked. When Sweetpea was present, the entire class was tense. When absent, the classroom climate felt lighter and less oppressive. Sweetpea demanded constant, consistent, and careful monitoring. Kerrie did not dare turn her back on him. When he was present, she was able to give little special attention to Ashton, and she made fewer efforts to engage him, as is indicated in observation notes and as Kerrie admitted in interview:

> I've definitely backed off on Ashton. . . . It's like [I'm] waiting for something to be the right answer, [for the right answer] to come . . . and it's not. . . . You know, if I sat down and took my time I probably could figure out what to do with him, but he's not in the right place. For one thing, that class! . . . There's no extra energy, especially for [helping] a passive child [like Ashton].

In mid-April, the situation changed dramatically. Sweetpea was removed from school, and Kerrie again shifted her energy to Ashton and began seeking ways of engaging him in class. The difference in the classroom once Sweetpea was gone was astonishing, and almost immediate. Class seemed more like it had been before his unwelcome arrival, as is indicated in observation notes made after his departure:

The bell rang signaling the start of fourth period, and I wrote a memo in my notes asking, "[Where is Sweetpea?]."

> The class is very quiet as Kerrie reads—only an occasional muffled brief bit of chatting [between two students] breaks the silence. . . . Kerrie stops reading. . . . (11:15) Quick transition. Kerrie reads two "I used to be" poems written by students. "Those two are good," she says. . . . Quick transition. "As I give you [your midterm report grades] you may leave for the computer lab." . . . Kerrie: "Ashton, what are you doing?" He says nothing. "I have a note for your mom. Can you take it to her?" He grunts and puts his head down. He gets up. "Mrs. Baughman, I'm going to the [school] activity." "Good. Did you pay your dollar?" "Yes." "Good." "I'm going swimming." "Great!" K writes the note. "Ashton, you wrote a haiku poem. Why don't you go type it at the computer." A: "No." K: "Yes." A: "No." K: "Why don't you type it up and you will get a VISA" (a card that recognizes students for good work). Now whispering playfully to Ashton. "Do you want a VISA? Do you want a VISA?" "Yes." "Okay, when you get to the lab you type it up. Here's the note for your mother that tells how you need to do your book report. Put it in your pack. [Your tracker] will help you type it or I will. Should we go upstairs [to the lab]?"

Kerrie was relaxed. Class was pleasant and productive. With Sweetpea gone, she again invested additional energy in Ashton.

The year ended, and Kerrie was still engaging in trial and error, seeking means for engaging Ashton. Had Sweetpea never been enrolled in the class, she may have made significant progress toward providing an adequate program for Ashton, as she did for the eighth graders generally, which will be discussed in the next section. Unfortunately, the context of fourth period was hostile to developing expertise, except perhaps expertise in working with disengaged and angry male students. The counselor bears much of the responsibility for creating fourth period. Clearly, some contexts bring with them more insistent problems than others, and teachers must make judgments about how to invest their energy. Ashton was passive; Sweetpea aggressive, demanding, and fully capable of preventing anyone else from learning. Kerrie put a large portion of her energy into containing and directing Sweetpea and in trying to make certain the class remained a productive place for other students, a point that will be further discussed in the next section. Ashton was not forgotten, he just received far less attention than he needed.

There is a knowledge dimension to the development of expertise that is well illustrated by Kerrie's trial-and-error approach to working with Ashton.

Since being certified, which did not involve any courses that addressed special education concerns, Kerrie had taken no fewer than thirty-six in-service and university courses, completed a master's degree, and obtained a certificate in gifted and talented education. Not one of these courses addressed severely handicapped children. Moreover, she received no help from the special educators working within the building, although in late spring district administrators assigned to work with Ashton a speech therapist who also helped him with class work. Nor was class size reduced. Ashton was assigned to Kerrie not because she possessed any particular knowledge about how to effectively teach him, but because she was increasingly coming to be recognized within the school, and by the counselors, as a caring and hard-working teacher who would do her best for students. In retrospect, Kerrie concluded: "The better you are [at teaching], the less help you get, even if it's in an area new to you." If the development of teaching expertise was an aim of either the administrators or counselors, and it should have been, then Kerrie ought to have received some instruction and a good deal of help within the classroom. She received neither.

Having both Ashton and Sweetpea in the same class nicely illustrates how problems interact, compound one another, and are prioritized and, further, how contextual events can conspire to constrain teacher development. To encourage the development of teaching expertise, careful attention must be given to making certain the contexts within which teachers work "provide support for the process of expertise" (Bereiter and Scardamalia 1993, 102). Such environments present conditions in which "progress or growth is a continuing requirement of adaptation to the environment" (Ibid., 244), but they do not overwhelm participants; instead, they invite them to work at the edge of their competence. Kerrie's fourth-period English class, at least when Sweetpea and Ashton were both there, was nearly overwhelming, even for an experienced teacher.

Teaching Writing

During Kerrie's first year of teaching at Rocky Mountain Junior High School, feeling swamped by the workload, she compromised the desire to have students write extensively and rewrite their work. Having compromised a fundamental value, she felt guilty but saw no alternative. Five years later, she reflected on this decision and remarked: "It is like, well, I [didn't] know what else to do, so I'm going to continue on and do the best I can and refine the things that I know I'm doing well" (Bullough and Baughman 1993, 88). Put succinctly, unable to make progress on the problem she set it aside, for a time.

As noted in Chapter 7, early in her fifth year of teaching Kerrie attended an International Reading Association conference and obtained a copy of Nancie Atwell's book *Writing, Reading and Learning with Adolescents*.

As she read the book, lights went on. She saw within Atwell's program, Writing and Reading Workshop, the possibility of shifting her program toward a writing emphasis and decided to change her entire curriculum. Spring term of her fifth year of teaching she implemented as much of Atwell's program as she could, changing it even as she did so. Kerrie remade the program to fit her context and values.

In some respects the schedule at Clarke was less compatible with Reading and Writing Workshop than was the schedule at Rocky Mountain Junior High. At Clarke, Kerrie taught social studies and English, not reading, which meant a significant reduction in the amount of time she had to work with students on writing, and Reading and Writing Workshop was time-intensive. As a "roving teacher," she did not have her own classroom, which meant there was no place to display "published" works. The English teachers shared a planning period and a textbook, and the expectation was that Kerrie's curriculum should represent departmental priorities. These problems, coupled with others associated with learning how to teach effectively within a new context, prompted Kerrie to set aside Reading and Writing Workshop, for a time. Her energy was expended elsewhere, in particular figuring out how things worked in the new school, finding her place, and getting to know inner-city students, as noted earlier. She was not concerned about developing expertise per se. It was a very difficult year: "The first year at the school was hard. I had to make a lot of changes in one year, and it was hard."

Her second year at Clarke brought another change in schedule. Her only English class was fourth period, Ashton's and Sweetpea's eighth grade class. As noted, she had not taught eighth grade before. Still, she felt she should emphasize writing more than she had with her seventh graders the year before. But how to do it? Drawing on her experience from Rocky Mountain Junior High, and her increasing knowledge of Clarke students, she decided to emphasize journal writing, along with frequent and more traditional writing assignments. In addition, she decided that before work was turned in, students should share it with others in the class, receive feedback, and engage in rewriting. She began routinizing the students to this process the first week of school, as she had done during her last year at Rocky Mountain Junior High:

"Okay, you're going to do peer response." Kerrie reviews the procedure. On the board she has written:

Peer Response
    1. Partners
    2. 1st person read aloud
        2nd person listen, take notes
    3. Trade

She continued: "Last, you need to read one another's paper and give feedback, so try and pick someone who is smarter than you . . . tomorrow you will write the final copies." In addition, Kerrie gave specific lessons on the parts of speech. On Mondays they studied grammar. Trying to make writing more interesting, she varied the writing assignments. One day, for example, they wrote picnic poems that were copied on paper plates, which were stapled to a wall over a red-and-white checkered, plastic tablecloth. Occasionally students went to the computer lab to work on their writing, the lab being available five days a term to each teacher. They did this in addition to reading and reporting on books through a variety of means such as the Clarke Filmstrip Festival, noted earlier.

Over the Christmas break, and looking ahead to the rest of the year, Kerrie thought long and hard about the English curriculum. Despite her struggle to find ways of teaching Ashton, and her difficulty with some of the boys in the class, she concluded: "If I really believe in writing, then that's what I'd better be doing [with that class]." She rethought the curriculum in light of her prior experience with Reading and Writing Workshop, what the students had thus far accomplished, and of the energy she thought she could put into the effort. Writing, she decided, would become the central focus of the class for the rest of the year. This decision was eased by her increased knowledge of district priorities—writing ability was tested—and of what other teachers within the building were and were not doing. She discovered, for example, that the computer lab was rarely used during fourth period.

After Christmas, Kerrie contacted other teachers and made arrangements to have the computer lab available for much of the rest of the school year. This was possible because only one other teacher was using the lab at that hour, and he only needed it occasionally. A chart went up on the wall:

    WHAT WRITERS DO:
    WRITERS:
        REHEARSE (FIND AN IDEA)
        DRAFT ONE
        CONFER
        DRAFT TWO/REVISE
        CONFER . . .
        DECIDE THE CONTENT IS SET
        SELF AND GROUP EDIT
        TEACHER EDIT
        FINAL COPY—PUBLISH

A new daily schedule was established. After giving students a list of types of writing assignments that would have to be completed during the term, class began, as at Rocky Mountain Junior, by Kerrie quickly reading the roll and noting what students were working on. The wall at the back of the room was set up for publishing, for posting student work. In addition, she began teaching the students new routines. For example, she expected students to read some of their written work to the class: "We have a problem with students leaving for the computer lab and not returning [for students to read their work]. It's okay, I want you to work in the lab, but some people are needing to read their writing to us, so we'll need to do that at the start of the class [not the end]. Is anyone ready to read to us?" Given the makeup of the class, making even minor adjustments in routines was difficult, but Kerrie persisted in refining her program while struggling to manage the troubling few boys in class and respond to Ashton's needs.

With these changes, Kerrie recreated at Clarke many of the features of her writing program at Rocky Mountain Junior High School. There were, however, important differences that stretched her teaching ability. Given greater time constraints and the availability of a computer lab, her approach to conferencing with students changed. Instead of calling students to her desk and talking through each student's paper, conferences took place at computer screens. Kerrie quickly read the writing on the screen, gave feedback, and later checked to see if changes were made. Conferences were brief, involved less coaching and goal setting, and seemed a bit less intimate than those held at Rocky Mountain Junior High. This was not only made necessary by time constraints but also by the need to carefully monitor Sweetpea, Ashton, and the rest of the class while in the lab. Generally greater emphasis was placed on self- and peer editing. In fact, Kerrie did not want to see a piece until the student was well satisfied with it.

In addition, the students seemed to need more help identifying topics, and a few students, Ashton and Sweetpea prominent among them, needed much teacher direction. Accordingly, some assignments were very specific, such as writing a cinquain. Listed on the board: "Cinquain title, 2 syllables. Description of title, 4 syllables. Action about title, 6 syllables. Feeling about the title, 8 syllables. Synonym for the title, 2 syllables." Others, such as making a map of the neighborhood, were intended primarily to stimulate thought and help students who had difficulty getting a writing topic. These were subtle but important changes without which this shift in Kerrie's curriculum may have caused more problems than it solved.

The importance of knowledge to the development of teaching expertise is again well illustrated in Kerrie's struggle to more effectively teach writing as it was in her attempt to better instruct Ashton. After all, had she not ever encountered Atwell's program she may have continued to tinker with her curriculum, never being fully satisfied with it. She encountered Atwell's work as a result of attending a conference, an opportunity that came because of her master's degree program. One might conclude that the writing and the English methods courses she took for teacher certification let her down, left her without knowledge of some of the better options available for the teaching of writing. Fortunately, her master's program did not.

Other issues emerge. Once again context becomes important. During Kerrie's last year at Rocky Mountain Junior High her writing program was running smoothly and well. Initial parental concerns gave way to praise. Indeed, because of her success she was invited to present her work at a district-sponsored conference. Other teachers sought her advice. While her desire to emphasize writing remained after moving to Clarke, she found it impossible to teach as she desired, and she fell back on earlier instructional practices, ones that required less energy and promised greater control of students. A change in context during her second year at Clarke—getting her own room in particular—encouraged a reconsideration of the curriculum and a reinvestment of energy in the problem of how to better teach writing, this despite the makeup of the class. What is noteworthy is that just as with the first change that led to her adoption and adaptation of Writing Workshop, this implementation was internally prompted; no one urged her to make the change. In fact, at Rocky Mountain Junior High there were a good many reasons not to adopt Writing Workshop, as already noted. Similarly, she was not compelled to alter her curriculum at Clarke to place a greater emphasis on writing. In this respect, neither context encouraged change.

In some respects, we brush lightly against the heroic dimensions of expertise here. When seeking to understand heroics, the first place to look is toward the person acting heroically. Kerrie's commitment to teaching writing was deep and abiding, as was her sense of needing to serve young people to the best of her ability.

> If you are going to be a teacher you really owe it to the kids to do a good job. You know . . . the reason why I'm teaching junior high is that there has to be someone who is willing to put up with the kind of stuff they do and get them through it. I've said this before, [you've got to] love them along and hang in there with them.

She was not unhappy with her approach to writing at Rocky Mountain Junior High, just not happy with it. The students were not performing as she thought they could, and it nagged at her. Immediately recognizing the "promisingness" of Atwell's program, she jumped at it, even though it would require a dramatic stretching of the boundaries of her expertise, a stretching she welcomed. What made her actions heroic was that she transcended the demands of the context. There is less of the heroic in the changes she made at Clarke, although this judgment is tempered by considering the makeup of the class. This change required only a little boundary stretching, but it still required additional energy, which was clearly in short supply. Most teacher-initiated changes are probably of this kind, where expertise is nudged along incrementally. Had a greater amount of energy been required to make the change, it is possible, perhaps even likely, given Kerrie's self-regulatory knowledge—knowledge of how far she could stretch—that she would not have made it. This is because of other demands of teaching and at home.

Clearly contextual differences are crucially important to developing teaching expertise. Differences in physical plant, formal curriculum, school and teacher culture, and philosophy are all important. To press personal competence boundaries in some contexts undoubtedly requires near-superhuman efforts. Neither school fits this category, however. Rocky Mountain Junior High may not have supported Kerrie's efforts to teach writing, but perhaps as important, it was not hostile to them. Nor was Clarke hostile. In fact, the existence of the computer lab provided a new way for addressing an old problem, and with it came an opportunity for Kerrie to extend her expertise, to work at the edge of her competence, as a teacher of writing. Considering this issue brings to light an ability of Kerrie's that may be related to the development of expertise. Although sensitive to contextual pressures, Kerrie had a knack for finding resources needed to achieve her aims, an expression, perhaps, of educated common sense. Of this more will be said later.

Planning ELP

> A lot of [planning] is in my head, but in ELP it's all written down on a master sheet that the four of us [on the team] have. . . . [Planning] has been a problem for me because here they are brainstorming and [the other new team member] and I are just sort of listening and saying, "Okay, I'll do that, I'll do that part." "Okay, be sure and tell me how to do that." Then, it's written down and it's in someone else's notes and you've got written down kind of what you think you're supposed to do. But later on, when it's the day before you're supposed to do it, I'm running down the hall to [one of the experienced teachers, the one] who *understands everything with perfect knowledge.* I talk with her and say, "Now, how am I supposed to do this?" . . . Now I need more lead time to think about it. . . . In the next planning meeting on Monday I'm going to be saying, "Whoa, slow down, I need to flesh this out and I need to write it down so I remember it." . . . I don't really care what [the other teachers think]. I need to know. I can't be deciding ten minutes before class what it is I'm supposed to be doing. I can't do that. It's when I have knowledge that I don't need a lesson plan—right now, I'm on the edge.

Working in ELP presented many problems to Kerrie, not the least among them balancing the extensive demands of teaching ELP with other

professional and personal demands. New to the program, Kerrie was unfamiliar with the experienced teachers' ways of planning and working together.
These teachers, intellectually powerful, articulate, and demanding women,
created the curriculum, and they expected it to be taught and taught well. As
a novice ELP teacher, Kerrie found herself scrambling to know what to teach,
and sometimes uncertain how to teach it. By comparison, her other experiences teaming had required modest investments of time and energy: "[All we
have to do for ELP] is mind boggling, just for one subject of two classes. It's
partly because we're teaming. It's much easier to plan when you can shut the
door and do your own thing." She found herself in a new situation, heavily
dependent on the two experienced teachers, and struggling to keep up her part
of the team's work. Planning sessions took place at lunch nearly every day, and
twice a week after school for a few hours. The demands were extraordinary.

> In ELP we plan big units and these are not turn the page and read the next
> page and answer the questions, [type units]. These are things where the
> teacher has to do research and then present things all the time. We plan
> twice a week, like on Monday we're going to go and plan probably through
> dinner [time]. . . . That's only the planning. That's not getting ready to teach.

The curriculum was fluid, plans often changed, and the work seemingly was
never ending.

Kerrie was not the only one having difficulty keeping up, however. The
other team member new to ELP also struggled, as will shortly be noted. Kerrie's and the other new team member's dependency on the experienced ELP
team members for ideas and ways of working is evident from the analyses of
the planning meeting tapes. At the same time, and in contrast to the other
new member, Kerrie's efforts to be a team player and to hold up her part of
the work are also quite apparent. For example, audiotapes coded for amount
of team member talk revealed that the two experienced teachers dominated
the conversation. In the tapes recorded in late winter and early spring, for
example, they spoke 79 percent and 81 percent of the time, respectively. In a
planning session following Christmas, forty-three questions were coded. Only
five of these were posed by an experienced ELP teacher, and the purpose of
three of these questions was to challenge another's point of view. Kerrie posed
twelve questions that were coded, six sought "clarification," one "confirmation"
of an idea (e.g., "They need to have an end task in mind, do you think, when
they start?"), and two "how" to do something (e.g., "How would we bring in
literature?"). The other new ELP teacher asked seventeen "clarification" questions (e.g., "Do they write their answers?") and five "how" questions. This pattern changed, somewhat, depending on whether or not both experienced ELP
teachers attended a meeting.

In a subsequent planning meeting sixty-five questions were coded. The pattern of the new ELP teachers asking "clarification" and "how" questions persisted. Experienced teachers asked primarily "challenge" and "confirmation" questions underscoring their possession of a large store of knowledge about students, the curriculum, and potential problems. This pattern was still evident in the spring meeting just noted, with both beginning ELP teachers' interaction being dominated by the need for clarification. Yet Kerrie's colleague participated in no other way in any of the coded meetings. In contrast, Kerrie amplified some ideas and clarified others, indicating that she sought to shape the program that would eventually emerge. The other new ELP teacher seemed content to have others tell her what and how to teach. This difference is important.

These roles—somewhat like the relationship of an apprentice to a master—were generally confirmed through discourse analysis. The experienced teachers, who created the curriculum and who had taught it previously, offered and explained their ideas in detail to their new colleagues, including those about how best to accomplish a desired outcome. They also sometimes defended their ideas or justified them, even though they were rarely challenged.

> What they have to do is write a four-page paper. . . . They have to write in the character's voice, a response to certain questions, like what do you think the nation should do about the slavery question? They have to answer as the character. Only one person in [each class] can be [any one character].

Unlike the other new ELP teacher, however, Kerrie presented and explained ideas, although not often. In one winter meeting, for example, the curriculum was altered to include a newspaper unit that drew heavily on her work in the past. This time, she did the explaining:

> [We tell the students], you're going to write up a newspaper—You're going to have things like two editorials, two advertisements . . .

In response to her explanation, the other teachers, including the two experienced ELP teachers, asked for clarification and amplified Kerrie's ideas: "So, basically we have three days to do this?" "How much is the newspaper worth?" "I think there should be individual grades and group grades." Although brief, this exchange mirrored those of the experienced ELP teachers when they presented ideas.

This exchange (and others like it) is important for understanding the development of expertise. The data suggest that both beginning ELP teachers were working at the edge of their competence. But unlike her colleague, Kerrie was pressing the boundaries of her understanding and ability here and there by seeking greater involvement in planning, including putting forth her own ideas for consideration, and perhaps rejection, by the team, even while she was learning about the curriculum and how to teach it from the experienced teachers. This stands in contrast to the actions of the other new ELP teacher, who assumed a passive role, one of responding to and implementing others' ideas. To be sure, by merely listening to the experienced teachers plan the curriculum much could be learned, but when there is no risk taking, no boundary pushing, there is no possibility of developing expertise.

The form or approach to planning ELP added an additional layer of complexity to the general problem of learning how to work with the team and plan an appropriate program for high-ability students. As part of her certification as a educator of gifted and talented students, Kerrie had to learn a new way of thinking about and organizing curricula, which also proved demanding. The approach had evolved over time and represented a modification of the model proposed by Kaplan (1986). The curriculum was organized thematically, and projects were developed that integrated the disciplines and emphasized "productive, complex, abstract, and/or higher-level thinking skills" and "self-appraisal" and "criterion referenced" evaluation (Kaplan 1986, 183). To assure development of higher-level thinking skills, the team sought activities at the upper end of Bloom's *Taxonomy of Educational Objectives* (Bloom 1956). Moving from simple to more complex, activities within units were "scaffolded," seeking eventually to engage students in synthesizing and evaluating knowledge. Kerrie valued this approach to planning, but initially felt that she and the other new teacher were "just really feeling our way along." She thought with time, it would "be much, much easier."

Kerrie's work in ELP illustrates a portion of the complexity of teacher problems. Problems come in interrelated clusters. Some problems are persistent and require constant attention, while others, once solved, remained solved. Learning how to plan using the Kaplan model is an illustration of the latter-type problem. Once Kerrie became comfortable with the model, she had little trouble using it, and energy was freed to engage other concerns. This is an example of progressive problem solving. Learning how to work with the team presented another cluster of problems that potentially could produce conditions that would facilitate progressive problem solving. The team itself potentially could become a "second-order environment" for team members, but only if the experienced teachers would agree to adjust the curriculum in more than superficial ways and be willing to give their expertise away to help the new teachers develop their own expertise. The openness with which the experienced teachers shared ideas suggests that they were willing to give their expertise away. In doing so, ultimately, their own burdens would be lightened and their development enhanced (see Bereiter and Scardamalia 1993, 24).

Expertise often is viewed as an individual possession, but there also is group expertise, "teamwork *is* expertise" (Bereiter and Scardamalia 1993, 21). For expertise of this kind to emerge would require not only that the experienced teachers give their expertise away but also to make room for the new ELP teachers to express and test their own ideas. Kerrie sought opportunities throughout the year to more fully participate in team decisions, indicating a desire to increase her expertise and to improve the team: "[I discovered] I needed to be more assertive [in meetings]. . . . Then I discovered the more I asserted myself, the more I got out of [teaching the curriculum]." In particular, she stated that she wanted to learn how to develop an integrated curriculum, which "I love. I think it's great."

In contrast to Kerrie, the other new ELP teacher showed few signs of pressing the boundaries of her expertise. Contextual demands and personal desire to develop obviously interact. Opportunities provided by a demanding and rich environment may be rejected, and personal striving may be met by hostility. Generally speaking, Kerrie found in the team a supportive environment that consistently presented new and interesting professional challenges.

There were limits to how many of these challenges Kerrie could accept, however. Boundary pushing is most likely to occur when there is a balance between ability and challenge, otherwise frustration and disappointment may set in (Bereiter and Scardamalia 1993, 102). Difficulties at home, or related to her other roles, lessened the energy she had available to grapple with new challenges, and balance sometimes was lost. During the winter, for example, Kerrie took a day off because she was physically and emotionally exhausted.

> Things have not been the smoothest between my husband and me for like a year. [These problems] take my mind out of what I'm doing. [I have difficulty concentrating]. Things pop into my mind—I think—I've got to get that out of my mind so I can give my effort [to teaching].

During this time, and as a means for coping, Kerrie planned activities outside of school to alleviate stress and revitalize her energy while cutting back on some work-related demands. These outside activities required additional time but were deemed necessary. She said she learned how to cope from growing up with a sickly mother. In interview, Kerrie reconstructed this pattern of thought, a pattern she said she followed when confronted with very stressful situations:

> I thought, What would have helped my mom? Exercise. Therefore, aerobics. And therefore, the play [I have a part in next month]. I've chosen to take steps to force me to do things; I've said "yes" to [requests] that I could just as easily [have refused]. I said "Yes." People think it adds to my stress, but really it alleviates stress.

Kerrie needed time away from work and away from family. These actions illustrate what Bereiter and Scardamalia would likely label "self-regulatory knowledge." "Self-regulatory knowledge [is] knowledge that controls the application of other knowledge" (1993, 60). It is highly individualistic knowledge of how one best works, of how to manage oneself.

Conclusion

The unevenness of Kerrie's professional development in general and teacher expertise in particular is striking. Often expertise is thought of as a state of being, when clearly it is more a matter of becoming, of pushing back boundaries here and there, and as energy is made available for identifying and confronting new and more complicated problems. Striving for expertise in teaching is complicated by the nature of education-related problems that are especially messy, overlap, and come in clusters rather than rows. As an experienced teacher, Kerrie brought teaching skill and understanding with her to Clarke from Rocky Mountain Junior High School, but there were no guarantees that this knowledge would serve her or her students well in the new setting and with the new challenges that setting would present. Having once shown expertise in teaching does not mean that one will continue to demonstrate expertise, especially in a new setting.

Getting to know students quite different from those she formerly taught at Rocky Mountain Junior High School was not least among the challenges Clarke presented to Kerrie. Kerrie had never worked with severely handicapped students. She could have defined Ashton as being like every other "dim bulb" she had taught, but she did not. She thought of Ashton as unique, different, and in need of a different curriculum. Unfortunately, she had no knowledge of how to teach such students, and without such knowledge she relied upon trial-and-error approaches to problem solving, just as she had done when first beginning to teach. With Ashton, Kerrie was a novice teacher. Moreover, the context of fourth period made it extremely difficult, if not impossible, for Kerrie to create the desired program, even if she possessed the appropriate knowledge. The conclusion is obvious: Teacher expertise best develops when the conditions of work support it, when there are "second-order environments" in place.

Planning ELP also presented a new set of challenges for Kerrie, ones that held the promise of calling forth greater expertise. In the context of the planning team, she could not function as she had in the past, by planning only in her head, like other experienced teachers commonly do. This option was not available; neither the team nor Kerrie would allow it: "I'm forced to go and plan ELP, I'm forced to go and plan," she stated in interview. She relished the challenge of teaching bright students, and, despite the huge time investment, she enjoyed the planning meetings, even though much of the time her role was limited to an apprenticeship. In these meetings she learned a great deal about curriculum and teaching, and with time one would expect to see the signs of expertise emerge as she presses for greater involvement in team decisions. Expertise in teaching does not come easily or quickly. In contrast to these challenges, establishing the Writing Workshop at Clarke, despite the presence of Sweetpea and Ashton, involved only a modest boundary stretching, but her teaching abilities increased nonetheless.

Kerrie's shifting and parceling out of energy from one problem to another seemed to take place intuitively. She did not formally prioritize problems. Rather, she seemed to respond to an internal vision of what a productive class was supposed to be and look like and made decisions about how much energy she could give to each class, minimally. This is important at a general and theoretical level, because developing expertise may be related to teachers possessing a deep and very basic understanding of educational purposes, of what schools are supposed to accomplish (see Copeland et al. 1994). Diversions from this ideal called forth an increased investment of time and energy, providing that such time and energy were available. Occasionally she was nearly overwhelmed by the demands of teaching and backed off from one or another problem for a time. We see an example of this when Sweetpea enrolled in Ashton's classroom. Although Kerrie continued to implement the writing program, she spent less time working with Ashton. Sweetpea got a lot of attention, perhaps at Ashton's expense, because he interfered with Kerrie's vision of fourth period. Sweetpea presented an overriding demand (because Kerrie knew how to deal with him, Sweetpea would not formally be considered a problem in Bereiter's and Scardamalia's sense), one that required a great deal of energy, even though there was no promise that the situation would improve significantly—perhaps the best that could be hoped for was that other students' learning would not suffer—or that it would extend Kerrie's expertise in any way. A good amount of a teacher's time probably is spent in just this way, on demands that are tiring and ultimately uninteresting from the perspective of professional growth, but nevertheless grimly insistent.

Kerrie had a knack for locating within the school opportunities for developing her expertise and for staying interested in teaching. Since her first year of teaching, involvement in the wider school community has been a central part of her conception of professionalism (see Bullough 1989, Chapter 10). In interview I asked Kerrie why she wanted to teach in ELP, even while knowing it would be very demanding of her time and energy. She responded:

> I always volunteer. I had a hard year last year but I also had it really easy academically. I was ready to do something else; it was a challenge, [although it's been] a lot of work.

Furthermore, she thought that professionals need to be "at the leading edge, working so that you're pushing the edge. . . . Why not be the best, and be experimenting and pushing so that you're preparing kids better for what they're going to see in the future?"

Her actions were consistent with her words. As noted, since certification she has taken at least three dozen courses, served on a variety of committees, and in other ways has been engaged in the profession and has expanded her teaching knowledge and improved her practice. "Professionals," she said, "are always growing." Not surprisingly, Kerrie's principal characterized her as a "progressive teacher," one who "stays on top of her profession." This said, ELP proved to be "a killer," and she expressed the need to back off from some of her other school commitments as a result: "[You] bite off a little and your mouth gets full really fast." But she enjoyed the work, finding in it the desired balance between ability and challenge (Bereiter and Scardamalia 1993, 102).

The quest for expertise in teaching plays out in the complicated interaction of person and place and can only be understood in relationship to a broad range of diverse personal commitments and shifting professional demands. Expertise, as Kerrie's story illustrates, is context-dependent and highly idiosyncratic. Some contexts—second-order environments—are more friendly to its development than others, and some persons are more likely to manifest expertise than are others. Moreover, expertise is surprisingly fluid and uneven, as Kerrie's work on the ELP planning team suggests, and may involve dramatic leaps in understanding and skill as well as small, almost imperceptible increases. Undoubtedly all teachers have gaps in their knowledge and in how to apply it effectively. Settled and secure, some teachers are comfortable living within receding boundaries. For others, like Kerrie, the discovery of such gaps is an opportunity to push boundaries here and there a little.

If this is true, then, one wonders whether or not the disposition to engage in progressive problem solving is a learned trait, an expression of temperament, or both, as this study in some ways suggests. A context may be rich in possibilities, but individual teachers must choose to act upon them if professional growth is to result. Conversely, a teacher enthused about the possibilities of developing new approaches to teaching and pushing out the boundaries of expertise can be worn down over time by an oppressive work context, an inappropriate teaching assignment of six periods of Sweetpea, for example, or serious and persistent problems at home. In all of this, the role of teacher education is unclear. Teacher educators are certainly concerned about providing a knowledge base for beginning teachers, despite recognizing the inevitability of significant gaps in that knowledge that will only become apparent once a first teaching position is accepted. New gaps will emerge with new teaching assignments, like Kerrie's move to Clarke. And, teacher educators claim to be interested in helping teachers becoming increasingly expert. Perhaps in the short run the most promising approach for teacher educators is to teach directly what is currently known about the development of expertise along with providing opportunities to utilize those tools, such as action research, that are useful for studying and improving one's own practice. The long-term aim, however, is much more ambitious, through partnerships for teacher educators to become part of the effort to study and create second-order environments, places that support teachers' ongoing quest to improve their practice without necessitating acts of individual heroism. Heroism ought not be necessary. Ultimately, the qualities of second-order environments ought to be the features that distinguish professional development schools from ordinary schools, just as a quiet hunger, like Kerrie's, to improve practice distinguishes expert teachers from ordinary teachers.

CHAPTER 9

Getting in Touch:
Dreaming, the Emotions,
and the Work of Teaching (2006)

with Dawn Ann Bullough and Pam Blackwell Mayes

Introduction

The study reported in this chapter originated following a remarkable, but perhaps not an uncommon, event. Taking a break from their preparations for the start of the school year, a group of elementary school teachers began talking about their dreams, nighttime narratives, about teaching. They giggled when imagining one another undressed and in front of a class of students or lost in a maze at a familiar supermarket while trying to find something, anything, to teach. Sharing the dreams was fun and in a sense liberating, a feeling prompted by recognition that as a teacher one is not alone when feeling frustrated or worried about school-related events. This is true even though some of the emotions arising in the dreams were unsettling and some dream actions disturbing to the teachers. As they spoke, it was apparent that the dreams of these teachers revealed something profound about teaching, about the context of teaching, and about themselves as teachers.

The connection between dreaming and the emotional life is now generally recognized as well established: "Past research shows that dreams most directly reveal concerns, interests, and worries [of dreamers]" (Domhoff 2003, 27). Some dream theorists have gone so far as to argue that one of the functions of dreams is the "possibility for recreating the emotional balance that has been lost during the day" (Vedfelt 1999, 317). This viewpoint finds support in what is called the "continuity hypothesis" (Van De Castle 1994, 363), that there is a "demonstrable correspondence" between the content of dreams and the life conditions of the dreamer, even when in waking hours these connections may be unrecognized. Accordingly, it is perhaps not surprising that the vast majority—upwards of 80 percent (Domhoff 2003, 165)—of emotions experienced while dreaming are reportedly "negative or unpleasant, involving emotions such as apprehension, anger, or sadness" (Van De Castle 1994, 298).

159

This conclusion is underscored by the teachers interviewed in this study who often referred to their dreams by the emotions that accompanied them: "It's my 'panic dream'; you know, worry dreams." In addition to a strong connection between life conditions and dream content, there is also correspondence between waking and sleeping cognition, which includes reliance on figurative thought. This is understandable, since most dreams are involved in resolving situations that have not lent themselves to daytime cognition and problem solving. Thus exploring dreams offers a means for gaining insight into and for checking one's emotional health, as well as an avenue for exploring the ways in which work contexts impede or enable teaching and teacher well-being.

The Study

The current exploratory study was planned to open up the lives of teachers for study in a new way that would permit making connections between work conditions and teachers' lives. It is important to note that the study is necessarily exploratory and suggestive rather than definitive, in part because images and symbols form the language of dreams, not words. But to be communicated, dreams must be told, verbalized. Hence, dreams are not accessed directly, not translated, as one might decode a text, but probed to be made meaningful. In this sense there is a strong connection between dream analysis and narrative analysis (Polkinghorne 1988), for narratives of dreams, which rely on a time sequence—this happened, then this—must be constructed and then interrogated, and interrogation may result in amplification, a retelling, and perhaps a transformation of the story told. The problem is hermeneutical.

Dream analysts approach their interpretative task by drawing on traditions that have proven therapeutically fruitful, but it is important to note that these traditions are evolving and in some respects competing. This said, here we tap well-established and widely recognized research conclusions. When therapeutic aims dominate analysis, the usual pattern is to collect or report dreams over an extended period of time, look for patterns and central story lines internal to the dream history, and then work to remove, reinterpret, or reimagine blockages or concerns and to restory self. Our aim is different. We seek to illuminate patterns in the dream reports of a group of individuals sharing a work and life context. Thus we sought breadth rather than depth in the data, seeking to paint a shared picture of teaching as experienced through and represented in dreaming. Even if we could, we are not interested in trying to tease out individual pathologies, if any were present. We believe the picture painted from the data provides a point of departure for educators who may wish to "turn inward" and explore the personal ontology of teaching as well as distorting aspects of the work of teachers.

Arrangements were made to conduct a set of interviews with a group of elementary schoolteachers teaching within the same school. Lincoln Elementary School is undergoing rapid changes that have profoundly affected the teachers' lives. As a result of the closure of a neighboring school, much of the faculty was new to the building, and a large percentage of the faculty was assigned new grade-level placements. Nearly every teacher was required to change classrooms, which was deeply disruptive. The student body also changed following school closure: Overnight, Lincoln became larger, much poorer, and, like other schools in the district facing the challenges of dramatically increasing legal and illegal immigration, much more diverse. For the six interviewed teachers transferred from the closed school to Lincoln, the transition was traumatic, even though their new colleagues mostly were welcoming. In most respects, Lincoln would be recognized as a typical elementary school, although class sizes are large (averaging about twenty-five to twenty-seven), and children are ability grouped in mathematics and may shift teachers and classrooms depending on teacher evaluations of student knowledge and ability. One unusual feature of the school program is a strong arts emphasis, which endures despite growing district and statewide emphasis on skills testing in reading, mathematics, and science. By interviewing nearly an entire faculty of one school, it was thought that a near-random sample across grade levels and levels of experience would be achieved, plus, given the shared context, it was believed making links between dreams and the work context would be facilitated.

Twenty-one interviews were conducted, audiotaped, and transcribed for analysis. Seventeen of twenty-two regularly employed teachers volunteered to be interviewed, along with four student teachers. Of the seventeen teachers, four had backgrounds in special education or were currently teaching special education classes. Of the teachers interviewed, two were male, one of whom was a student teacher. The modal number of years teaching for the regularly employed group of teachers was twenty (the range was from just beginning to teach to thirty-one years of teaching experience). All names are fictitious.

Interviews were conducted at Lincoln during August, shortly before the beginning of the school year. A member of the faculty solicited her colleagues' participation and explained the study before a time was set for the interviews. In this way the teachers had time to think about their dreams, usually for a day or more before being asked to share them in interview.

Dreams can be accessed in many ways. Given our aims, the focus is on "memorable dreams" (Domhoff 2003, 77), dreams that were of sufficient emotional power to be relatively easily recalled. To this end a rather open interview format was developed, which would encourage the sharing of dreams and stimulate recall of past dreams. Accordingly, after asking a few demographic questions (e.g., "How many years have you taught?"), each interview began with a general question, phrased in different ways depending on the interviewer's sense of the situation—"Do you have any teacher dreams, dreams about teaching?" With the exception of one student teacher, all teachers reported having such dreams. The one student teacher who reported not having such dreams may only have been saying that she did not recall them. Questions were then asked that invited the teachers to tell the story of their dreams, which were probed for details and for story line and theme. As the teachers talked about their dreams, often additional dreams were recalled and details emerged. Questions were asked about the timing, pattern, and content of the dreams (location, participants, and actions taken), thoughts and feelings recalled, and any additional details that could be remembered.

Transcriptions of the interviews were analyzed to identify themes (Delaney 1997) and prominent imagery and to consider possible meanings in light of the wider literature on dreaming and dream analysis (see Van De Castle 1994). In addition, connections between the dreams, emotions, and work of teaching at Lincoln were sought. Theoretically, this approach holds promise, because "most dreams are like dramas or plays in which the dreamer acts out various scenarios that revolve around a few basic personal themes" (Domhoff 2003, 34). As a narrative, like a drama, a dream usually has four components: "(1) an opening scene which introduces the setting, characters, and initial situation of the main character; (2) the development of a plot; (3) the emergence of a major conflict; and (4) the response to the conflict by the main character" (Van De Castle 1994, 165–66). Generally the teachers claimed their dreams had no clear ending; often they would awaken from a dream, then laugh, or feel relieved upon realizing that it was "only a dream." Likely this sense of dreams having no ending comes from the manner in which images tend to flow into one another, from one subject to another to another, each needing some sort of dream-time intervention.

Dream Themes

In our discussion of themes we will attend to differences in the pattern of dreaming and salient aspects of the teacher's work assignment and professional standing (student teacher, first year, well experienced). The themes include preparation; control, which is of two sorts, issues over which teachers have direct responsibility and those over which they have relatively little influence; being judged by others; mulling over problems; and making a space. After considering the themes, we will stand back and look at the data set as a whole and identify general patterns and two outliers. By way of anticipation, and echoing conclusions reached in Chapter 6, there is a dominating mood of vulnerability that cuts across most of the dreams.

Preparation

Most of the teachers said they had dreams about not being prepared to teach and that feeling unprepared produced anxiety and worry. Five of the experienced teachers, all women, had dreams of teaching in one or another state of undress. Karen is a thirty-year veteran whose dream is representative. For many years she had dreamt of coming to school having forgotten to dress for school. "I'm in [my pajamas and] I'm a little panicky. I'm trying to hide [from the children], but I don't know what to do because I don't have clothes on, just my pajamas—I sleep in a T-shirt, a long T-shirt. I'm telling [my students] to do Workshop, because they come into my class and start Workshop [first thing in the day]. Do Workshop. And I'm trying to call someone to bring me some clothes. Then, I just wake up." Despite having had this dream for many years, which is an indication of its strong emotional weighting (Domhoff 2003, 28), she wakes up and feels a deep sense of relief when she realizes "that that didn't really happen." Such dreams tend to express an "anxiety and a worry about feeling overexposed, feeling terribly vulnerable, and feeling that you'll be criticized and not have any defenses at your disposal" (Delaney 1997, 26). These are feelings widely shared by teachers whose work is very public. While the teachers are concerned about being undressed, the students in the dreams do not seem to notice; mostly they want to go about their business.

The majority of the teachers dreamt of being late or unprepared for class. Maggie, the only first-year teacher in the group, reported dreaming of walking into the classroom, being late, and realizing that she "didn't have any plans. I was standing in front of the class and I couldn't say anything. I felt dumbfounded." Having no plans and having nothing to say, Maggie looked out on the class which, before her bewildered gaze, became "chaos," and the theme of the dream shifted to lack of control. A recurrent dream for a seventeen-year-veteran focuses on events of the first day of school. While at school Janet realizes that she has "forgotten to order all of [her] supplies. I didn't have a thing to teach. So I had to run over to [the local supermarket]. I thought, 'Well, what can I do? Okay, I can run over to [the store] and at least get some paper and pencils.' Somehow, in my dream, I found a convenient way [to leave] . . . I darted over to [the store]—which I actually did in real life a few times—and once I get there it turns into a maze [and] there was no getting out of it. . . . I frantically go up and down the aisles, searching to find a way to get out. I don't know [if I found the pencils], I just know that I was searching, searching, and thinking, 'Oh, no, the kids have come back from recess and I'm over here and I can't get over there—will anyone notice? Will any of the other teachers know? Will I get caught?'"

The themes of both of these dreams shift as they unfold. In the first, what begins as a preparation dream becomes a dream about control, underscoring the close connection between being well prepared in teaching and being able to successfully manage large groups of children. Being well prepared for teaching is essential to feeling secure and comfortable, but it is impossible to ever be fully prepared for teaching, since a teacher cannot anticipate all eventualities, which Maggie seems to sense. Also beginning as a preparation dream, the second dream shifts to fear of being negatively judged by others, another of the shared themes arising in the dreams. The maze in this dream may hold several meanings. We mention two: It may indicate uncertainty about which directions to take when planning the curriculum, that no clear end is in sight and no guidance forthcoming. It also may indicate a struggle to resolve conflicting expectations and opinions about what teachers should be doing in the classroom and, with the shift to being judged negatively by others, a fear that the decision made will not be recognized by others in the school as a reasonable or good one.

Control

Control dreams take several forms: not having a substitute teacher for class, being behind schedule and not being able to keep up ("I just can't keep up"), missing class, yelling at students ("I was screaming and trying to get them under [control]"). With the exception of the male student teacher who had extensive teaching experience as an aide, the other two student teachers who reported having teaching dreams had control dreams. Rachel remarked that she had a "kind of funny dream" the origin of which she directly linked to a comment made by a methods teacher who, when discussing classroom management, quipped, "If you don't have control there's [a] 24 to 1 [student to teacher ratio] and they can tie you up if they want." She began dreaming of students, second graders, gathering around her and tying her to a chair with a rope. As they bind her, she is helpless. Having completed their task, the students simply wander off. The dream, which she has had several times, begins with "the kids kind of all bouncing off the walls. A couple of them are tying me up, and I'm just sitting there and can't do anything." During the dream, Rachel is "terrified. I have no control over these kids." When asked to describe exactly what is terrifying during the dream, she said: "I'm going to lose my job because I don't have control of these kids or I won't get a job." Rachel believes, rightly or wrongly, that the ability to control students is perhaps the most important teaching ability she can possess, and that to gain control requires student cooperation. Students have power.

As noted, some control dreams stretch a teacher's abilities to direct a situation and sometimes reach well beyond those abilities. Two of the experienced teachers reported very emotionally loaded dreams of losing children, one slipping away while waiting for the bus and another child disappearing on a swimming field trip. As part of teaching, Betsy, a twenty-eight-year veteran teacher new to the school, offered students the opportunity once a year to "earn" a swimming field trip for "being outstanding in the classroom." With parental permission she would take the children, third graders, to a nearby gymnasium. She had two vivid dreams tied to this outing. "We were all in the swimming pool and then I turn around, and you know, a couple of 'em are gone and I don't know where they've gone. I get out of the pool and I go into the dressing rooms [looking for them]. I come back and then they're all together [again]." Another time she dreamt that while looking for the missing children, "one of them drowned . . . I woke up with this horrible feeling." She said that following this dream, she no longer took children swimming, and she is relieved that swimming field trips are not an option at Lincoln Elementary. The fear is that the dream might come true.

Betsy had another control-related dream. Like a few of the other teachers, she had dreams related to the annual standardized tests which, under federal mandate, are reported and used to grade the school. Her dream was especially vivid and disturbing. She said that she and her class "worked really hard" to prepare for the tests, particularly the math portions. She wanted to make "sure that everybody would go into the test having learned and having been taught all the skills [needed to do well]." She dreamt about preparing the children for the tests, including mapping skills. In the dream the children "had to identify a playground on a map. We hadn't covered that, so they didn't know east, west, north, south. . . . They had to identify where the swings were, which direction that the swings were. Then there were some slides, and the school. Then there were hop scotches and things like that. They had to identify where [everything was]. I walked around in my dream and there were some kids that got it. [But] I was just downtrodden over all the kids [I'd] taught, but they just weren't getting it on the test . . . I wanted to go over and shake this child and tell him, 'You know this, you know this! Fix it! Erase your answer! Fix it! We've got to have right answers on the test!'" In this dream, Betsy had done all she could to prepare her students for the tests, but nothing she did changed the outcome. Many children failed, and in failing, Betsy was shaken.

Figuratively, Betsy's second dream is rich and provocative. In the dream she confronts her inability to get the students to perform as she hopes, but more importantly she seems to reveal her feelings about the tests themselves. It appears that for her the test is silly and the content to be tested trivial, requiring her students to mark on a map the location of swings and slides on the playground. In the dream Betsy realizes she had not taught the proper content, while at the same time it appears that the content is not worth teaching. She is deeply frustrated, feeling compelled to teach topics unworthy of her or her students. But being unwilling to teach such subjects means the students will do poorly on the exam, which reflects badly on her, the school, and the students. All that is important, finally, is that in the dream the children mark the correct answers, so it would seem Betsy can once again resume teaching content that matters. The situation is unresolvable in the dream and, we wonder, perhaps in Betsy's and the other teachers' professional lives.

While most of the teacher dreams carried negative emotions, not all did. The four teachers whose backgrounds were in special education had decidedly different dream experiences, underscoring important differences in the nature of their work and school lives. Dreams connected to a special education assignment did not include images of having difficulty managing classes of usually faceless children. In part, it would seem, this difference arises because special education classes are by comparison very, very small. For this group of teachers, the control theme is related to vivid dreams about trying to help an individual and very troubled student but not being able to alter the situation. The teacher feels powerless. The teacher confronts the limitation of her influence and ability, and the situation is beyond her control.

In contrast to the other teachers, the special education teachers' dreams generally included children with faces, and often they recognized some of the children in their classes, suggesting a different level of intimacy than that achieved by teachers in regular classrooms. Sometimes individual students drift through nonschool dreams, like a "shadow" that catches the teacher's attention momentarily. "I have dreams about kids that I worry the most about, that I don't feel I'm reaching or I'm successful [with]. They tend to show up in my dreams. . . . I had one boy . . . I really struggled with. He had a brother who was diagnosed [with] a behavior disorder but it turns out that he had a brain tumor and he had lots of behavior problems. He ended up dying. I had his younger brother. . . . This kid had a lot of problems besides a learning disability. I always felt like [I had a] connection with him but I wasn't able to [get him] into [a regular] classroom. He would show up [in my dreams]. . . . A family event and he'd just be a participant . . . like a shadow, just there." In this dream, Laura had unfinished business with this child, business that could never be finished. This child left her classroom without making significant progress emotionally or intellectually, and his image lingered hauntingly.

Penny, who taught special education for twenty-five years before transferring into a regular classroom, often dreamt of a boy who, she said, looked like the Pillsbury Dough Boy, a child diagnosed with a "failure to thrive." He was "very pale, passive, very unengaged, noncommunicative." Penny dreamed "over and over again" about this child, large and lying in a crib, wearing diapers and baby clothes. In the dream she tried and tried to get him to come with her, but she "couldn't get him up. He'd just lie there." She kept trying, but she never was able to get him to move, to leave the small and closed world of his crib. This is her most memorable dream, and it remains emotionally laden and disturbing.

Being Judged by Others

Eight of the teachers had dreams that included adults—three of these teachers had backgrounds in special education. All three of the teachers with special education backgrounds had dreams that included teachers with whom they had worked over the years, and for two of these teachers the emotions were positive, of being reconnected to missed friends and participating in delightful events, such as a camping trip. For the third teacher, the memories were painful, of intense, persistent, and unresolved disagreements over how best to serve individual students. For four of the five remaining teachers who reported seeing adults in their dreams, being judged was the central theme (as it was for a few additional teachers who, although no one was present in the dreams to judge, still worried, in the words of Janet, about "being the fool").

Penny, mentioned earlier, reported having an especially difficult class: "I had some really, really, hard kids, particularly a bunch of little boys that were really devilish. They were stinkers. I can remember their faces, just two of them. . . . I dreamt that I was in this classroom, and I'd be asking them to do stuff and they wouldn't do it." In response to their defiance (a control theme), she said, "I just stood there." What made the dream memorable was that she recalls the principal watching. She connected this event to a situation some years before when "I had a principal that I felt was not very supportive of me . . . I can remember her sitting [in the class] with this disapproving look on her face—that's the first time I ever felt the kids were out of control, that I couldn't bring them back quickly." In the dream, the principal sits and scowls. Upon awaking from the dream, Penny said she first felt like crying, then anger arose because, she said, drawing on her actual experience, a principal should be supportive, and this principal was not. Although not recurrent, the feelings associated with the dream persist. Betsy had a very similar dream to Penny's, and she said that her fear was that she would not "live up to the expectations of my principal or my colleagues." In many of Betsy's dreams she does not meet expectation, and comparing herself to others, she worries: "I haven't planned out this unit and everybody else is teaching it and I haven't started teaching yet." She was asked: "In your dreams, do you ever win, are you ever ahead?" She replied: "No, I never do. I always feel like I'm behind or I haven't met expectation. Maybe," she mused, "I set my expectations too high for myself."

Mary's was the most remarkable of the dreams falling under this category. In her dream she is lecturing to all four second grade classes and the children were lined up neatly in front of her. As she is lecturing, Rosalynn Carter, the then First Lady, and wife of President Jimmy Carter, ominously walks into the classroom with two or three school "district people," stands, and looks on without saying anything. She departs the classroom after watching

Mary teach but having said nothing leaves Mary wondering why she came. Perhaps there was nothing really to say: Mary was competent and probably able to handle more significant responsibilities than those she then had. She is in control of the situation, and the children apparently were learning. Then, a sense of puzzlement overcomes Mary. "How," she wonders, "could these people have gotten to her classroom from the outside of the school building without coming through the office?" Apparently, they had direct access to her classroom. There are multiple interpretative possibilities for this dream. At the risk of pushing Mary's figurative thinking a bit too far, we mention two. Mary's puzzlement about how Mrs. Carter and the administrators could enter her room through some surreptitious means may point toward a range of work-related issues. The arrival of the administrators and Mrs. Carter could suggest that despite Mary's best efforts to manage district mandates and administrative demands, she could not prevent their intrusion: Administrators could marshal power, in the form of Mrs. Carter, that could not be contained or managed, and sufficient to assure Mary's unwilling compliance without the need of a word or warning. Alternatively, the arrival of Mrs. Carter, a well-recognized and influential human rights advocate, might suggest that Mary had doubts about how children were treated in school, lined up, and lectured to. It is apparent that to uncover what troubles Mary would take a good deal of probing, but the odds are that Mary could locate the issue herself.

Mulling Over Problems

When dreaming, it often seems that the dreamer is engaging in solving problems that stalk waking thought. Domhoff (2003) has discussed the difficulties with this conclusion, suggesting that in dreams, what actually takes place is a kind of reflection on problems, and that solutions arise as "waking realizations that are based on thinking about the dream" (159). In dreams, problems are mulled over, turned around and seen in new and sometimes provocative ways, and dramatized. As Mary remarked, in dreams, "my brain seems to process a lot." Iris described how her dreams operate in this way: "I ruminate over things, you know, when you're kind of half awake and half asleep, and solve some problems that way." There is an abundance of dreaming of this sort in the data set, which, consistent with the continuity hypothesis, indicates teachers simply do not, when asleep, turn off the problems and issues that concern them, and that they are anxiously seeking inspiration.

Curriculum dreams also occur, as when Sandi awoke singing a song that immediately seemed just right for her class to learn. In his dreams, Mitch has thought carefully about his learning centers, awakened and jotted down ideas that came to him. Another teacher made connections between subjects she taught in previous years and current units, including one on the water cycle. Laura dreamed about group work, Samantha of regrouping to alter and improve the classroom learning climate. Rachel, a student teacher, dreamt of ways of presenting mathematics on the playground, "trying to find angles or shapes." There are dreams tied to making decisions about specific classes, and sometimes specific children, like the child who looked like the Pillsbury Dough Boy, mentioned earlier. The emotional tone of these dreams is one of urgency, and sometimes anxiety, that something must be done and done quickly. Occasionally the dreams are recognized as funny. Samantha was so pleased with how the students responded to her regrouping that she decided to reward them by taking the entire class to a restaurant for lunch. Unfortunately, a group of retired teachers showed up and came along. "[In the dream], I let [everyone] have whatever they wanted for a treat, [which] was crazy. This is going to cost $1,000. How can I do this?, I thought." Samantha had no way of paying the tab and she knew it, but she still was determined to reward her students. Perhaps, symbolically, Samantha, who was in fact contemplating retirement, was worrying about the loss of income that would follow retirement.

Making a Space

As previously noted, several of the teachers were new to Lincoln, and nearly all faculty were forced to change rooms and/or grade levels. There was, in short, a great deal of dislocation. The teachers frequently mentioned dreaming about their rooms not being ready to receive the students, and until this issue was settled, all others waited. On their part, several of the teachers in fact did spent hours each day over several weeks relocating—packing, unpacking, hoisting, and hauling. In her dream Samantha came to school and found all of her classroom furniture in the hallway, "kind of in the shape of a small rectangle. There were no walls. My bookcases were lined up, so it made a perimeter for a space, and that was going to be my room for the year." She looked at the situation and felt despair. In the dream, all day long the teachers paraded through her space to get to their mail boxes. The principal was unconcerned about the situation, thinking it would be "fine somehow." In the hallway there was a "little glassed-in space" that was to be Samantha's office, a space everyone could peer into and no one could avoid seeing. She was told that after school another class would occupy her assigned space, such as it was. Awaking with a start, Samantha was distressed, confused, and felt disoriented. Betsy dreamed that her room was filled with unpacked boxes, which in fact it was, and she fretted over where she would put the students when they arrived. She also worried about the presence of intruders. Sheila dreamed of being transferred to another school. David, a student teacher who assisted his cooperating teacher in her move, also dreamed about moving from one to another school building: "All the boxes were filled, but we still had more stuff but not enough boxes." Not having enough boxes was upsetting. What to do?

For teachers who seek to nurture the young, teaching spaces are profoundly personal and intimate locations, for some taking on womblike importance, while for others they are homelike. Lacking a space that is recognized as their own produces feelings of dislocation among teachers, as though they are visitors to the school rather than members of it. Having a space means being at home, feeling protected and secure. Samantha's vulnerability is apparent not only in the glass walls of her office but in the lack of protective walls, walls that both she and her students desperately need for their nurturance and reassurance. It does not seem unreasonable to conclude that those who made the decision to shuffle teachers as they did had little interest in nurturing the young or in the well-being of teachers. Thus Samantha's principal may represent the insensitivity of the entire district administrative structure that proved itself disconnected and unconcerned.

Standing Back

Looking at the data set as a whole, it is apparent that there is a general, albeit rough, rhythm to the dreams of the twenty-one teachers, a rhythm tied to the school year. Not surprisingly, most intense dreaming takes place in the days and weeks immediately preceding the start of school, and for some teachers these dreams intensify the closer they are to the first day of classes. Dreams about school become less frequent once school begins, although specific events might trigger intense dreaming episodes: end-of-the-term grading; the first grade play; the arts fair; a tense disagreement with a colleague; a student acting out unexpectedly; a parent-teacher conference; and end-of-year testing. A few dreams that veteran teachers had early in their careers were well remembered, and some of these dreams persisted, in one instance for twenty-five years. While there may be some differences between the dreams of beginning teachers and well-experienced teachers, the general patterns seem to persist, although frequency and intensity may vary, which is consistent with recent dream research (Domhoff 2003). In part, this may be a reflection of a simple and nagging fact about teaching, that problems are seldom ever fully resolved and often remain insistent across an entire career. The connection between dreams and waking life is often strong, and the emotional intensity of dreaming is readily apparent, indicating the strength of the waking concern, interest, or problem that underlies the dream. Finally, while not all dreams are meaningful, many are, but meaning is often obscure. For this reason, attending to the figurative thinking of some dreams opens up potential avenues for understanding of self and of context that may be hidden during waking hours and may reveal promising but unexpected courses of action.

Connections between dreaming and work conditions are quite apparent, as are differences in how the teachers understood their role and responsibilities. As differences between the special and regular education teacher dreams suggest, concerns related to classroom control are likely linked to large class sizes and to the difficulty of establishing teacher-student intimacy under such conditions. There is a potential trade-off: Not knowing one's students well may result in dreams of faceless class control but prohibit the deeply troubling dreams linked to a specific child of the sort experienced by the teachers with a special education background. On the other hand, dreams involving mulling over images and emotions tied to a specific child offer the possibility of the emergence of a determined and particular course of action. Dreams about being unprepared to teach were not simply a matter of not planning but of having insufficient materials for teaching and, importantly, of curricular uncertainty. Tensions born of being watched and judged were heightened by administrators who paid relatively little attention to the well-being of teachers and, once in place, concerns of this kind seem to linger. Given the dramatic and rising presence of standardized testing and the increasing emphasis on accountability, it is conceivable, although uncertain, that in the future teachers will experience a growing number of dreams and of great intensity related to fear of failure and of being negatively judged and punished. The trauma felt by several of the teachers over moving classrooms was not wholly necessary and was worsened by exclusion from the decisions made. Better district planning and more generous and early support may have lightened these teachers' burdens considerably.

No doubt, even with improved work conditions, the teachers would still have had troubling dreams, but perhaps not the same ones or of the same intensity. The temptation is to hope that with improved work conditions teachers will have mostly happy dreams. Human nature, and a large body of research, suggests otherwise. Regardless of the work context, individual and peculiar problems would persist and inevitably become the object of dreaming, and some problems and concerns that form the content of dreaming are simply part of teaching and working with children, although they need not be dominating concerns. More to the point, had better work conditions prevailed, perhaps a greater measure of the positive energy of dreaming tied to setting and exploring problems and identifying alternative courses of action may have been released, and this would have positive outcomes for both teachers and students. This is energy that holds creative potential, that is enlivening, the stuff of which good and productive—but not necessarily happy—dreams are made.

Outliers

Reviewing the data set, two outliers emerged that require consideration. Occasionally dreams are had that are quite remarkable, and one of these emerged in the data. Of these, a "dream which correctly represents unlikely future events is called a precognitive dream" (Van De Castle 1994, 405). Joan reports such a dream, which she characterized as a "great dream." In her class she had a child with severe learning disabilities arising from her mother's drug usage during pregnancy. Joan dreamed a solution and an outcome to this child's reading problems that came true; Joan witnessed in her dream events well before they happened. The dream energized Joan, confirmed the value of her innovative approaches to teaching reading, and helped her stay the course, despite good reasons to give up.

The second outlier stands in stark contrast to Joan's dream and points toward the importance of dreaming to teachers' well-being. This dream proved very disturbing to the dreamer because, she said, what she did in the dream was so very uncharacteristic of her as a person but seemed to suggest that she had reached a limit. The dream invites interpretation and cautious speculation.

> I've had dreams where the class has been out of control. I can't get them under control. I'm very frustrated. Yelling at them, but they won't listen, they won't pay any attention, they don't care that I'm the teacher. Really frustrating. I [had another dream]. Not only am I very frustrated, and to the point where I'm yelling, but I end up hitting a kid. It puzzles me after I wake up. I have never felt like hitting anybody. It puzzles me. . . . That's real troubling to me. I don't understand why I feel that, because I have never felt that [way] in the classroom . . . I never have had an experience teaching where the kids didn't do what I asked them to do. I've felt frustrated, but not ever out of control, that I can't handle it.

Hitting in a dream may mean many things. When viewed figuratively, who receives the hit in the dream, the unrecognized but out-of-control child, may not be the intended object—a member of one's own family may be the actual object. It also is possible that the teacher was striking at herself, lashing out at a growing frustration linked to not being able to do something desired for a child or class of students, of being blocked from doing what she needed and wanted to do. If the violence in the dream escalated, which reportedly it did not (the dream was had only twice but remained highly charged in memory), then other issues arise, suggesting that the teacher may be in serious psychological trouble, that her ability to cope with difficult work conditions was deteriorating. Nevertheless, the dream may represent an unrecognized warning, a need to turn inward and seek help or alter work relations.

Conclusion

At a time when high standardized test scores are the *sin qua non* of good teaching and a source of growing teacher anxiety, there arises the danger that the importance of teaching technique and being businesslike with children to achieving set ends will eclipse other valued elements of good teaching, particularly those associated with teaching as a form of pedagogical relationship that involves intimacy and caring (van Manen 1999). At its extreme, in the quest to make certain no child is left behind, there arises a threat to all children, that to prove the value of schooling and of teacher worth, children will increasingly be treated as things that can be used—measured, categorized, prodded, pushed about, and toward some ends set somewhere by an unknown and distant someone. Treating others as things, as Paul Tillich (1967) writes, profoundly and negatively affects the state of one's soul: "If one uses a person one abuses not only him but also one's self. . . . If I use a person as a thing I myself lose my dignity as a person" (95). Surely no teacher enters the profession expecting to lose dignity; rather, teaching is thought to be a venue for fully expressing or claiming it. Yet the demands of teaching call forth contrary acts that bruise the teacher's soul—teaching contrary to beliefs and commitments, and suffering as a result. Under such conditions, teachers dream of being watched and judged negatively, of failing to teach students items on standardized tests, and of faceless and threatening children.

Several years ago, Arthur Jersild (1955) argued for the importance of teachers "facing [their] own emotions" (85). The challenge remains as vital today as when Jersild first made it. Like Palmer, Jersild was concerned with the well-being of teachers and their search for meaning through teaching. He recognized that teaching was anxious and often lonely work that produced in some teachers feelings of hostility and anger. Meaninglessness was then, and remains now (Ball 2003), a concern—and so Betsy struggles in her dreams to teach what she believes is not worth teaching, let alone learning. Jersild argued that for teachers to help pupils have meaningful experiences in school, the teacher must "face the problems of his own life": "A teacher's understanding of others can be only as deep as the wisdom he possesses when he looks inward upon himself" (83). Like Palmer, Jersild asserted that teachers need to look inward and then have "the humility to accept what [they] may find" (ibid.).

The dreams of some teachers may suggest the need for therapy. But for the vast majority, the turn inward is probably best and most sensibly facilitated through simple and more straightforward means, like talking about teaching with other teachers and even sharing dreams. A good deal of research (Bullough and Baughman 1993, 1997; Giles and Wilson 2004; Wilson and Berne 1999) has pointed toward the importance of ongoing and consistent teacher talk to learning to teach and to building a supportive professional learning community (DuFour, Eaker, and DuFour 2005). More specifically, teachers can engage in their own dream work. By writing out and visually rehearsing new endings, disturbing dreams actually can be eliminated (Domhoff 2003, 37) and energy redirected elsewhere. It should be noted, however, that this process does nothing to change the underlying conditions that may have prompted a nightmare, such as the desire to hit a child. When external conditions cannot be changed, talking, managing the emotions, and learning to cope may be all that is left (Alfi, Assor, and Katz 2004).

Dreams provide a window through which to see and take stock of one's emotional health, the condition of the teacher's soul, and for better understanding the nature and impact of work conditions on the self. Taking stock is important not merely to enable better coping but also to help teachers remain centered and positive about the children and their future. Ullman (1987) makes the point clearly:

> I have come to look at our capacity to [dream] as a way nature has of giving us the opportunity to examine whatever may be impinging on the state of our connectedness to others, for good or bad. While dreaming, we seem able to explore both the inner and outer sources of any change in the state of these connections. It is as if, while awake, we tend to lose sight of our basic interconnectedness, focusing more on our discreetness and our separateness. Asleep, we turn our attention to the reality of our interconnectedness as members of a single species. (129)

Within the dreams of teachers may reside the deepest and heartiest seeds of resistance to the growing dominance of instrumental reason in schooling and the threat of performativity (Ball 2003) that turns children into things and, sometimes, when stood on their head, reveal their deepest ambitions for themselves and the children they teach. These seeds require nourishing to avoid the "surrender" and death of burnout (Coles 1993, 141) that may grow from the loneliness and frustration that Jersild noted. Often, embedded in teacher dreams are calls to action—although not yet fully formed—and not just to reflection, calls for teachers to take charge and reshape their world and themselves to better realize, as Ullman writes, their basic interconnectedness and their desire to more effectively nurture and care for the young.

PART **4**

Program Studies

CHAPTER 10

Rethinking Portfolios:
Case Records as Personal
Teaching Texts for Study in
Preservice Teacher Education (1993)

Introduction

Like a good many teacher educators, for years I had my students keep journals about their experience in teacher education. And, like others, I have found the practice somewhat limited and frustrating. Knowles (1991) observes that beginning teachers often find the time demands of journal keeping prohibitive; that frequently the journal is shaped by a desire to echo professor talk; and that journal writing is often superficial, and, I would add, narrowly introspective and unfocused. I have struggled to know how to respond to journal writing and have had great difficulty finding the time to enter into anything approximating a written conversation with my students. Given these difficulties, I gave up requiring journals and began searching for other means for encouraging students to think about and explore teaching and their development as teachers.

At about the same time I gave up on journals, portfolios were beginning to garner attention in education. A portfolio is a "purposeful collection" of student work intended to "measure and reflect student performance" (Paulson, Paulson, and Meyer 1990). From the K-12 teacher's perspective, the portfolio's value is threefold: It facilitates teacher evaluation of student work, it is a good means for demonstrating to parents what the child has accomplished, and, when the student is involved in its creation, it may become a means for the teacher to assist the child to consider areas that require greater work and attention and to set personal learning goals (Vavrus 1990).

Portfolios in teacher education typically are utilized for the first and second purposes, both of which emphasize evaluation to satisfy external audiences—a certifying agency or board (see NBPTS 1991), or a supervisor or an administrator looking to hire a new teacher. There is, however, potential in the concept to do much more (see Richert 1990). Rather than be thought of as a "showcasing of the best work which an individual feels he can collect" (Lewis 1990) for external audiences, I realized that a portfolio might be thought of as

177

a record of one's development as a teacher, warts and all, collected with an eye toward gathering data that would enable development and encourage purposeful reflection. Viewed from this perspective, a portfolio might be thought of as an evolving text for continuous study and elaboration, a personal teaching text (PTT). Given the close association of portfolios with external evaluation, it is important to note that this shift represents more than just an expansion of the concept; it is a fundamental change.

Yin's description of the use of cases as a form of record keeping "used to facilitate some practice, such as medicine, law, or social work [and that] the criteria for developing good cases for practice are different from those for designing case studies for research" (1984, 14) proved helpful when beginning to think through what a PTT might be and include. Following Yin's lead, I met with a highly skilled veteran intensive care nurse and with her explored how cases are used in medical practice. From this conversation, and my reading that followed, three important insights emerged that proved especially suggestive for my work in teacher education: First, nursing case records include a detailed history of the patient. All clinical judgments are made in light of this history. Second, data of different kinds are gathered systematically and frequently, and some data are gathered at intervals to enable comparisons to determine if and in what ways change has taken place. Third, which data are gathered is determined by the knowledge that nurses and other medical practitioners have, not only of the patient but about the type of medical problem he or she has. Put differently, the patient is seen not only as an individual but also as a representative of a type, which provides some guidelines for treatment and for future data gathering.

Case Records as Texts

The kind of text I have in mind is both similar to and different from journals, portfolios, and nursing cases but draws upon each. Like nursing case records, PTTs should represent careful, systematic, and ongoing data collection. The data need to be organized in a manner that facilitates self-analysis and comparison, not external evaluation, as is now commonly the practice with portfolios. The data ought to enable problem diagnosis and planning. What is included in the text, and in contrast to my prior experience with journals, ought to be determined by an understanding of what kinds of data are most likely to facilitate beginning teacher development and not merely by whatever a beginning teacher feels a need to write about on any given day or what might impress an external evaluator or hiring administrator. Data arising from a diversity of activities and experiences representing a variety of encounters with self, content, and teaching context need to be included. And, analysis of the data needs to be guided.

It should be noted that the analogy between case records in nursing and teacher education breaks down rather quickly if pressed. Despite sharing the challenge of enabling clinical decision making within fields where the "conversation of practice can be learned but not taught" (Yinger 1990, 92), the aims of the nursing and teacher education case records differ in some very important ways. Achieving health as an aim differs fundamentally from facilitating personal and professional development. In nursing, the focus of a case record is the patient; in teacher education, the focus is the novice teacher, who develops and analyzes the case but with guidance.

Reflection as a Program Aim

Like other teacher educators currently working in the field (Clift, Houston, and Pugach 1990; Grimmett and Erickson 1988), I am seeking a means for encouraging the development of reflectivity among my students (Bullough 1989). The knowledge and skills needed to frame productively and resolve situationally specific teaching problems are essential not only to provide responsive and educationally defensible programs for young people but also to teachers' professional development; they are central to teacher empowerment, the ability to choose oneself as teacher.

I seek to encourage reflection of both an interpretive and a critical kind (Gore 1987), and the development of PTTs has become an important part of this effort, as reported in this chapter. As Kagan (1992) observes, generally speaking teacher education has ignored the biographically embedded personal beliefs and images of teaching and self as teacher that novices bring to teacher education and through which they make their programs more or less meaningful. Yet these beliefs and views of self are of crucial importance to teaching and teacher development (Nias 1989). Reflection of an interpretative kind aims to reveal these meanings, beginning teachers' tacit knowledge (Polanyi 1958), and make them explicit. Journals have been used as a means for accessing this knowledge, but often journal writing only represents a reflective turn inward of one kind or another. Something more and different is required; to engage in critical reflection necessitates getting outside of self: Drawing on social reconstructivist aims, "the teacher's attention is focused both inwardly at their [*sic*] own practice (and the collective practices of a group of colleagues) and outwardly at the social conditions in which these practices are situated" (Zeichner and Tabachnick 1991, 8). Reflective teachers engage in both turns, inward and outward.

Program Background

In the first and second quarters of their year-long program, certification students met on Tuesday and Thursday mornings for three hours. In the fall term, curriculum-related issues were addressed. In the winter term, the focus shifted to instruction-related issues. During this quarter the students taught a short course (a single unit) lasting up to three weeks in the classroom where they eventually student taught. In the spring term they student taught and attended a weekly seminar that I coordinated that addressed the immediately pressing problems of practice teaching. The cohort organization allowed the program to be focused and activities to be coordinated, and it enabled the continuous interweaving of topics and issues across the year. The instructional pattern was for a topic to be introduced on campus, studied in the field, and reconsidered again on campus. In this way, practice and theory were linked.

The year began by my having students write "education-related life histories." These are less elaborate creations than what Goodson (1981), for example, has in mind, but they have proven to be useful means for starting to identify beginning teachers' preconceptions about teaching and self as teacher (see Introduction and Chapter 3). Based on their life histories, the students identified in writing "personal teaching metaphors" that were intended to help them think about themselves as teachers (see Chapter 11). Throughout the year we returned to the metaphors and "updated" them in writing and discussed what was happening to their thinking about teaching and themselves as teachers and tried to identify sources of change. In addition, we explored some of the ethical dimensions of holding to one or another metaphor. What does it mean, for instance, for pupils and what they are allowed to do in the classroom when a teacher embraces an expert metaphor? A teacher's definition of self as teacher brings with it a definition of the proper student role and responsibilities.

Additionally, the beginning teachers conducted interviews of experienced teachers to discover their views about teaching and the teaching profession. They did a "shadow study" of a pupil that involved following one student throughout an entire school day to understand what school was like from a young person's point of view. They conducted a series of classroom observational studies seeking to understand what norms governed teacher-student and student-student interaction, how time was used, and how engaged students were in learning. They analyzed and had their pupils analyze their performance in the short course. They read about some of the more serious political, cultural, and social issues confronting American public education and reacted to these readings based upon their views of teaching and the purposes of education. In student teaching they conducted an action research project (Kemmis and McTaggart 1988), engaged in peer observations, and solicited pupil feedback on their teaching. All written work was read and commented on. The purpose of the comments was to nudge along student thinking and to raise questions that might otherwise be ignored. In addition, a good deal of discussion took place within which issues were raised and explored.

Content of the Personal Teaching Text

All written assignments, including the feedback given from pupils and peers on teaching, became part of the case record, the text. The metaphors and metaphor "updates" forced the students periodically to turn inward and think about their thinking about teaching and themselves as teachers. The importance of the metaphor updates arises because a change in metaphor signals a change in thinking (Russell and Johnston 1988), and thus the updates provided an evolving, comparative record of development. In addition, at the end of each term, the students were required to review and in writing analyze their texts. The year-end assignment read as follows:

> Reread the content of your Personal Teaching Text for the entire year. Based upon this reading, assess your development as a teacher. Are you pleased with what you have accomplished this year? Any disappointments? Has your resolve to become a teacher strengthened or weakened? Why? Has your view of yourself as a teacher changed during the course of the year? If so, what has prompted the change? If not, why not? Are you on track for becoming the kind of teacher you imagine yourself capable of being?

The reviews, like the metaphor updates, were compared directly, and changes were readily identified. When thinking through program activities that result in the products that form the content of the personal teaching text, careful attention was given to both reflective turns, inward and outward. The turn outward is more fundamental than is sometimes acknowledged: There is no meaning without context (Mishler 1979). Thus case records need to include data that describe the context within which meaning about teaching is to be made or remade, and this may well involve the study of the context's history. Essentially, the PTT contains slices of an evolving life story tied to the quest to become a teacher; it is an account of growth toward and sometimes away from an imagined future. As such, the work is representative of that being done by the third group of educators interested in pursuing reflectivity as a central aim of teacher education, described by Grimmett, MacKinnon, Erickson, and Riechken (1990). These educators "argue that experience, as embodied in one's personal biography, constitutes both the content and consequence of reflective thinking. That is, reflection shapes and restructures one's personal knowledge about teaching as well as about life" (1990, 31).

The Study

An initial, tentative study of the value of the PTTs was conducted. Based upon the results of that study, adjustments were made in the approach and plans made for a second study, reported here. At the conclusion of the year, the reviews of the PTTs of twenty of twenty-three secondary education students in the same cohort, ages twenty-one to fifty-one and representing various academic disciplines, were photocopied, with their permission, for analysis. In addition, a questionnaire was administered, which included specific questions about the value and use of the PTT. After grades were turned in, interviews were conducted by a teaching assistant with ten students. Interview questions sought to identify the strengths and weaknesses of the approach. All interviews were transcribed for analysis. Data are not included from three of the students, because one joined the cohort late in the year, and two did not complete the questionnaire.

Because of my interest in the development of reflectivity, a content analysis of reviews of the PTTs was conducted. I believed that because this was an open writing assignment what the students chose to write about—the issues and concerns they raised beyond the focus on self—and how they wrote about these issues and concerns would be reasonably good indications of the degree to which program aims were met. Results from the questionnaire and interviews are presented first.

Questionnaire and Interview Results

Twenty students responded to the questionnaire. Of these, fifteen were very positive, finding the process of writing, reading, and analyzing the PTT useful and interesting. One student, representative of the group as a whole, wrote:

> Yes! [it's valuable]. I have been able to identify how I perceive my role as a teacher. . . . I would have had a much more difficult time putting myself in a classroom as a teacher without it. I can look back and see how I have changed and grown.

Another wrote:

> It gave me a focus and made me think ahead and reflect on my progress as a teacher. I also have something I can look back on with pride and say, "I survived," and even thrived during my year in the cohort. (I'm pretty proud of some of those papers.)

No students were negative, although five were less than enthusiastic about the assignment. Typical comments from these beginning teachers included: "I'm not sure of its utility, but it was an interesting way to try and measure or compare development. Its utility may yet lie in the future." And, "It is of some help in the growth process. . . . Maybe if I read through it more frequently, it would help my reflection."

Interviews were conducted with two of the students who were less than enthusiastic about the process and eight who found it very helpful. The interviews took place after the completion of student teaching, and one of the less enthusiastic students had, by that time, become quite positive. Why her view changed is uncertain. Four basic reasons for valuing the PTT were articulated over and over again in the interviews.

1. The students appreciated having a record of their development because it let them know that they had made progress in their thinking about teaching, and as a result they felt increasingly confident:

   > I hated it while I had to do all the assignments. I grumbled about doing the assignments when they were due, all the writing assignments, but it has helped a lot to be able to look back and see what I was thinking about at that time and what I was struggling with. . . . You do change your thinking, drastically. It helped me a lot.

This is an important outcome given the frequent claims made by teachers that they found little of value in their teacher education programs and that programs are fragmented and disjointed. Perhaps the problem is partially that they are not fully aware of how much growth has taken place. Clearly, the cohort organization and the texts proved crucial to providing these beginning teachers with a sense of program coherence.

2. The students valued and enjoyed engaging in self-evaluation; generally they saw themselves as producers of legitimate knowledge about teaching and as not being dependent on experts.

   > I loved going back and looking over [my text]. I loved having to really think about my reasons for teaching. I liked having to think about the issues of teaching besides just how you are going to do a lesson plan, because that is a very, very small part of teaching [as] I've learned. There are politics involved, power plays. . . . I think it has made me a lot more aware of what I am doing and why I'm doing it.

3. They found the texts a useful means for looking backward so that they could project themselves forward. Put differently, most thought the PTT was valuable for gaining insights useful for directing their future professional development; it helped them plan ahead: "I know I am going to refer back to it a lot. Just reading over it, I thought, 'Boy, I've learned a lot.' I [need] to keep adding to [it] so that . . . I can keep learning from it."

4. Finally, echoing Solas (1992, 212) when he observed that "writing modifies the movement of our lives," some of them saw value in the process of writing itself: "Unless you [write your thoughts] down on paper . . . you

don't really get a chance to think through everything. If you have to actually write [your thoughts] down and arrange [them], then you can really go
into depth. So [the PTT] has been really good for me." The students valued their PTTs, seeing in them an important tool for considering their
development as teachers, although some complained about the amount of
work involved in producing them. They thought of them as a useful means
for focusing their thoughts, encouraging reflection, and thinking about
their future development as teachers.

Reviews of the Personal Teaching Texts

The reviews of the PTTs (papers written at the conclusion of each term) were
analyzed through the creation of a series of matrices (Miles and Huberman,
1984) to determine what, if any, kind of evidence was present of reflection and
development in thinking about teaching. Consideration was given to the
kinds of issues raised—what questions demanded attention—how they were
treated, and whether or not there was evidence of increasing complexity of
thought about teaching and self as teacher.

Regarding kinds of issues, virtually all of the students, as one would
expect given the nature of the assignment to review the text, discussed a variety of issues related to self: their feelings about teaching, their uncertainties,
and their inadequacies.

> I thought I knew about teaching before this year, but the more I learned the
> more I realized how much more there was to learn as well as how little I
> actually knew before. . . . I do not have much . . . idealism [left].

Another beginning teacher recognized at the conclusion of the first
quarter that the views she brought with her to the program about teaching
were heavily colored by her social class background:

> There are many thoughts I have not committed to paper until now that I feel
> need to be meshed with the experiences in my personal teaching text. The
> first is that I was raised in a politically conservative household that rolled its
> eyes every time the teachers started complaining about working conditions.
> Coming from a working-class family, I couldn't understand why teachers
> complained about low wages. I have now come to the conclusion that things
> are as bad as [the teacher association] paints them: We really do "stack 'em
> deep and teach 'em cheap." I was appalled at how crowded the classrooms
> are, at the fact that there are not enough sophomore English textbooks of the
> new edition, and that teachers are expected to spend so much of their own
> money . . . to do a decent job.

In addition, virtually all mentioned, and explored, a variety of technical issues: "[I need to work on] writing tests that correlate very closely with
what I have been teaching." Among these, not surprisingly, management
concerns were most prevalent. In sum, there is an abundance of evidence of
engagement in reflection of technical and interpretative kinds (Gore 1987),
where control and clarity of meaning are the aims.Of greater interest was
the presence of evidence, admittedly in varying amounts, in twelve of the
texts of the turn outward, of critical reflection. This runs somewhat counter
to a significant body of research that suggests that beginning teachers are so
consumed with themselves and the problem of establishing and maintaining
control that they are unable to think contextually about the social conditions
that surround and influence practice. Ultimately, for these beginning teachers, the turn inward necessitated a turn outward in order to understand better the nature of their experience. It is important to note that the beginning
teachers need not have included talk of a critical kind; the assignment did
not require it. Rather, it was included because it represented their thinking.
One student, for example, located the source of her frustration in "low standards and [large] class sizes [which] reflect the nation's, the administration's,
and the parents' hypocrisy. The priorities in this country," she said, "and particularly in education, are all backward." Most of the twelve were critical of
the manner in which work conditions limited what they were able to accomplish for their students. Others struggled to understand better cultural and
political influences that complicated their work in the classroom and
affected student opportunities to learn. And some explored the purposes of
education. Another indication of getting outside of self was the surprising
degree to which the twelve beginning teachers were concerned about student learning. It was with respect to facilitating student learning, and only
secondarily of maintaining control, that they thought about curriculum and
instruction.

Of the remaining eight beginning teachers, six were generally consumed
with themselves and with exploring technical issues. "I need to have control,
and I can't allow disrespect for the authority a teacher should have. I've come
to the conclusion I'll have to be tough like [my cooperating teacher] until I've
earned the students' respect."

It is impossible to determine to what degree the PTT can be credited
or blamed for these outcomes. Based upon a reading of students' life histories,
it is quite apparent that some students entered the program predisposed to
engage in critical reflection, while others were not. Moreover, the program
itself included a variety of efforts, in addition to the PTT, to encourage reflection, including emphasis on the discussion of issues in class and the modeling
of critical reflection in instruction. Still, it is most certainly true that the texts,
as the students claim themselves, encouraged reflection of all three varieties.

Depth and Complexity of Thinking

One indication of depth and complexity of thought was that issues were explored contextually and in relationship to other issues, as was evident in the writing of the twelve students noted earlier. But depth and complexity are not exclusively the domain of those who engaged in critical reflection. Technical issues also might call forth complex and deep thinking aimed at discovering better ways of doing something. For example, one beginning teacher wrote at length about his difficulty establishing classroom routines. He thought carefully about the problem, seeing it not as a matter of needing to increase control over the students for the sake of control or for his sanity but rather to free up time so that he would be able to "[plan] lessons that are interesting; I want students to learn something in my class." For this student, control was understood not as a good in and of itself but as a means for achieving desirable educational aims.

Most but not all of the twenty beginning teachers' reviews of their PTTs contained rich and complex explorations of issues of various kinds. Only one of the beginning teacher's texts was void of evidence of depth or complexity of thought, even about technical issues. This person seemed to drift through the program and encountered significant problems in practice teaching.

Most importantly, all of the beginning teacher texts, excepting the one, evidenced increasing complexity of thought about teaching and self as teacher over the course of the year, although in varying degrees:

> The thing that most stood out to me after rereading my personal teaching text is that the best and most important part of teaching is not in my . . . text—at least not directly. The teaching that [I talk about] in the text is the "dissemination of facts" kind of teaching. This quarter has shown me that dissemination of facts is only the tip of the iceberg when it comes to teaching. Something else happens when you teach—when you are doing it "right"—that's like . . . magic.

One not too surprising outcome was that as the beginning teachers' thinking about teaching became increasingly complex, there was a concomitant decrease in their "unrealistic optimism" about themselves as teachers (Weinstein 1989):

> I enjoyed reading [about] my outlook on teaching throughout this school year. I started the year with a hope and a dream of what my teaching encounters would be like. . . . I think I had an unrealistic view of how most students experience school.

Increasing knowledge of students was the most significant factor forcing this readjustment of views. Naive optimism was replaced by a more mature and grounded understanding of teaching and students. Again, it is not possible to know to what degree this outcome is attributable to the PTT, but that it did contribute seems certain. The evidence supporting the usefulness of the PTT as a means for facilitating beginning teacher development and reflection is indirect and, ultimately, a matter of student self-report. This is so because the PTT was part of a larger programmatic effort, and it is not possible to isolate its influence from that of other program elements. Nevertheless, the claims of the beginning teachers that the texts were valuable are supported by the analysis of their written reviews. Together the analyses of these sources of data—the questionnaire, interviews, and text reviews—suggest that it is a useful and (for some beginning teachers) a powerful means for enabling development and encouraging reflection.

Problem Areas

In interview, where the beginning teachers were asked to critique various program activities, including the PTT and in the questionnaire, three problems were mentioned by a few students: brevity of writing, author honesty and trust, and limited data sources during practice teaching. I identified three additional, related difficulties that appear to have limited the educational value of the PTT: lack of closure, text content and integrating content, and my personal role.

Brevity

That some of the entries and in particular the reviews were brief should not have been surprising. As noted, teacher educators who have used journals and other forms of student writing as a means for encouraging reflection have commented on the difficulty of getting students to write, and to write thoughtfully (Knowles 1991; Weinstein 1990). It was surprising, however, to have the problem identified by two students, both of whom mentioned it as a personal problem but then offered a justification for their actions. One remarked: "There were several comments I wrote in the mid-year review that . . . I didn't write in detail. [I wrote] just so that I could check up on some things to see how they went, how things progressed. They went okay." In effect, this student was saying that I should not have been concerned that what was written was so brief, that the text still had its desired effect. But brevity cannot be so easily dismissed as a problem. Although brevity and superficiality are not necessarily synonymous, brevity can lead to superficiality, and this is a significant issue. Fortunately, it appears as though the diversity of assignments weakens the problem somewhat. While not every assignment engaged all of the beginning teachers, nearly all of them found some of the assignments worthy of serious effort. Nevertheless, as a teacher I cannot compel the students to engage in rich and interesting analyses; it is laughable to think it is possible to compel the "good." To use the threat of grades would seriously undermine the value of the texts and perhaps set the stage for sophisticated but dishonest student writing. I can urge, invite, and in other ways encourage the students to take the assignments seriously, but I cannot compel them to do so.

Honesty and Trust

A few students noted that initially they had a struggle being honest in their writings. They wondered if they were writing for me or for themselves: "I know I can write to myself and it doesn't really matter. I'm not writing to please [you]. I'm not sure all the students have those same attitudes." And another student wrote: "I have sat in front of my computer for better than an hour at times not wanting to be open about how I feel." Undoubtedly, some students were guarded in their writing, and this also is not uncommon as teacher educators who require student journals know. Being socialized as a student brings with it the knowledge that caution is the prudent course when grades are at stake.

Anticipating this problem, I avoided the temptation to grade student responses. Instead, all work was accepted for full credit if turned in, and if a reasonable amount of effort was expended. When effort seemed minimal, some students were asked to redo one or another assignment. Through written and oral comments, I attempted to encourage the students to write more, to go deeper, and to risk. Whether or not these efforts had the desired effect is uncertain, but my impression is that most of the beginning teachers were honest in their writing.

Limited Data

During student teaching it became increasingly difficult to get the beginning teachers to complete assignments fully and well. Work became increasingly shoddy—with some notable exceptions—as their time was taken up with matters related to teaching. I anticipated this problem and cut down the number of assignments initially planned; I simplified others, such as the action research project. Ironically, while the students originally appreciated having their workloads lightened, at year's end some expressed disappointment. When they went to write their last review of the PTT they found comparatively fewer materials to analyze and the value of the analysis weakened as a result. As one beginning teacher remarked disappointedly in interview: It was a "limited text." The case record was, simply stated, incomplete.

There are no obvious solutions to this problem. That some students expressed disappointment underscores the value of the texts and of maintaining a reasonably healthy workload, despite student complaints. I anticipate continued experimentation seeking a means for generating data that do not place unreasonable demands on student time and energy yet provide useful information. Meeting this challenge will have a significant bearing on the ultimate value of the texts.

Content and Content Integration

As noted, I struggled over what kinds of assignments and sources of data would be most useful for generating a record that would facilitate reflection and nudge along development. Functioning a bit like a nurse responsible for putting together a case record, I decided what data to include based upon a working hypothesis that proved in some ways faulty. Not all of the assignments were equally valuable. With this group, action research, for example, in part because of the tremendous time and emotional pressures associated with practice teaching, was of surprisingly little worth, particularly compared to how useful it was for the first group that created PTTs. Others have had similar difficulties (Gore and Zeichner 1991). The difference was that this group student taught for only ten weeks, while the first group taught for fifteen. Given the pressures of a short, intense practice teaching experience, and group and context differences of various kinds, every assignment must be carefully scrutinized. In contrast to my disappointment with the action research projects, peer observations of teaching were of extremely high value, as were the pupil evaluations. These assignments encouraged the beginning teachers to step outside of themselves and consider their teaching from the perspectives of others. Assignments of this kind, when structured around the exploration of questions of a nontechnical kind (e.g., asking pupils to address questions about fairness in grading and teacher-student and student-student relationships), encourage the reflective turn outward.

After considering each assignment and its apparent educational value, and from the perspective of honoring both reflective turns, an adequate case record probably should include the following, each a source of data useful for analysis:

- personal history and descriptions of the context within which practice will take place
- records of efforts to identify and explore personal beliefs, values, and understandings about teaching collected over time

- examples of problem diagnosis and framing, especially during practice teaching
- copies and evaluations of plans generated to solve problems
- an organization for the materials that facilitates the ongoing analysis, reinterpretation, and sharing of data.
- periodic written analyses of the text's contents that represent the novice's assessment of his or her development and projection of self into the future

An additional problem has to do with content integration; content was not interwoven as well as it should have been, and thus some of the value of the text as a means for providing program coherence was lost. For example, one student remarked that he was surprised to discover upon rereading his life history that it had changed: "The educational [life] history was really interesting . . . my perception of it has changed." Unfortunately, I failed to have the students explicitly return to some of their earlier work to reconsider it in light of current thinking. Instead, I gave the more general review assignment. Perhaps a more skillful tillerman, one who could have better directed turns inward and outward, may have increased the text's value, and perhaps more evidence of critical reflection would have resulted. This discovery is intimately connected to the last area of difficulty.

Closure

The disappointment I noted in a student's remarks about the text being "limited" underscores the importance of coming to closure. The pressure of student teaching, as year's end approached, was joined by pressures to get a positive evaluation from cooperating teachers, to set up interviews, and to get a job in a tight market. The students, soon to be teachers, were on edge, their nerves worn. It was within this context that I tried to pull all of our work together for the year. Unfortunately, the closer the last day of student teaching came, the less time we had in seminar for anything but what loosely might be called "therapy." While I had hoped to spend a full session reviewing the year and then discussing the final text review, we ended up having only time for a brief critique of the cohort. A few days later, a picnic and celebration followed. Although the final review is an important part of bringing closure to the certification year, it needs to be complemented by other activities designed to get the students thinking about where they were in their thinking and development at the beginning of the year, where they are, and where they would like to be. This also is essential to coherence. The importance of sharing the data and the associated analyses cannot be underestimated. There is a tendency among teacher educators who seek to develop reflective practitioners to think of reflection as essentially an individual and private undertaking (Bullough and Gitlin 1989; Cinnamond and Zimpher 1990) and to ignore its social and moral aspects. Reflection is inherently and inevitably a social affair.

Role

I struggled with my role. I felt part of my task, roughly similar to a nurse's, was to assist the students to diagnose problems arising from the data contained in the texts, to help them plan ahead, and then guide them as they sought solutions. I used the seminar, notes to students on their work, and personal meetings for this purpose, but by year's end I realized that the role was more complicated and difficult to fulfill than I imagined it would be. To be sure, working with twenty-three students was much more difficult than the ten I worked with when first exploring PTTs. I became a helper and sometime cheerleader who, having pointed the novices in a direction and given them a rather vague map, was available primarily when a traveler was in danger of becoming completely lost.

Conclusion

Personal teaching texts represent a useful but complicated means for encouraging beginning teacher development. Generally speaking, and despite being guinea pigs, the students were pleased with what was accomplished in the program and through use of the texts. The texts allowed the beginning teachers to keep in touch with their development; increased their self-confidence; enabled them to see themselves as producers of legitimate knowledge; helped them to consider, thoughtfully, their values; enabled them to take greater control over their professional development; and gave them a sense of program coherence. Additionally, the texts facilitated teacher reflection of various kinds. While some of the problems associated with student journal writing persisted with the PTT, on the whole, the results are encouraging.

CHAPTER 11

Exploring Personal Teaching Metaphors in Preservice Teacher Education (1991)

Introduction

The question of the impact of teacher education is a continuing concern among teacher educators (Cole 1985). Zeichner and Tabachnick (1981) have posed the question, are the effects of teacher education "washed out" by teachers' experience in schools? Many reasons have been given for the apparent lack of impact of teacher education, including lack of rigorous course work and limited program quality and length (Carnegie Forum on Education and the Economy 1986; Holmes Group 1986). A constructivist view of learning suggests an additional reason. Teacher educators typically ignore the novice's prior knowledge about teaching and instead approach the task of teacher socialization and development as though the beginner were a tabula rasa (Britzman 1986; Crow 1987). Functioning as a teaching schema (Bullough, Knowles, and Crow 1991), prior knowledge about teaching serves as a filter through which the student responds to teacher education. Content and experiences that tend to confirm the schema and related conceptions of self as teacher are accepted, whereas those that do not are rejected (Zeichner, Tabachnick, and Densmore 1987). Questions are framed and answers are investigated and evaluated through this background knowledge. Thus teacher education should have greater impact if the novice's background knowledge about teaching is incorporated into instruction in teacher education (Clark 1988). Much of the novice's background knowledge, however, is tacit. Its power to shape understanding comes because it is embedded in our language and hidden from view. The challenge for teacher educators is to make this knowledge explicit (Weinstein 1989). Only by expressing tacit meanings can they be subjected to analysis and through scrutiny find justification (Polanyi 1958).

While gathering data for *First-Year Teacher* (Bullough 1989), I encountered this issue with Kerrie, the teacher whose experience is reported in that book. As we explored her thinking about teaching and the impact of her teacher education, I began to understand the pattern that gave coherence to her conception of teaching. Her life experience had led her to think of teaching as essentially an extension of mothering, a form of nurturing. Kerrie made teaching sensible through this self-understanding, attending to that part of teacher education that confirmed her outlook while discounting the rest. Her metaphor of mothering led me to consider the use of metaphor in preservice teacher education. In this chapter, the development of the use of metaphor analysis to help preservice students examine and refine their conceptions of teaching is described.

Teaching Metaphors

There is growing interest in the study of the metaphors that teachers use to reveal their self-understanding (Hunt 1987; Miller and Fredericks 1988; Munby 1986; Provenzo, McCloskey, Kottkamp, and Cohn 1989; Russell and Johnston 1988), what Bandman (1967) earlier called "picture preferences" (112). Metaphors represent teachers' understanding about teaching and their conceptions of themselves as teachers, what Pajak (1986) calls their "professional identity" (123) or persona. This view is based, in part, upon the belief that metaphor is the primary means by which humans come to terms with experience.

> Just as in mutual understanding we constantly search out commonalities of experience when we speak with other people, so in self-understanding we are always searching for what unifies our own diverse experiences in order to give coherence to our lives. Just as we seek out metaphors to highlight and make coherent what we have in common with someone else, so we seek out personal metaphors to highlight and make coherent our own pasts, our present activities, and our dreams, hopes, and goals as well. A large part of self-understanding is the search for appropriate personal metaphors that make sense of our lives. Self-understanding requires unending negotiation and renegotiation of the meaning of your experiences to yourself. . . . It involves the constant construction of new coherences in your life, coherences that give new meaning to old experiences. The process of self-understanding is the continual development of new life stories for yourself. (Lakoff and Johnson 1980, 232–33)

Although metaphor is frequently criticized for simplifying phenomena, I have come to see simplification as a virtue (Dickmeyer 1989). This characteristic of metaphor appeared to be a partial solution to my quest for a means for making the experience of preservice teachers more accessible to analysis.

An Initial Testing of Ideas

During the 1988 academic year, I began testing a few tentative ideas about the use of metaphor analysis with a group of fifteen secondary, preservice graduate certification students in my student teaching seminar. These students were proceeding as a cohort through a year-long, full-time program. In the spring seminar that parallels practice teaching, I intended to help them become aware of the metaphors they used to interpret teaching and teacher education and to explore the origins of those meanings. The purpose of the seminar was to assist the student teachers in thinking about the problems of student teaching. In addition to addressing the challenges they were experiencing, we explored some of the literature on the typical problems of beginning teachers. I stressed that we would examine the problem of coming to know oneself as teacher, and to that end we would identify and explore personal teaching metaphors. The students began by identifying a root teaching metaphor that captured their "core self-perception" (Ball and Goodson 1985, 18). They wrote about these metaphors and discussed them in seminar, exploring the similarities and differences between metaphors and experiences. For example, three of the women and two of the men thought of teaching as an extension of parenting. Immediate bonds were formed among them as they, with half smiles, knowingly nodded their assent to each other's comments. For one of these student teachers, however, the discovery revealed an inner tension that negatively affected her relationship with her students. She found herself parenting young people but not wanting to do so:

> I find there is a lot more parenting in my teaching metaphor than I would like, perhaps because I am a parent and have chosen the parenting metaphor in other areas of my life. . . . That metaphor is so very strong; it reaches over into the teaching area. . . . I don't want to permanently parent anyone other than my own children. . . . I fight against becoming so involved with any student that I am personally affected by his behavior.

In response to this discovery, she began seeking a new metaphor.

As student teaching proceeded, we returned three times to the metaphors to identify changes that had occurred in their thinking and especially to the factors that prompted these changes. Through our discussions, it became apparent that Connelly and Clandinin (1988) were correct: It "makes a great deal of difference to our practice . . . if we think of teaching as gardening, coaching, or cooking. It makes a difference if we think of children as clay to be molded or as players on a team or as travellers on a journey" (71). The students found the analysis of metaphors a valuable process. As one student stated:

> This whole idea of [producing] a teaching metaphor has really been a powerful [vehicle] for [thinking about] myself. . . . It comes at a time when I am experiencing a personal crisis over the age-old question of "Who am I?" Just when I thought that my [teaching] identity was fairly secure and well established, I am being subjected to yet another identity crisis.

Although much went well with this initial use of metaphor analysis, it was far from satisfying. Much that was written and said was superficial or glib; for some students, metaphors came too easily and did not represent the thoughtful self-examination for which I had hoped. The pressures of student teaching encouraged shallowness. While thinking about this problem over the summer, I realized that I might have avoided this superficial response by encouraging the students to link their metaphors to their biographical roots and personal histories. As Woods (1987) advised, "Demands for change . . . that go to the roots of one's construction of self are very difficult to meet without some examination of how that self has come to be constructed" (131).

Therefore, one of the first assignments I gave to my group of secondary, graduate certification students that fall, prior to engaging in any fieldwork, was to write education-related life histories. Drawing on Measor's (1985) work, I gave them the assignment to "identify those critical incidents that prompted the decision to become a teacher and have most profoundly influenced how you think of yourself as teacher." The second assignment was to identify, based upon their written history, a metaphor or metaphors that best captured how they thought of themselves as teachers. Life-history writing preceded the identification of the metaphors.

Three Examples

Although I was not fully satisfied with the results, the connections that nine of the eleven students made between life history and metaphor were strong, interesting, and rang true. Three examples follow, chosen because they are interesting, generally representative of the students' experience in the seminar, and theoretically provocative:

> I was thirteen when my younger brother Tommy, almost ten, died in an accident near our home. With his boundless energy and inexhaustible inquisitiveness, Tommy constantly presented me with challenges which threatened my position as the wise, if insecure, older brother. When he died, suddenly I was left with all the rotten things I had done to him, all the chances I'd had to express my love to him irretrievably lost. Tommy's life and death have taught me more about the value of life than anything else I know. In many ways, he provided me with the inspiration to teach and share my energy and love with others. . . . Now I feel that every moment of life is part of an exquisite work of art. Whether running, parenting, writing, doing the dishes, or teaching, I am only truly fulfilled through knowing that I am doing my best to share my soul with others.

The writer, a mountain runner in his middle thirties and father of two young children, went on to explore other experiences, especially in nature and with young people. From these experiences, he derived the metaphor of teacher as husbandman of the young. During the second week of class in September and well before he began working in the schools, he wrote:

> Every student who enters my classroom will have been tended and nurtured, perhaps hindered and tortured, by a unique process of caretakers, some compassionate and humble, some prescriptive and authoritarian. As husbandman to a group of growing human beings, I see my role as teacher being most importantly one of providing the very best climate in the classroom for the maximum growth and development of each student. . . . My experience as teacher will be one of ongoing discovery, a succession of mistakes which will help me understand not only who needs more or less light, more or less water, or who needs to have the weeds pulled up from around them, but also what methods for administering this care will contribute the most to healthy growth. As husbandman I will cultivate an appreciation of the intrinsic dignity and beauty of the living beings I will be entrusted to care for. Students, indeed, all of us, are "state of the art" human beings; they are the best hundreds of millions of years of evolution can offer. . . . I feel a natural affinity toward the role of husbandman for human life, as well as all earthly life.

Another student, in her early forties and the mother of two elementary schoolchildren, thought of herself as "devil's advocate," one who challenges the taken for granted, and she wrote:

> Dad was my best teacher in my early years. School days were full of indifference. Learning was easy but not interesting. The worst days were the ones in which everything seemed indifferent; the teacher, the other kids, the spelling words, math problems, even recess. The best days were the rare and sacred days in which two plus two miraculously did not equal four. The pleasure of unpredicted experiences!

A third preservice teacher education student, a very shy, introspective woman of twenty-four, wrote:

> [Teaching] is in my blood. It's what I always wanted to do. And now, here I am, a teacher trainee, trying to identify what led me to where I am. I've been interested in teaching ever since I was a child, when I would hold make-believe school in our family room. My two younger brothers would gather up the neighborhood children every week and would bring them over to our "classroom." I taught my two brothers and some of the other kids how to read and write a little bit before they even entered kindergarten. . . . I put together a workbook made up of construction paper and staples. I made up

games, stories, and crossword puzzles. My pretend schoolhouse lasted a couple of summers, until I was in the fifth grade. At that time I began tutoring first and second graders at the school. Tutoring was such a rewarding experience that I continued to tutor all through junior high and high school. Tutoring was rewarding because not only were the students learning from me, but in turn, I gained a lot from them such as companionship, trust, respect, and patience. Tutoring made me feel good about myself.

This student used multiple metaphors in thinking about herself as teacher; one was "teacher as butterfly." This metaphor seemed to capture a much broader view of herself than just teacher, and, as she later asserted, it represented especially well how she thought about herself as a person:

> My second metaphor is kind of silly, but it has meaning to me. It is teacher as butterfly. I have viewed myself throughout my undergraduate years as a cocoon, growing inside and striving to achieve beauty. As a graduate student I feel as though I am finally breaking free from that safe cocoon and becoming ready to emerge as a butterfly. I identify with this because butterflies are very delicate and fragile on the outside, yet are strong willed and enduring on the inside. Butterflies are free and beautiful. They explore and experience everything around them and bring beauty and enjoyment to others. I hope to be able to spread my delicate wings and bring some beauty and knowledge into the lives of others. However, a butterfly's wings can be broken very easily.

Return to the Metaphors

After the initial writing assignment and during student teaching that began second term and lasted until the end of the year, we returned approximately every two or three weeks in seminar to consider the metaphors. At these times I had the students write about their metaphors, and we discussed any changes that were noted and attempted to identify sources of the changes. Just prior to student teaching, the three students asserted that their metaphors had remained intact but were being elaborated as they observed and worked with their cooperating teachers and as we read about and discussed teaching. The "husbandman" said that his metaphor "intensified during the quarter." Similarly, the "devil's advocate" said that her metaphor was "still intact," but she was beginning to wonder about whether or not such a vision of self was appropriate for school settings:

> I'm more skeptical about being able to fulfill my expectations. Two of the structural problems in the school working against my metaphor are the short class periods and the crowded classrooms. The other problem I've become

aware of is the need to structure the classroom so that as few as possible of the students are "lost": Spoon-feeding appears to be helpful, but creative spoon-feeding is so difficult.

What was especially striking about this student's response was that seven weeks earlier she had asserted that she could not believe that anyone's views could or would change: "Frankly, I'm feeling more certain as our group continues to discuss the readings that we are all very much set in our ways, that our metaphors won't change much, if any." Her discovery was quite to the contrary. She was changing, but not entirely in ways to her liking.

Metaphors and Student Teaching

Early in the beginning of their five months of half-day student teaching, we returned to the metaphors, and this time, in the thick of student teaching, the students faced the difficulty of negotiating a role in the school that was both personally satisfying—close to the ideals implied by their teaching metaphors—and institutionally fitting. The "butterfly" found herself struggling for a clear image of herself as she attempted to negotiate a role with not only her students but also with her cooperating teacher:

> Some days I feel like teacher as policewoman or teacher as bitch. . . . I'll leave school feeling awful about what transpired that day. But on other days I have felt like teacher as nurturer or mother . . . and teacher as friend. I feel like a chameleon—I like that: teacher as chameleon! Always changing and trying to find a spot where I am most comfortable.

Threatened by both her cooperating teacher and the students, this beginning teacher, like so many others, retreated into conservative practices (Zeichner and Grant 1981) and coped with the situation through strategic compliance. Eventually she settled into a role very much like that of her cooperating teacher. To obtain student conformity, she returned to her cocoon and emerged a poor imitation of her cooperating teacher, strict and surprisingly harsh.

This unhappy situation persisted until near the end of the year, when she felt confident enough to begin in small ways breaking away from the set practices of her cooperating teacher. This change suggested she might, eventually, find herself as teacher. On the last day of school she reflected on her experience in a concluding interview in this way:

> I wasn't quite sure what I wanted to be [as teacher]. . . . [I] was just kind of trying to find my little niche, what was comfortable for me, and I think I changed a lot. . . . I feel like I'm getting there. . . . It is going to take me getting a job to really work out [who I am].

The fears of the "devil's advocate" were realized: The context of teaching, including the large number of students in her classes, the large number of non-English-speaking and low-ability students, paperwork, and the short class periods, made it difficult for her to come near to achieving her metaphor. Moreover, she was frustrated by the role of student teacher, because she perceived it as artificially constrained. After all, the students and classes were not her own:

> "[I feel]," she said, "[like] a character in someone else's play. I am exhausted, overwhelmed, and feeling a premature need to be the real teacher. I want to have the freedom a real job would give [me]. . . . There are so many aspects [of student teaching over which] I have no control."

Yet despite her frustrations, and unlike her cohort colleague, she resisted the press toward conservatism, although she was necessarily engaged in a variety of compromises of her image ideals.Of the three preservice teachers, the "husbandman" felt the most continuity between what he was doing in the classroom and his view of himself as a teacher. He was determined to make the context fit his metaphor, but his aim was not easily realized. In the early spring, he wrote this:

> I have been experiencing an intensification of my metaphor of teacher as husbandman. This intensification is emerging as I continue to scatter seeds, but I am learning more about how to prepare the soil and climate in the classroom so that an ever-greater number of seeds may actually sprout and flourish. This is not to say that I have witnessed a widespread greening among my students, but I do feel that by being alert to the natural tendencies for growth and development in my students, I am making progress toward realizing my role as a good husbandman.

Three weeks after this writing, the situation for the husbandman-teacher had changed, however. In keeping with my belief that the "most effective evaluation for learning is self-evaluation" (Johnston 1989, 523), I required each teacher to conduct a series of studies loosely following the "action research spiral" (Kemmis and McTaggart 1988). For the purpose of gathering data on classroom performance, this teacher audiotaped several class sessions. After listening to the audiotapes, he was deeply disturbed. The teacher he heard talking to the students on tape was not the nurturing and responsive teacher he imagined himself to be. Describing this discovery in seminar, he remarked that rather than being characterized by open conversation, the classes were dominated by monologue; he was imposing his will on the students: "I noted totalitarian tendencies. . . . I sort of take [over] the show. . . .

The problem is, I'm good at monologue." He was visibly shaken but remained determined to eliminate those elements of his practice that were inconsistent with his metaphor, even though the students responded positively to his monologues and obviously felt comfortable with this approach to instruction. For him, to be a husbandman meant that teaching could not be synonymous with telling, the imposition of ideas. Although optimistic that he could purge the "teller" within him, he recognized the difficulty of the challenge: "Virtue," he said in seminar, "is one thing, but the practice of virtue is another.... There is so much more [to becoming a teacher] than I ever dreamed of."

The weekend following the seminar, during which he shared this disturbing revelation, he began to rethink some aspects of his practice. He discovered that the set of principles he was using to guide practice was at odds with his husbandman metaphor. Writing in seminar, he stated:

> I have tended to adopt a standard of measure [of my performance] that would be simple and manageable; but this tendency appears likely either to diminish the potency of [my] metaphor or to require its abandonment altogether.... Abandoning my metaphor I must not, cannot, and therefore will not, do.

The standard he was using, he asserted, was deeply embedded in the American culture, and he had been seduced:

> For those of us raised in an industrialized society the tendency to [judge performance by] a simple standard of measure is overwhelming. We have been eager to buy unconditionally the economists' pitch that innovation and competition would solve our problems, and that we would ultimately accomplish a technological end run around the biological realities of the human condition by applying ourselves to one standard: the standard of productivity.

A narrow conception of efficiency, tied implicitly to student conformity and content coverage, had crept unnoticed into his teaching, and he did not like the results. Another standard, one consistent with his desire to be a husbandman of children, needed to be created and put into practice if his metaphor was to be preserved.

The principle that emerged through contrasting his metaphor with his practice and that became pivotal in curriculum and instructional decision making was tied to a husbandman's conception of human nature:

> A good husbandman is a dialoguist or a conversationalist in that he asks nature which of his actions will be permitted without diminishing nature, and he waits for nature's response, knowing that its response will impel only thoughtful and kindly use and that his [response] will, in turn, impel an

unforeseeable response which will, in turn, change the user. This conversational approach, immitigably two-sided and mysterious, necessarily takes on a life of its own, a life that binds the user to his surroundings in a manner which grows and changes to no preconceived end and therefore is irreducible to such a simple standard of measure as that of productivity.

In his quest for principles to establish congruence between practice and personal metaphor, a second and complementary metaphor for teaching emerged, teaching as conversation. As winter turned to spring, this metaphor, with its attendant teacher images, played an important role in producing the desired coherence that remained to year's end.

A Return to the Problem

Becoming a teacher is an idiosyncratic process reflecting not only differences in biography, personality, and conceptions of teaching (Zeichner 1983) but also differences in context (Wildman, Niles, Magliaro, and McLaughlin 1989). From the perspective of schema theory (Rumelhart 1980), beginning teachers inevitably pick and choose what they will respond to in teacher education. Drawing on their past experience, they seek first and foremost confirmation of what they assume to be true about themselves as teachers and about teaching. When this view of themselves and of teaching proves faulty, as it often does during student teaching, beginning teachers face a difficult decision to accommodate to the situation, what Lacey (1977) labeled "internalized adjustment," to engage in one or another coping strategy that aims at self-preservation (Rosenholtz 1989), or to remake the situation. In so doing, they may develop in directions quite different from those predicted by the widely discussed progressive-traditional shift (Zeichner and Grant 1981) and in ways quite at odds with those often sought by teacher educators.

Regardless of what course of action is followed, it is generally pursued tacitly and in reaction to the context of teaching. That the process is tacit presents a problem to teacher educators that requires a rethinking of both the structures and processes of teacher education. A first, necessary step is to establish a means for helping beginning teachers make explicit the grounds upon which they interpret and understand their experience of teaching and of teacher education. It is here that the identification and analysis of teaching metaphors, coupled with life history and action research, are of particular importance.

In interviews conducted at the conclusion of the teacher education program to assess program effectiveness and to identify problems, the teachers indicated that the analysis of teaching metaphors was important to their development as teachers. They asserted that it helped them think about themselves as teachers and the values they held and identify and frame problems. I believe, therefore, that the approach has the potential for increasing the influence of teacher education. Although the "chameleon" had yet "to settle on a clear vision" of herself as teacher, she remarked in interview the following:

> [Metaphor analysis] forced me to think about my role as a teacher and what I do want to be as a teacher. . . . It made me think, reflect back on what I was doing, and look at what kind of person I think I am or what kind of a teacher I think I am.

Moreover, sharing the metaphors in the group helped her see that there were numerous legitimate ways of coming to terms with being a teacher, not just one way, as she had initially believed, based upon her prior experience as a student:

> I thought everybody had to be the same as a teacher [which] was a big thing at first. I thought that all teachers were the same. [But] when I heard what some of the other metaphors were, I thought, "This is so different from what I've been doing or what I've been experiencing," and I liked that.

The "devil's advocate" found metaphor analysis especially helpful. She used it to make judgments about curriculum and instruction and to help her identify and frame problems. For example, she remarked that being a devil's advocate forced her

> to not be routine [in her teaching], to ask questions, and I've had a very hard time with asking questions, especially considering the metaphor. . . . [Learning how to ask provocative questions] will be my focus next year. . . . My metaphor should mean that I'm questioning a lot, that should be a big part of my teaching, but it was so tough for me to form good questions.

Overall, she concluded, the emphasis on metaphors was "really a good idea. . . . I think that it would be nice if all teachers thought of a metaphor for their teaching." The "husbandman" had similarly strong feelings about the usefulness of the approach, which was, he asserted, of "tremendous value for me," serving as the basis for his analysis of practice. In addition, it helped him begin to identify the school conditions necessary for him to be the kind of teacher he wanted to be.

Conclusion

Although promising, metaphor analysis is not without problems. One problem is that it may encourage an overly narrow focus on self (Bullough 1987).

Beginning teachers need to reach beyond self and engage in a broader consideration of the context of teaching and of schooling than is presented in this chapter; self must be seen in relation to the identification and creation of conditions needed for professional development. Such a critique is only foreshadowed in the words of the "devil's advocate," as she criticized the conditions under which she was working.

With respect to this issue, the experience of the husbandman deserves further consideration. The pressure he felt coming from the context of teaching, and especially the students, was to embrace the dominant teaching metaphor of the faculty: Teaching is telling. To teach in this way, however, would have been a conservative response to the situation. Feeling secure about his metaphor, he chose not to comply but rather to engage in critique. The problem was located not in his conception of self as teacher, his persona, but in the situation and in his lack of ability to realize his self-conception in context, a problem of enactment. He strategically redefined the situation. In this instance, metaphor analysis assisted him in framing the problem and responding to it in a manner that strengthened his already strong sense of self. Such an outcome may be encouraged if metaphor analysis is coupled with a greater effort to engage in context analysis. Clearly reaching beyond self and the immediate concerns of the classroom to analyze wider schooling-related issues is essential to professional development.

Given her weakly held teaching persona, the "butterfly" presents quite a different problem. When a student teacher lacks a clear conception of self as teacher, it may be developmentally impossible to get beyond the concern for self to engage in a critique of the context of schooling. For such teachers, the pressure to comply may be overpowering.

While working to create methods and establish conditions in teacher education that help novices develop the capacity and inclination to engage in critical reflection, it is tempting to seek shortcuts and to try to build in right answers and forget the importance of respecting the neophyte. As Wilshire (1990) reminded us, this will simply not do if education and not training is our aim. Occasionally I have had to remind myself that I must be respectful of the teacher metaphors; educationally, there is no escaping from them, only building upon them or assisting in their reconstruction, as Dewey (1916) suggested. If teacher educators learn this lesson, and learn it well, then the influence of teacher education might be significantly increased.

CHAPTER 12

Teaching with a Peer:
A Comparison of Two Models
of Student Teaching (2003)

with Janet R. Young, James R. Birrell, D. Cecil Clark,
M. Winston Egan, Lynnette B. Erickson,
Marti Frankovich, Joanne Brunetti, and Myra Welling

Introduction

Increased field experience has become a centerpiece of teacher education
reform over the past several years. In Europe and North America, there is
a veritable "celebration of experience" (Buchberger, Campos, Kallos, and
Stephenson 2000, 14); the value of school experience to teacher education
is, as Johnston argues, "accepted almost on blind faith" (1994, 199). At the
same time there is a growing recognition of the shortcomings of traditional
patterns of field experience, particularly of student teaching, and awareness
of how little is known about what is actually learned in the field (see Wilson, Floden, and Ferrini-Mundy 2001). The typical pattern of student
teaching has remained little changed for fifty years: A teacher education
student is placed in a classroom with a single cooperating teacher for varying lengths of time, a term or perhaps a semester. As quickly as possible the
student assumes complete responsibility for classroom instruction and
management and, while soloing, "practices" teaching. "The university provides the theory, the school provides the setting, and the student teacher
provides the effort to bring them together" (Wideen, Mayer-Smith, and
Moon 1998, 152). Not surprisingly, this model gives cooperating teachers
tremendous power over teacher education students' learning (Wilson et al.
2001). The challenge for student teachers is clear: "survival appears upper-
most in their minds, with risk taking being minimal and the need for a
good grade essential" (Wideen et al. 1998, 156). While the model has
remained essentially the same, the challenges of teaching have dramatically
increased.

There is a growing need to rethink student teaching and to generate alternative models of field experience. In particular, given the increasing difficulty and complexity of teaching, there is a need for models that enhance teachers' "collaborative problem-solving capacity" (Buchberger et al. 2000, 49). Howey and Zimpher echo the point: "Most fundamental to the improvement of teacher education is addressing how all teachers are prepared to work with one another" (1999, 294).

The Study

In light of these considerations, and following a careful examination of our own institution's approach to student teaching, which stresses solo teaching, a proposal was made to one of the urban school faculties associated with the university to explore an alternative model: rather than place one student teacher with a single cooperating teacher, we suggested placing two student teachers together in one classroom and with one teacher. Approval came. We then set out to answer the general question, "What are the benefits and possible shortcomings of partnered student teaching as an alternative model of practice teaching?" To begin to answer this general question, a set of more specific questions was posed that will be used to organize the findings: (1) What kind and quality of relationships will develop in the two models of student teaching between cooperating teachers and student teachers and, in the partnership model, between student teachers? (2) What differences in roles and responsibilities will emerge for cooperating teachers and student teachers in the two models of student teaching? (3) What value will the student teachers and cooperating teachers find in their experience? What impact will the student teachers have on the classroom, the cooperating teachers (including their workload), and pupil learning? To answer these questions, it was necessary to create a research design that enabled comparison of single placement and paired student teaching experiences.

School Context and Participants

Western Horizon (fictitious name) and Brigham Young University have been linked in a wider school-university partnership since the school's opening, and there was a very positive working arrangement. The school has been open three years and has a student population of 670 students, of which two thirds qualify for a free or reduced lunch. Western Horizon is located in a very diverse section of Salt Lake City, and nearly half the student population is categorized as either non-English speaking or limited English speaking. Forty-three percent of the students are Hispanic.

Teachers and student teachers from an elementary education cohort volunteered to participate in the study. Placements were made randomly. No effort was made to match partners. Of the ten teacher education students who participated in the study, all female, four were assigned to single student teaching placements and six were paired then placed with a cooperating teacher. Each of the participating cooperating teachers had previously served in this role, all were veteran teachers, and all agreed to work with either a single or a pair of student teachers. Pairs of student teachers were assigned to teach in the second, fourth, and sixth grades, thus allowing for the possibility that younger and older children might have different experiences with partnership teaching. Singly-placed student teachers taught in the second (two classes), third, and sixth grades, but we draw upon data from only one of the second grade and the third grade classes for reasons that will shortly be noted.

Cooperating teachers were given few directions about how they should work with the student teachers. They were encouraged to develop their own way of working that made sense to them and that would be beneficial to the student teachers and children. In part this decision was justified by knowledge that mentoring is highly idiosyncratic (see Martin 1997), and in fact diverse approaches did emerge.

During student teaching, two of the four solo student teachers were necessarily reassigned to different cooperating teachers. Reassignment came in one instance because the teacher completely disengaged from the classroom to work on a district assignment, leaving the student teacher without any assistance and only minimal guidance. In the second instance, a change was made because the cooperating teacher had serious difficulties with classroom management herself, as well as with organizing a program of study for the children. This teacher was an experienced teacher who had returned to the classroom after a long break from teaching. Data from these two student teachers are not used. All three teaching pairs remained together in their original assignments throughout the eight weeks of student teaching (one of two student teaching placements).

Data Gathering and Analysis

Data were gathered using a variety of sources. Time logs allowed comparison of the activities of the student teachers. Student teachers turned in all literacy and social studies lesson plans. This source of data proved of little value, however, as no clear differences in written plans emerged between the two groups. Planning meetings were taped early and late in the term. Unfortunately, some teams failed to tape both meetings. Nevertheless, some useful information emerged from meeting transcripts. A set of interview questions was developed to examine the children's attitudes about having multiple student teachers in their classroom. Children from each of the classrooms within which pairs of student teachers taught gathered in small groups around a tape recorder and a member of the research team asked them questions about the advantages and disadvantages of having multiple student teachers.

Interview protocols for the cooperating teachers and student teachers were developed. Questions asked of the student teachers varied slightly, depending upon the nature of their placement. Interviews were conducted early (second week) and late in the term. Each interview was recorded and transcribed for analysis. Interviews were conducted by members of the research team who had no formal connection to Western Horizon or to the cooperating or student teachers. Each student teacher or partnership was observed teaching a minimum of twelve hours, four half-day observations, two early and two later in the term, by a member of the research team, who also was responsible for interviewing that cooperating teacher and student teacher(s).

Data analysis consisted of calculating from the logs the kinds and amounts of time spent in various teaching activities by the student teachers. Single and partner placement comparisons were then made. Interviews, including group interviews with the children, were transcribed and analyzed first through open and then axial coding (Strauss and Corbin 1990).

Similar questions were asked in each interview. Drawing on these data sources and observation notes, case studies were independently written by the research team member who conducted the observations for each partnership and each individually placed student teacher. The cases were written explicitly to give a sense of development over time and to capture the nature of the participants' experience and the sense they made of that experience. The attempt to portray development in the cases and to make certain that differences were not lost when comparing single and partner-placed student teachers resulted in some variation in the organization of the cases. In order to address the general and specific questions underpinning the study, a cross-case analysis (Yin 1989) was conducted and themes and shared patterns were identified for each of the two models of student teaching.

Two cases follow. The story of the singly placed student teachers is mostly a familiar tale, but it is told here because it enables comparison and discussion. Although independently written, the partner teaching cases proved remarkably similar. To simplify our findings and to better enable comparison of the two models of student teaching, the decision was made to present the most representative case, that of the sixth grade partnership, and to note within this case consequential differences among the cases where they emerged. Attention will be drawn to similarities across the cases when they have particular importance to the research questions.

Single-Placement Cases

Single-Placement Participants

Both cooperating teachers, Mr. Oakes and Ms. Gardiner (all names are fictitious), were experienced teachers. Recently named district teacher of the year,
Mr. Oakes had taught young children for nearly three decades and mentored
over that time at least ten student teachers. Ms. Gardiner had worked with
three student teachers over her nineteen years of teaching. Characterized as
"soft-spoken and just easy going," Ms. Gardiner believed that mentoring student teachers was "important for [teachers] to do as part of [their] professional responsibility." Both cooperating teachers had school-related assignments in addition to their role as classroom teachers. Mr. Oakes served on a
district team responsible for observing and assisting a struggling, senior-level
teacher on probation. This responsibility required him to be absent from the
classroom on a regular basis. Ms. Gardiner was the school technology specialist and was therefore called upon from time to time to help other teachers in
the school with computer problems. Mr. Oakes described Jerriann, his student
teacher, as "very easy to get along with. I think [she wants] to please others."
She was also fiercely independent. He noted that "a lot of times, I'd just ask,
'are you ready for the day? What can I do to help you?' and I know she had
things to do. . . . I got the same answer all the time, 'No problem.'" In addition to doing her student teaching, Jerriann was still completing some of her
course work on campus, so she often had to hurry off at the end of the school
day to make the hour-long drive to the university for a late afternoon class.
She also was engaged to be married at the end of the semester. These circumstances, coupled with Mr. Oakes's frequent absence from the classroom,
framed Jerriann's student teaching experience, severely limiting opportunities
for Mr. Oakes and Jerriann to plan for upcoming instruction or to engage in
any sort of dialogue about teaching.

Like Mr. Oakes, Ms. Gardiner found her student teacher, Joni, "easy to
work with." From the beginning, Ms. Gardiner saw Joni as one who was "very
receptive to ideas . . . always taking initiative and [being] prepared." Although
Joni's prior teaching experience had been in upper-grade classrooms and she
was initially concerned about her ability to teach younger children, by the end
of her student teaching she was cautiously optimistic about her capability. "I
feel like I've ended with a better experience than I started with."

Relationships

The relationships that developed between the student teachers and their
cooperating teachers differed considerably in these two single-placement

classrooms. In Ms. Gardiner's classroom, Joni felt supported at every turn and spent extended periods of time planning and reflecting with her cooperating teacher. Even toward the end of Joni's student teaching, after Ms. Gardiner had withdrawn from the classroom for the majority of the day, interaction continued.

This sense of support was not as strong for Jerriann. Almost from the beginning of the semester, even when he was in the school, Mr. Oakes was generally not in the room when Jerriann taught. Rather, he moved in and out, spending much of his time in the office area adjacent to the classroom. Opportunities for communication were at a premium: "One of us was always rushing someplace, so we didn't get to spend a lot of time planning. . . . It was always a fight for us to meet together to talk about things." When they did plan together they usually focused on the upcoming week's teaching activities and their scheduling, with Mr. Oakes making suggestions about activities and materials, or occasionally critiquing Jerriann's teaching. Mr. Oakes's and Jerriann's relationship was pleasant and professional but could not be described as particularly close. As Mr. Oakes remarked, "[Looking] at the perspective of student teachers that I've had in the past, we were just acquaintances instead of really working together." Jerriann described her relationship with Mr. Oakes in this manner: "We got along fairly well. I think we struggled with communication . . . but generally speaking, we got along."

The conditions within these two teams contrasted in some important ways, most notably the time available for conversation. Opportunities to interact were far more common for Joni than for Jerriann, so the relationships that developed within the teams were quite different. Additionally, there was some difference between the two cooperating teachers' confidence that their student teacher would prepare adequately to carry out instruction. Both found it easy to get along with their student teachers, but Ms. Gardiner saw Joni as well prepared and on top of things. Mr. Oakes did not share that same confidence in Jerriann. It is not surprising to find variation in the quality and depth of interpersonal relationships, and these two cases likely exemplify rather typical relationships that develop between cooperating teachers and student teachers (see McNally, Cope, Inglis, and Stronach 1997).

Roles and Responsibilities

The roles enacted by the two single-placement cooperating teachers were very similar. Both shared a view that the role of a cooperating teacher was to provide a classroom where the student teacher could practice teaching and to give some support in the form of feedback and guidance in planning. They also shared the view that their role included helping the student teacher locate instructional materials. Both considered it appropriate for the cooperating teacher to maintain responsibility for major curricular decisions in their class-rooms. Transcripts of the planning sessions clearly indicated that from the beginning of student teaching to the end, both Mr. Oakes and Ms. Gardiner were the decision makers, although they allowed some flexibility. In Ms. Gardiner's classroom, for example, Joni was given some control over how the topics and concepts could be presented, but within established guidelines. "[Ms. Gardiner] has a lot of influence, but then she also asks me [for my input]. . . . I say 'I'm hoping to go through subtraction and addition with regrouping,' or 'I'm hoping to teach penguins' and then she'll say, 'so you'll want to look at the [state] core and kind of think about that.' . . . So she's kind of given me guide-lines and then I choose what I want to teach and when I want to teach it." While Jerriann's experience in third grade left her more alone in her planning and preparation than Joni, Mr. Oakes was nonetheless in charge of what was to be taught.

Intentional absence from the classroom on the part of both cooperating teachers signaled a strongly held belief that solo teaching is the best prepara-tion for teaching. When contemplating the instructional possibilities created by the presence of two teachers in a classroom, Ms. Gardiner welcomed another "trained adult" to help in reading groups. Yet she, like Mr. Oakes, asserted that such an arrangement was unrealistic in public school classrooms. She struggled with finding a balance between working in the classroom with her student teacher and giving her a "realistic" experience in the form of solo teaching. She seemed settled with her decision to transfer the responsibilities of teaching as quickly as possible to Joni. For Jerriann, Mr. Oakes's withdrawal was abrupt and came early in the term. Jerriann's time logs reveal no differ-ence in the amount of time spent observing Mr. Oakes teaching at the begin-ning to the end of the semester. She was given considerable responsibility for instruction within the classroom early in the semester, and that continued. Early on she was responsible for setting up and managing learning centers, teaching mathematics, opening the classroom day with calendar, weather, and pledge of allegiance routines, dealing with discipline issues, and closing each day. She also was responsible for correcting assignments, giving and monitor-ing homework, and moving children during the day to lunch, recess, and other out-of-class activities. When Mr. Oakes was in the room he tried not to inter-fere with Jerriann's teaching. During those times he reported that he found it difficult not to "jump in," to say something, or to take control when he felt uncomfortable about what he observed. The version of a "team" that emerged was one where Mr. Oakes attempted to guide Jerriann from behind the scenes during occasional planning sessions, but he stayed out of her way in the pres-ence of the children.

In Ms. Gardiner's classroom, withdrawal was more gradual, but it was nonetheless intended to prepare Joni for the solitary world of classroom teaching. Initially, Ms. Gardiner taught most of the day while Joni observed, took notes, or occasionally assisted with student questions or off-task behavior. Eventually the roles changed. After the third week Ms. Gardiner spent less and less time in the classroom, finally leaving Joni to manage and teach the students independently. After she had eased into full responsibility for instruction, Joni maintained Ms. Gardiner's class routines, including daily oral language, sustained silent reading, mathematics, two reading groups, attendance, pledge of allegiance, all subjects, and transitions to recess, lunch, and music. She also planned lessons and schedules with her cooperating teacher and developed and implemented a management plan.

Perceptions, Expectations, and Assessment

The overall concerns expressed by both student teachers and cooperating teachers were those commonly acknowledged in the literature (see McNally et al. 1997). Mr. Oakes had difficulty turning the teaching of his students over to another: "I just hate to give my kids away [during] prime teaching time in January and February. And I always worry. I'm too possessive of my kids." This reluctance was amplified by his concern about Jerriann's daily preparation. "Because of her outside influences with the two classes and getting married, she was flying by the seat of her pants a lot of the time. She'd get the kids working and then run over to the computer to get a worksheet ready for that afternoon, which should have been already run off." Ms. Gardiner also worried about her children, but she sought opportunities to give them additional help: "I have so many kids that are on the low end of the academics and [having a student teacher] will give me a chance to give them a little bit more individualized attention." Perhaps Ms. Gardiner's release of her class to the care of a student teacher was made easier by her confidence in Joni.

For Jerriann there was a need for more interaction with Mr. Oakes but little opportunity for extended conversations, feedback, and planning. Because much of Jerriann's teaching was solo teaching in Mr. Oakes's absence, she received little scrutiny. "I felt like I was being critiqued with not as much support in helping me grow." She was, however, appreciative of her cooperating teacher's help when offered. "There were a few times when the planning went really well, and we were actually able to talk and plan together. I remember when we were working on the fairy tale unit. . . . [For] an hour and a half we were able to bounce ideas off each other and that was incredibly valuable because I got his feedback and suggestions." For both, there seemed to be some level of professional respect for the other, but neither was elated about their experience. As noted, limited time was a serious issue for Jerriann, as it was for most of the student teachers.

Joni's expectations for student teaching were more closely matched to those of her cooperating teacher than was the case with Jerriann and Mr.

Oakes. Ms. Gardiner perceived herself to be a nurturer, a facilitator, and the director of her classroom curriculum, and Joni felt those roles were appropriate for a cooperating teacher. In her opinion, her cooperating teacher was "responsible to know what's required of me and to be able to help me work through that." Additionally she indicated that the cooperating teacher should "answer any questions that I have and kind of guide me through the process of student teaching, . . . take note of what's going on so she can give me pointers and feedback, and then . . . to always kind of be there in case I need help." Ms. Gardiner's view of her role aligned with Joni's perception: "It's important for me to give her praise for the things that I see she is doing well or that I think are being successful with the students, and then to give her ideas on the things that aren't working so well." With this match of perception and expectation, Joni and Ms. Gardiner worked harmoniously. Both were pleased with the contribution and performance of the other.

Partner Placement Case

As noted, we use the case study of the sixth grade partner team to present our findings. Not only does this case well represent the others, it has the additional advantage of involving two very dissimilar student teachers. Indeed, it would be difficult to imagine two more unlike personalities than Rebbie's and Emma's, the two paired student teachers. In contrast, the student teachers in the fourth grade team were characterized by the cooperating teacher as a "perfect match," because they had "similar personalities." While for a time Rebbie and Emma struggled with their relationship, eventually they became very close friends.

Partnership Participants

We begin with background on Mrs. Kenny because, as Graham (1997) argues, "personal histories have a profound influence on the mentor teacher-student teacher relationship" (516). Rebbie and Emma were assigned to student teach with Mrs. Kenny, a sixth grade teacher with sixteen years of elementary school teaching experience. A self-confessed "control freak," Mrs. Kenny had mentored over fifteen student teachers in two school districts. She characterized her previous experience as a cooperating teacher as "a mixed bag." Before volunteering to participate in the study, she had "mixed emotions" about working with two student teachers rather than one. Her concern not only was whether or not having two student teachers would increase her workload but more generally tied to the potential negative impact of any student teachers on the children: "[Some] of these kids are so low [academically] that it's really difficult [to give up my class]. . . . The kids have to go to seventh grade next year; I always feel a [need] to get them where they need to be to move on." She thought being taught by student teachers might impede their progress. Understandably this is a common view among cooperating teachers. The cooperating teacher of the second grade team felt much the same way, that student teachers would harm the children. Mrs. Kenny approached participation in the study cautiously, expecting to carefully monitor the children's performance and be fully ready to continue to play an active role in the classroom to make certain no harm was done.

According to Mrs. Kenny, Rebbie "had a little chip on her shoulder" at the beginning of student teaching. Apparently she wanted to student teach at Western Horizon but hoped she would not be placed with a partner. She wanted her own classroom, but did not get one. Of the six student teachers placed with partners, only Rebbie and Lou, a member of the fourth grade team, initially expressed doubts about partner teaching.

Characterized by herself and by Mrs. Kenny as relatively "easy going" but a very serious student, Rebbie brought to student teaching an unusually rich academic background, particularly in mathematics and the arts. Emma, Mrs. Kenny said, was not as "strong" academically as Rebbie. Their personalities, she said, were opposites. Emma was playful and seemed much younger than Rebbie, was "cool," very concerned with the latest fashions, hair fads, and music groups, and very confident and outgoing, not reserved at all. In contrast to Rebbie's solid, calm, more grown-up bearing, Emma was flighty, less steady, and, according to Mrs. Kenny, "superficial" and much less reflective. As Mrs. Kenny remarked, "Those personalities are so different." Yet they were assigned to be partners.

Like the other partner-placed student teachers, Emma and Rebbie did not know one another well prior to their assignment as partners. As Rebbie said about Emma: "I really didn't know anything about her. . . . [We've had some classes together but] I've never done any group projects with her at all. So it was really different being paired with her. I wasn't sure how it would turn out."

Relationships

At the beginning of the term, and throughout, planning together was ongoing. At the end of each day, Mrs. Kenny, Emma, and Rebbie met to discuss the day's events, consider problems, and make certain everything was ready for the next day. The upcoming week was planned on Fridays. At the start of the term, like each of the other cooperating teachers, Mrs. Kenny shared the established curriculum with her student teachers. The school had adopted reading and mathematics programs, and the expectation was that these would continue in place. In science, the sixth grade studied light. In social studies, the topic was the Middle Ages. Vocabulary and spelling were part of each week, as were physical education and music, both taught by specialists. Art activities took place every week, and in this one area there was no assigned curriculum.

During the first two weeks, Mrs. Kenny was heavily involved in every aspect of teaching, but this soon changed. She noted, "At the beginning of the student teaching experience [as a cooperating teacher], I do a lot of spoon-feeding. A lot of talking. With the two [student teachers] in the classroom, I feel like it's been more discovery [than in the past]. I'll tell them, this is your topic . . . and you go figure it out. Bounce ideas off each other and come back to me and then I'll help you tweak it before or after you teach it. It has been different [from my previous experience]."

Before Mrs. Kenny withdrew from the classroom, Emma and Rebbie thought of her as fully part of the team, albeit a senior member. Rebbie remarked: "There's no separation. It's all three of us. Always. Every time the kids are gone, we're talking. . . . She's part of the team. She's a strong part of the team." But as the term progressed and Mrs. Kenny withdrew from the classroom, though not from the ongoing conversation about teaching, Emma and Rebbie became increasingly interdependent and simultaneously independent of Mrs. Kenny. Quickly they realized that they were invested in one another's development, and that success was dependent upon fully and openly sharing ideas and resources and helping one another in any way possible. In response to the question, "When something goes wrong in the classroom, to whom do you go for help first?" both said their partner. "I go to Emma first. We talk about it, especially if she's noticed a problem, then we'll go to Mrs. Kenny. I like to talk to Emma about [a problem] first to see if maybe we can work it out." They used one another as sounding boards, sources of ideas and feedback, and support. In turn, Mrs. Kenny became a much-valued resource and guide. As Emma said, "She's awesome to work with. She's very helpful. If we need resources, she'll help. She'll explain ideas. She talk[s] with us . . . and gives us advice . . . and suggestions. But then she hands [everything] over to us." This interdependence was present in other partner-placed teams of student teachers as well.

Roles and Responsibilities

Mrs. Kenny transferred full responsibility for the classroom over to Emma and Rebbie more rapidly than she initially thought she would or could. As she did so, her role quickly changed. She continued to give feedback, struggling, as she said, to be "critical," but she saw herself, particularly with the language arts curriculum, as one member of a team. Given Emma's and Rebbie's knowledge of writing instruction, for the first time in her career Mrs. Kenny decided to organize learning centers. All three of the team members took responsibility for a center through which the children moved each day during the time scheduled for the language arts. There were four centers, including one designed for independent work on spelling and vocabulary. This represented a dramatic change in Mrs. Kenny's program, one noted and valued by some of the children, as one child remarked in a group interview: "At first we didn't have centers. . . . But now . . . we have these centers where we have literacy; it's a rotation." Another commented: "I just like to get into the writing [centers]."

Emma and Rebbie assumed complete responsibility for the curriculum by the end of the third week. This change is indicated in the time logs where they reported from week two to week six that the amount of time spent on planning and preparing to teach nearly doubled. While planning patterns varied, planning and preparing to teach remained a time-consuming activity across the term for each of the three partner teams. Throughout the term Rebbie and Emma met each day with Mrs. Kenny, who observed regularly but spent progressively less time in the classroom. Observation notes reveal that Rebbie and Emma shared the day, and even when one had major responsibility for an activity or a lesson, the other remained significantly involved. For instance, Rebbie assumed major responsibility for the Friday arts lessons, but Emma actively participated in them by helping the children. Similarly, as the term progressed, they became increasingly willing and able to slip into and out of one another's lessons, offering suggestions, support, assistance, and, from time to time, correction. For example, around midterm, Emma and Rebbie had planned to introduce a new book when the children returned from morning recess. The decision was made because they felt that the children had lost interest in the book they had been reading to the class, Lloyd Alexander's *The Book of Three*. The plan was for Emma to make the transition to the new book and to begin reading. The students protested; they wanted to finish the story. Standing together in front of class, Emma and Rebbie quickly conferred, and roles were switched—Rebbie led the class. Roles were likewise traded with ease during the weekly class meeting. During a vocabulary activity and without embarrassment Emma turned to Rebbie for help pronouncing an unfamiliar word that caught her by surprise. This pattern was also typical in other partner placements. Our observation notes of the second grade team include the following comment similarly illustrating how closely the three teachers worked together: "Erica engages in supportive interaction, while Susan (the cooperating teacher) switches between correcting papers and monitoring. Erica shifts from supportive interaction to full teaming with Liz directing [a] game." Within each of the teams, roles became fluid.

Mrs. Kenny offered a way of thinking about how Emma and Rebbie taught together, which applies to each team. Early in the term, as she transferred responsibility to them, she said: "You can team teach or you can tag teach, which are two different things. You need to decide which you want to do." By teaming, she meant that each was fully involved and equally responsible for a lesson or an activity. By tagging she meant turn taking. As our observation notes indicate, Emma and Rebbie did both, mostly "tagging" in the morning and "teaming" in the afternoon, but always, Mrs. Kenny said, "collaborating."

The transfer of responsibility for the classroom to the student teachers was handled somewhat differently in each of the three teams. In the sixth and second grade teams the cooperating teachers withdrew from most active classroom participation relatively early. The cooperating teacher of the second grade team felt able to give over more responsibility for the classroom faster than she had when working with previous student teachers. This was her plan:

> We began working as a team right from the first day. At first [their teaching] was a little bit limited because I wanted to give them some time to learn the routines. . . . I'm gradually moving them from a team situation [with me] into a situation where they're taking over more of the responsibility.

As the term progressed, this cooperating teacher, like Mrs. Kenny, was often out of the classroom. In contrast, the cooperating teacher of the fourth grade team was seldom out of the room unless she was working with students in the adjacent pod area. She remained much more actively engaged instructionally: "During the day she mostly stays out of things when we're in charge, maybe taking kids aside who need individual attention. We divide the kids up in small groups and she takes a group." This difference may help account for Marsha's conclusion that, in contrast to Lou, her partner student teacher, and the other four partner-placed student teachers, she would not teach in a partnership if she were to have the opportunity of reconsidering her initial decision.

Perceptions, Expectations, and Assessment

Early in the term Mrs. Kenny would only say that having responsibility for two student teachers was "very different" from having one. She refused to answer the question, "If you had a choice between having one competent student teacher, and two promising student teachers [assigned to you], which would you choose?" Then she was uncertain: "That's kind of a loaded question. I don't want to make that decision [yet]." However, like her two colleagues, she clearly valued working with student teachers: "I think a limited amount of [work with a student teacher] is good. It helps me stay fresh as a teacher. They bring things to the table that are interesting, that help me." The other two cooperating teachers did not share her initial doubts about partnership teaching. From the start, the fourth grade cooperating teacher was thrilled at the prospect of having additional adults in the classroom: "We don't need lower class size, we need more adults in the classroom!"

At the end of the term, Mrs. Kenny's doubts about partnership placements were gone: "I had mixed emotions about it at first, but I think this has been a much more positive situation for the students than what I've seen in the past." She thought the benefits to the student teachers were significant, but she dwelt on the benefits for the children, her primary concern:

> It's been much more supportive for the kids. To have an extra body in the classroom [is a plus]. . . . Because of [the student teachers'] planning and collaboration, the kids have really gotten good material. . . . They are getting richer experiences. I think that if you just throw a single teacher in there all day, the children are going to get some good experiences, [perhaps] a super math lesson, and that would be it for the day. The [teacher] then just kind of gets through reading or spelling. . . . [In contrast] this team [makes it so] they're getting rich experiences every time. . . . They do so many exciting, high-energy kinds of things, that when I go back into the classroom the kids are going to die. . . . They've really kept the kids moving.

The fourth grade cooperating teacher supported this view and added an additional insight: "Man, it's wonderful. . . . They have covered in eight weeks much more material than I would ever cover."

Early in the term, a downside emerged for Mrs. Kenny—her workload increased beyond what, based upon her extensive experience, she thought was normal for mentoring a single student teacher. "At the beginning, I felt a little bit overwhelmed." But this situation changed as the term progressed: "In some ways it is more and in some ways it is less [work]. I don't think [it's a bad trade-off]. I don't think it's been more work; it's [just] been different. . . . It's more at the beginning, and less now." The fourth grade cooperating teacher disagreed: "I have a [reduced] workload. They do a lot. They are very competent. It has been less work for me, because it has been a team effort. . . . The kids got more instruction."

Despite having doubts of her own about being placed in a partnership, Rebbie concluded the term very enthusiastic about teaming and about her student teaching experience.

> Emma and I, we're great together! If we have a suggestion, we feel free to make it. If she is doing something that isn't going well, I feel free to step in and she does the same with me. You know, if we notice something, or if we talk about a lesson plan before and say, "You know, I don't know if this is going to work," we aren't afraid to step in. Because we're here to help each other.

Emma echoed Rebbie's assessment and added: "[In our partnership] the lessons are really thought out and well planned because there are at least two people working on them, and figuring things out. . . . It adds variety." She said that she felt that her creativity had "been increased" by working with Rebbie. Then Emma spoke specifically of Rebbie and the support she offered: "It's nice to have somebody else that understands exactly what you're going through. We can talk about different kids and the problems they're going through. How are we going to get this student to learn better; I have somebody that knows my situation, that is there every day, that I can discuss issues with." Because of Rebbie, Emma felt "more security" when student teaching.

At the beginning of the term, Emma expressed concern that her participation in a partnership during student teaching would be viewed negatively by future employers: "Just what is a future employer going to think? If they know [I] team taught, does that mean that I can't [teach] on my own? In a way that kind of worries me, but not [a lot because] I've had two semesters that it's been just me and [a cooperating] teacher [in the classroom]." At term's end, this concern was entirely gone, having been overwhelmed by her positive experience with Rebbie and her growing appreciation of the value of teacher collaboration: "I think it's important to collaborate with other teachers. . . . [From collaborating] you get more ideas, more depth in lesson planning, it's just better." When asked if she would partner teach again, Emma responded: "I loved having a partner"; she would recommend it to others. Then, pausing to think, she offered a qualification: "There are some personalities that I think would have been difficult to work with. But then, maybe not. Maybe not. I thought so at the beginning [of student teaching]."

Rebbie shared Emma's assessment of partnership teaching. Despite being pressured in interview to identify negative effects, she did not. She was asked: "If you could go backward and do it all over again, would you prefer to work with another student teacher, or would you rather be on your own?" She replied, "I would work with another student teacher again." She said this despite her initial concern. "Convince me, why? Imagine that I'm a student and I have to make a decision about student teaching." Rebbie responded:

> Because having Emma in here has [provided] extra support to where I felt more daring, more courageous to do things I may not have done with a class before. Neater activities, something that might need a little more monitoring going on from a new teacher perspective. I've been able to do things that I might not do with my regular classroom. . . . I'd say, do it!

Neither student teacher was concerned about having to share a class and a cooperating teacher. They felt equally powerful and fully responsible for the class. As Rebbie said, "I feel responsible for the class, even when Emma is in charge." Nor did they feel they did not receive a sufficient amount of time soloing, being wholly and individually responsible for the class. While this was not a concern for Emma or Rebbie, it was for Lou and for one of the second grade partner teachers:

> It's not realistic. We had three people to help [the children] and that won't happen in a real class. . . . I like working in the partners for the students' sake because it gives a lot of them a bit more variety in teaching. . . . But probably for the student teacher's sake, [teaching] singly would be a little bit [better preparation] in aspects of management. But working with others and trying to figure out ways to creatively approach the curriculum and the things you need to teach—pairing is probably better.

Discussion

The discussion is organized around the following set of questions that guided inquiry.

Question 1: What kind and quality of relationships will develop in the two models of student teaching between cooperating teachers and student teachers and, in the partnership model, between student teachers?

As noted, only one of the six paired student teachers said she would not want to work with a partner if again given the opportunity. However, she also said that the experience of partner teaching was valuable, just not "realistic." This comment underscores a persistent tension within teacher education: "The need to free prospective teachers to develop powerful educational visions and to imagine new possibilities, although important, may come into conflict with the need to prepare them for schools as they currently exist" (Kahne and Westheimer 2000, 380). The belief that to teach is to work in isolation, to plan lessons alone, to solve problems alone, and to stand alone in front of a classroom and talk to children is a recognized and major impediment to educational renewal.

The concept of "collaboration" frequently appears in the school reform and teacher development literature as an unqualified good: "Research has shown collaboration to certainly affect the level of commitment to the school organization, the level of motivation and job satisfaction among teachers, and the professional development of teachers" (van Veen, Sleegers, Bergen, and Klaassen 2001, 190). Despite these results, the nature of professional relationships that facilitate development and enhance performance is much more complex than is typically suggested. Clement and Vandenberghe (2000) convincingly argue that collegiality and autonomy both have a place in teacher development, that they most productively exist in a "circular tension" where "learning opportunities . . . and learning space are attuned to one another" (92). They warn: "Even modest learning experiences originate more easily in a school characterized by a circular tension between autonomy and collegiality. Such circular tension cannot be created by enforcing collegiality through, for instance, the establishment of structural forms of collaboration" (98). Partnership placement is a structural form of collaboration. Did it encourage collegial relationships?

Our data indicate that student teachers placed in a partnership teaching arrangement came to appreciate the value, when learning to teach, of working closely with other teachers. A member of the second grade partnership nicely captured the common view: "I've learned that others can be very helpful to me and I will . . . get other teachers' input and avail myself [of their knowledge]." Each of the paired student teachers became heavily invested in her partner's development and success.

In varying degrees, the partner-placed student teachers felt the tug between autonomy and collegiality. When Mrs. Kenny urged her student teachers, Emma and Rebbie, to decide how they wanted to work together, tagging or full teaming, she offered a model for thinking about and negotiating their relationship. She presented both approaches as legitimate and valuable. Her concern was to help her student teachers think through their relationship prior to encountering difficulty. Each of the partner-placed student teachers wanted opportunities to test her own ability and ideas, and for this a measure of autonomy was needed; each also wanted critical feedback and opportunities to talk about her teaching, and for this collegiality was required. Within the partner placements the circular tension described by Clement and Vandenberghe (2000) was much in evidence, but it was embedded within a shared understanding that they could not succeed alone. They needed one another.

Creating a desirable tension between autonomy and collegiality in the single placements was more difficult. The absence of Mr. Oakes from the classroom left Jerriann alone to make the best she could of her autonomy. Teachers often confuse isolation with autonomy; Jerriann faced loneliness, a common and debilitating part of the lives of many teachers (Koeppen, Huey, and Connor 2000). She did not feel connected to Mr. Oakes; she just happened to be assigned to student teach within his classroom. In fairness to Mr. Oakes, his approach to mentoring is more typical than not: "Under the individualistic culture of teaching, mentors are hesitant to offer suggestions to their novices, and they worry about intruding into the autonomy of their novices" (Wang 2001, 52). In contrast, Joni came to value Mrs. Gardiner's consistent support and her suggestions and feedback. Through this experience she came to understand the important place another teacher could have in her own development as a teacher. However, her view was colored by her formal relationship with Mrs. Gardiner: novice (student) to cooperating teacher (and evaluator). Having a partner who also was a peer opened up opportunities for development unavailable to single-placed student teachers, with the additional value of enabling risk taking both singly—where the boundaries of one's autonomy are pushed outward—and unitedly.

Question 2: What differences in roles and responsibilities will emerge for cooperating teachers and student teachers in the two models of student teaching?

For the most part, singly placed student teachers began as assistants to their cooperating teachers charged with carrying out an established program, and then they assumed virtually all of the responsibilities of teaching, but within the established activity structure. Functioning as supervisors, cooperating teachers gave feedback and advice as they could. The student teachers taught and listened when given feedback. The relationship was clearly one of expert to novice. In contrast, although in varying degrees, partnership-placed cooperating teachers and student teachers became interdependent members of instructional teams. Among partners and cooperating teachers conversation about teaching was frequent, consistent, and open. Since partners had the opportunity to plan and then to observe one another teach, they had abundant opportunities to jointly analyze their teaching which, as Roth and Tobin (2001) argue, provides rich opportunities to learn about and better understand teaching not available to a teacher working alone in a classroom. Thus in partnership placements not only the cooperating teachers but peers become critics of teaching. But since they were joined in a common commitment to provide an enriched education to a specific and shared class of children, feedback was less one-directional, more conversational, and decidedly focused on mutual interests.

Working with two student teachers prompted cooperating teachers to rethink their conceptions of their role as mentors, understandings based upon their prior experience with solo student teaching. They found it relatively easy to allow a greater measure of risk taking in the classroom and greater involvement in curriculum decision making because they trusted their paired student teachers and their joint ability not only to manage the classroom but to provide an enriched curriculum. Trusting the student teachers made it easy for cooperating teachers to slip into a supporting instructional role if they wished, perhaps to assist an individual student or a small group of children. Remarkably, we found no evidence of serious competition between partners nor any indication that the active involvement of the cooperating teacher with children was threatening.

Question 3: What value will the student teachers and cooperating teachers find in their experience? What impact will the student teachers have on the classroom, the cooperating teachers (including their workload), and pupil learning?

According to the cooperating teachers, all of the student teachers performed well, with no exceptions. However, cooperating teachers to partner-placed student teachers thought their paired student teachers (based upon prior experience mentoring individually placed student teachers) were better able to take risks, developed richer, more interesting, and varied lessons, and were able to be more helpful to children. They also learned how to collaborate: "When one slips up, the other one catches it, and they don't seem to have any problem taking up the slack for the other. They work equally hard at what they're doing. They try and make sure that each succeeds. Whatever the lesson is, the other one is over there getting materials, making sure it works." In sum, the cooperating teachers concluded that the experience was more beneficial than traditional student teaching, but not only for the student teachers. The children, they said, were also better off. Based upon previous experience, the cooperating teachers had some concern about working with student teachers, generally arising from fear of potential negative impact on the children. There also was some concern about working with pairs of student teachers, as Mrs. Kenny observed. At the end of the term, however, each of the cooperating teachers, excepting Mr. Oakes, echoed words about the value of mentoring commonly reported in the research: Mentoring a student teacher has a "significant impact on [the cooperating teacher's] own teaching," reduces "isolation because they share students and lessons with another adult," brings "new ideas, strategies, and up-to-date research directly into [the classroom]," and provides "enthusiasm, excitement, and encouragement to try new things" (Hudson-Ross 2001, 438). None of these statements is unique to mentoring pairs of student teachers.

However, partner teaching did impact the classroom in three somewhat unique ways: First, given increased human resources, cooperating teachers with partnered student teachers engaged in unusual and extensive curricular and instructional innovation. Recall that Mrs. Kenny organized learning centers for the first time. With her student teachers, the second grade cooperating teacher organized small groups and consistently tutored individual pupils who, she said, had been lost or neglected before as she sought to keep her class on task and moving through the curriculum. Moreover, the cooperating teachers asserted that the curriculum became much richer, beyond what was possible with only one student teacher, and this impacted how Mrs. Kenny thought about the future and what she would teach. As noted, Rebbie brought her expertise in art and mathematics from which Mrs. Kenny learned, while Emma created an after-school dance program, which Rebbie and Mrs. Kenny enthusiastically supported.

Second, classroom management was dramatically altered, which reflected a change in the power structure of the classroom and, we believe, in the quality of human interaction. To be sure, established management routines were kept in place, and with two or three adults in the classroom, these likely had a greater effect than usual. However, we observed interactions and patterns of interaction that are rare in a typical classroom, even when a teacher's aide is present. While one of the partners was guiding a lesson, another lingered with a single student for an extended period of time or actively scanned the classroom for signs of confusion and then responded immediately. This was possible, in part, because the teachers thought of themselves (unlike an aide) as equally responsible for the classroom. Although debate continues over the value of reduced class size, with some researchers noting that the key to improvement is the quality of teaching (see Stone and Mata 2000), we witnessed some of the possibilities.

Third, the cooperating teachers asserted that the children learned more, and more quickly. This result is similar to that reported for team teaching generally: "According to the literature, team teaching encourages multiple perspectives, promotes dialogue/increased participation, and improves evaluation/feedback" (Anderson and Speck 1998, 673). In group interviews the children gave compelling reasons why they liked partner teaching. Like each of the three cooperating teachers, the elementary schoolchildren found significant benefits in partnership teaching. Rebbie's and Emma's students especially appreciated having a teacher always available to offer assistance and liked the variability of the curriculum: "I think it's good because all the lessons are different." Another commented favorably on instructional differences: They have "got their own techniques." The children spoke of specific lessons they enjoyed, including art lessons Rebbie taught on Monet and another on Georgia O'Keefe. Another liked the faster pace: "We can get through a subject a lot faster." All children, without exception, said they liked having multiple teachers in the room. These comments were typical. Second graders supported their older peers' views and added their own insights: "We can do more centers." "When I get mixed up on something, someone comes to help me." "One teacher gives one assignment, and another teacher gives another assignment, and I like to have different assignments." Only two drawbacks to partnership teaching were noted by the children in Emma's and Rebbie's classroom: Sometimes there was a little confusion about which teacher to go to for help ("Sometimes it's confusing, because if you have a question about a lesson that one of them's teaching, you might go to the other one [and] they can't really help you") and the children said there was too much homework ("We have a lot of homework now").

Considering the impact of partnership teaching on the children, the cooperating teachers expressed one concern, best captured by the second grade teacher:

> It's taken me a half a year for [the children] to feel really safe and comfortable with me, and now we've brought in some other people who are taking

primary responsibility for [teaching] now. . . . All at once [they'll go back to having one teacher]. I think it will be hard for the kids. They'll have to wait [for help]. I wish that didn't [have to] happen. They could get questions answered immediately [when the student teachers have been here].

She went on to say: "It's going to be hard for me to go back to teaching a room by myself, because that's not how I like to teach. I like to teach with other people. I don't think I have everything that a child needs, and the more people I can bring into a room to offer things for the children, the better off they are going to be."

Cooperating teachers had mixed views about whether or not having a pair of student teachers was more work than having responsibility for a single student teacher. One thought it was less work; another, Mrs. Kenny, thought it was more work at the beginning of the term, although on balance the trade-off was judged worthwhile. This difference in cooperating teacher perceptions might be connected to the increased complexity that is involved when trying to forge a team with two very dissimilar student teachers such as Emma and Rebbie.

Conclusion

Cooperating teachers who worked with pairs of student teachers were enthusiastic about the practice and hopeful that it would continue. With one exception, the paired student teachers agreed. Yet there is some reason for caution. Most of our students came to teaching sharing a moral orientation to the world grounded in a shared religious commitment. They were dedicated to teaching, saw teaching as a moral act and form of valued service, and tended not to be confrontational when faced with a differing point of view, a point noted by Mr. Oakes about Jerriann. Thus while we felt relatively secure randomly assigning students to either a pair or single placement, under other circumstances success might be dependent, as Emma suggested, on who one is paired with. Some student teachers might make poor candidates for a partnership. Similar attention probably should be given to selecting cooperating teachers and schools. We were fortunate at Western Horizon to have a sufficient number of teachers volunteer, albeit only barely, so we could conduct the study at one site. Even then, as noted, challenges emerged, with two cooperating teachers assigned to work with single-placed student teachers. The teachers were experienced as cooperating teachers. They were not easily threatened by the presence of university faculty nor multiple student teachers. Additionally, Western Horizon is an urban school with a faculty and principal comfortable with the language and values of collaboration. While these teachers were predisposed to support the idea of partner student teaching, some still had doubts. Other faculties might well be hostile. After all, beliefs about how one best learns to teach differ and are often intense and very personal.

For purposes of this study we intentionally did not conduct in-service meetings on mentoring. In the future, we will. Had we done so perhaps Mr. Oakes would have had less difficulty giving feedback and Mrs. Kenny might not have struggled to be helpfully critical of student teacher practice. Further, we did not consider the potential impact of partnership teaching on the university supervisor's role. In their co-teaching model, which also involves peer teaching, Roth and Tobin (2001) include the supervisor as a participating member of the instructional team, another teacher, who needs to be involved in the classroom in order for his or her participation in the conversation about teaching to be grounded and valuable.

Of the four single placements with which we began the study, as noted, only two stayed with the same cooperating teacher throughout the term. We have wondered what would have happened if the two student teachers who encountered difficulty had been placed with a partner. Perhaps with a partner to offer support and feedback a change would not have been necessary. Then again, perhaps a change in placement would have been necessary for other student teachers, those placed with a partner, had they been assigned alone.

The charge that student teaching with a partner is not "realistic" is a serious one. An adequate response requires clarity and agreement about the aim and purpose of student teaching: If to learn to teach is to learn to manage by oneself large numbers of children, then partnership teaching has an obvious disadvantage. However, if student teaching's primary purpose is to learn how to develop innovative curricula and expand one's knowledge of methods and of children while learning to engage in collaboration, then partnership teaching has an advantage. We give Mrs. Kenny the last word: "It's been a really, really positive situation for the girls, and I hope in the future [the university] continues [to support partner teaching]."

Afterword

The view is widely held that teachers are born, not made, and that learning to teach is simply a matter of teaching. But practice does not make perfect. Aristotle told only part of the story: "For the things we have to learn before we can do them, we learn by doing them" (in McKeon 1947, 331). Some experiences, as Dewey (1938) argued, are "miseducative" and actually impede future growth (13).

The studies contained in *Counternarratives* are part of an ongoing personal quest to make ever better sense of the experience and practice of teaching and teacher education. As Dewey (1916) reminds us, for experience to have educational value, one must "extract its net meaning" through reflection (7), and in fact doing without "undergoing the consequences of doing" does not count as having *an* experience at all (323). The process of re-searching teaching and teacher education and of composing narratives to describe the results has helped me recognize and better understand how institutional structures and social practices shape meaning and action. It also has increased my understanding of the models and metaphors, the theories, that commonly sustain the practice of teaching and teacher education, including my own personal theories.

Robert Coles reminds us that the "critical root" of the word theory is "'I behold,' as in what we see when we go to the theater" (1989, 20). Through studying the practice, and also the history, of teacher education, and reflecting on my experience, my beholding has evolved. I hope in positive ways. For the personal theories underpinning the practices of teaching and teacher education to become open to change, when change is warranted, such theories must be made explicit. When they are not, common sense reigns supreme and for good or ill practice reproduces itself and lives on as habit. Thus teacher educators face the challenge, as David Hunt (1987) suggests, of becoming our own "best theorists," and best theories come from studying practice, else "they will not apply to practice" (ibid., 109). A philosophy of education, as Washburne (1940) argued, ought to be "living."

Becoming our own best theorists requires making our implicit theories explicit and necessitates a joining of what Griffiths and Tann (1992) call "public theory" with private theory in intense conversation (Korthagen, Kessels, Koster, Lagerwerf, and Wubbels 2001). This is so for the reason Dewey

asserted: "Theory [referring to public theory] is in the end . . . the most practical of all things, because [of the] widening of the range of attention beyond
nearby purpose and desire" (Dewey 1929, 17). Studying my practice and
reflecting on my experience in light of public theory and history, with the help
of many thoughtful students and colleagues, have helped me know what to
look for and helped me to better see, make changes, and anticipate consequences when teaching or developing a program. Freire's *Pedagogy of the
Oppressed* (1970) played such a role early on when I taught high school, and
Dewey's writings, among many others, continue to challenge and inspire my
thinking.

I first reported on my working assumptions a decade ago (Bullough
1997b), believing that identifying and then going public with them would be
useful personally and, recalling Feyerabend (1975), prove provocative professionally, offering an occasion for others to compare, criticize, and perhaps
reconsider their own theories and practices in relationship to my own. A principle, Hullfish and Smith (1961) argue, is a "vehicle for bringing to bear upon
what is at issue a large body of digested experience which is not, at that time,
directly under question. A principle—never tells one what to do; it merely
helps one find out what to do" (95). Offered cautiously, the following set of
principles—"digested experience"—represents not just an update but in some
respects a rethinking, and as such it provides an appropriate but a tentative
conclusion to the studies contained in this collection. My aim has remained
the same: to help educate teachers who are disposed to be students of teaching, who are morally grounded in the practice of education as the practice of
freedom, who are at home with young people, who possess the skills and
knowledge needed to design potentially educative environments characterized
by civility and tolerance, and who invite the young to work at the edge of their
competence. At present, my principles include the following:

1. Teacher identity—what beginning teachers believe about teaching and
   learning and self as teacher—is of vital concern to teacher education.
   Operating as a "mediating force between structure and teacher agency"
   (Flores and Day 2006), identity is the basis of all meaning making. This
   speaks to the "who" question that Parker Palmer poses—"Who is the self
   who teaches"—that was briefly addressed in the Introduction. Well supported by multiple chapters, the principle is this: Quality teacher education involves the exploration of the teaching self and the commitments
   that characterize the self and their consequences (Tickle 1999).
2. Because selves are formed in context, the exploration of identity and the
   teaching persona necessitates the critical study of the practice of schooling (including its history, as indicated by Chapters 1 and 2) and the wider
   social milieu within which schools operate to reveal how meaning is both

enabled and limited, knowledge privileged and suppressed, and action constrained and facilitated (see Chapters 3, 6, 7, 8, 9, and 12). This knowledge is foundational to developing the skills of enactment, of knowing how to shape a context to better support one's better judgment. The footsteps of various critical theorists sound here.

3. To identify and critically consider the ways in which contexts enable and limit meaning requires clarity about aims, especially an understanding of the social philosophy and the evolving purposes of education in a radically pluralistic democracy (see Chapter 2). As Boyd Bode warned: "Educational practice which avoids social theory is at best a trivial thing and at worst a serious obstruction to progress" (1937, 74). Relatedly, miseducation follows when effective methods are used to achieve unworthy aims.

4. Reflecting a lifetime investment, biographically and culturally embedded self-conceptions are deeply resistant to change, as my determined early flight from the problems of teacher education illustrates (see Chapter 3). Change requires self-study. Teacher education must be powerful enough—and this means long and intense enough—to encourage a change in beliefs when potentially miseducative results may follow.

5. Self-study can be risky, as indicated in Chapter 5 on action research and Chapter 11 on metaphors and teaching. While challenging, the immediate context of teacher education both preservice and in-service also must be supportive and respectful of students as adult learners—individuals capable of making reasonable and productive judgments about their own learning and the direction of that learning (see Pinnegar 1996; also see Chapter 2), a point central to Kerrie Baughman's development as a teacher (see Chapter 7).

6. All education is ultimately indirect, as Dewey argued; teachers can create the conditions for learning, while learning itself is the responsibility of those who choose either to embrace or reject the opportunity. The principle is this: The "good" cannot be forced, but it can be encouraged (see the Introduction and Chapters 2, 4, and 6—on the emotions—Chapters 8 and 12). Abundant and consistent teacher talk about teaching can be powerfully encouraging (see Chapters 7 and 12).

7. Each person makes teacher education meaningful in his or her own way, a point illustrated by my professional journey and in each of the case studies I have written of beginning teachers. Professionals study their own practice; like Kerrie Baughman, they learn *in* as well as *from* experience (see Chapters 3, 7, and 10–12). *However*, public theory, including the results of empirical research and historical studies (see Chapters 1 and 2), greatly enriches personal experience and enables productive beholding and thoughtful action. (The value of literature reviews in action research is a case in point; see Chapter 5.)

8. Quality programs—in schools and in teacher education—arise from and are sustained only and best by "continuous experimentation" (see Chapters 2, 5, and 10–12) that attends to the genuine concerns of teachers and students.

9. Program continuity is not just a matter of sensibly sequencing courses and content but of creating means that enable students to forge their own sense of continuity through attending—systematically, over time, *and with others*—to their experience of teacher education and development as teachers and in relationship to their ideals. (This point is consistently supported by the richness and diversity of the personal teaching texts; see Chapter 10, and in Chapter 12, "Teaching with a Peer.")

10. Part of building a trusting and respectful learning environment is to openly articulate the reasons lying behind program decisions, a point central to the success of the Commission on Teacher Education projects, described in Chapter 2, and the personal teaching text, described in Chapter 10. Purposes, I have learned, must be open to scrutiny if they are to be found compelling.

11. While program purposes should be explicit, educational outcomes are inevitably unpredictable—probably unmeasurable, or only indirectly so. Nevertheless, because of teachers' ethical responsibilities to serve and to actively care for young people, quality judgments of teaching must be made (see Chapters 4 and 12). This is so despite there being no one best teaching style, personality, or model that can serve as a stable standard for evaluation. The most powerful and useful of quality judgments ultimately are those arising from data-driven self-assessment.

12. Seeking to develop teaching skills, and eventually artistry in teaching, necessitates opportunities to test and explore programs, methods, and techniques with the active and invested involvement of thoughtful and knowledgeable others and over an extended period of time, including in-service (see especially Chapters 4 and 12). As is evident in Chapter 4, year-long internships are promising when skilled and committed mentors work with novice teachers. All teachers require a "repertoire of habits and rules of thumb [that] help [them] move efficiently through their lessons without having to think about every move along the way, and . . . help them quickly find appropriate responses to unexpected contingencies" (Kennedy 2006, 210), and this requires training—practice and informed feedback.

13. Lastly, expertise in teaching is context-specific. Teachers are not interchangeable. Change a teacher, including a teacher educator, and change a program.

Operationally, like Kerrie Baughman's principles, discussed in Chapter 7, these principles, working as hypotheses, are not distinct nor fully comprehensive. The principles intertwine, wrap around, and shape my experience of teaching and how I think about teacher education. As noted, the cohort program organization early provided a context within which many of these principles started to take on life and also played an important role in creating the "shared ordeal" (Lortie 1975) so often missing in teacher education and for teacher educators (a point seldom noted, but something I have experienced). Within this structure and with the involvement of the students themselves, it became possible for me to explore questions of purpose, content, process, and relationship. In addition, I have been fortunate to have had colleagues who have shared my concerns, interests, and desires and have actively joined with me in the quest to become students of teaching.

In the Introduction to *Counternarratives*, I expressed concern about the narratives that now dominate teaching and teacher education. Although not writing to educators or about education, Michael Polanyi (1958) offers a fitting response to the diminishment of the individual teacher that follows triumph of standardization and Big Science narratives, a triumph that raises the specter of performativity (Ball 2003):

> This then is our liberation from objectivism: to realize that we can voice our ultimate convictions only from within our convictions—from within the whole system of acceptances that are logically prior to any particular assertion of our own, prior to the holding of any particular piece of knowledge. If an ultimate logical level is to be attained and made explicit, this must be a declaration of my personal beliefs. I believe that the function of philosophic reflection consists in bringing to light, and affirming as my own, the beliefs implied in such of my thoughts and practices as I believe to be valid; that I must aim at discovering what I truly believe in and at formulating the convictions which I find myself holding; that I must conquer my self-doubt, so as to retain a firm hold on this program of self-identification. (267)

The principles, the "convictions," as Polanyi states, "which I find myself holding," represent a piece of who I am and offer a partial answer to the question of why I do what I do when teaching. They also provide the basis for locating points where educators are prevented or diverted from doing what they most want and need to do when teaching. Tensions emerging between conviction and established and emerging subject positions, and between experience and role expectations, open doorways to institutional criticism and invite a pushing back. But clarity about one's own principles comes first, and this requires a "program of self-identification," as Polanyi argues.

Polanyi's warning about the danger of self-doubt to self-discovery is crucially important. Facing constant and very public performance reviews and rising expectations, no educator ever feels fully competent. Vulnerability grows, and signs of a fearful and cautious conservatism appear. For veteran educators, including teacher educators, feeling compelled to engage in various forms of impression management leaves a lingering and unpleasant taste of duplicity, the double-mindedness discussed earlier. The soul is wounded and guilt results when otherwise dearly held educational ends are set aside in favor of self-preservation. Putting on a deathly persona, one loses or perhaps forgets who one is or once was. Thus education deans hang their heads and worry about the future, while teacher education faculty grumble about, but comply with, irrational, diversionary, and increasingly misguided assessment and accreditation requirements (Johnson, Johnson, Farenga, and Ness 2005).

Self-discovery requires courage. But courage also may require the recovery of self—perhaps a recalling of the motivation that initially inspired the decision to teach or to become a teacher educator. Local studies serve both aims and help shore up programs of self-identification. They do this by displaying how beliefs and convictions matter in human interaction, even if they do not count in the arithmetic of accreditation; how, in the complexity of the moral relationship that is teaching, an educator's commitments shape lives; and they do this by revealing promising and potentially meaningful avenues for action and engagement. Clearly, the commitments we display—in what we invest our lives—and how we are invested—the courage we demonstrate— indicate the kind of persons we are and our moral standing as teachers and teacher educators.

References

Aikin, W. M. 1942. *The story of the eight-year study*. New York: Harpers.

Alfi, O., A. Assor, and I. Katz. 2004. Learning to allow temporary failure: Potential benefits, supportive practices and teacher concerns, *Journal of Education for Teaching* 30(1): 27–41.

Allender, J. S. 2001. Teacher self: The practice of humanistic education. Lanham, MD: Rowman & Littlefield.

American Council on Education. 1938. *Major issues in teacher education*. Washington, DC: Author.

Anderson, R. S., and B. W. Speck. 1998. "Oh what a difference a team makes": Why team teaching makes a difference. *Teaching & Teacher Education* 14(7): 671–86.

Arizona Group: K. Guilfoyle, M. L. Hamilton, and S. Pinnegar. 1997. Obligations to unseen children. In *Teaching about teaching: Purpose, passion, and pedagogy in teacher education*, ed. J. Loughran and T. Russell, 183–209. London: The Falmer Press.

Armstrong, W. E., E. V. Hollis, and H. E. Davis. 1944. *The college and teacher education*. Washington, DC: American Council on Education.

Ayers, W. 1993. *To teach: The journey of a teacher*. New York: Teachers College Press.

Bagley, W. C. 1918. The distinction between academic and professional subjects. *National Education Association Journal of Proceedings and Addresses* 229–34.

Ball, S. J. 2003. The teacher's soul and the terrors of performativity. *Journal of Educational Policy* 18(2): 215–28.

Ball, S. J., and I. F. Goodson. 1985. Understanding teachers: Concepts and contexts. In *Teachers' lives and careers*, ed. S. J. Ball and I. F. Goodson, 1–26. London: Falmer Press.

Bandman, B. 1967. *The place of reason in education*. Columbus: Ohio State University Press.

Beck, C., and C. Kosnik. 2001. Reflection-in-action: In defense of thoughtful teaching. *Curriculum Inquiry* 31(2): 217–27.

Beck, C., and C. Kosnik. 2002. Professors and the practicum: Involvement of university faculty in preservice practicum supervision. *Journal of Teacher Education* 53(1): 6–19.

Beijaard, D., P. C. Meijer, and N. Verloop. 2004. Reconsidering research on teachers' professional identity. *Teaching & Teacher Education* 20(2): 107–28.

Bellah, R. N., R. Madsen, W. M. Sullivan, A. Swidler, and S. M. Tipton. 1985. *Habits of the heart: Individualism and commitment in American life*. Berkeley: University of California Press.

233

Bereiter C., and M. Scardamalia. 1993. *Surpassing ourselves: An inquiry into the nature and implications of expertise.* Chicago: Open Court Press.

Berliner, D. C. 1986. In pursuit of the expert pedagogue, *Educational Researcher* 15(7): 5–13.

Berliner, D. C. 1988. Implications of expertise in pedagogy for teacher education and evaluation. In *New directions for teacher assessment: Proceedings of the 1988 ETS Invitational Conference,* 39–67. Princeton, NJ: Educational Testing Service.

Berliner, D. C. 1990. Characteristics of experts in the pedagogical domain. Paper presented at the International Symposium on Research on Effective and Responsible Teaching, University of Fribourg, Fribourg, Switzerland, September.

Bloom, B., ed. 1956. *Taxonomy of educational objectives: Handbook I. Cognitive domain.* New York: David McKay.

Bode, B. H. 1937. *Democracy as a way of life.* New York: Macmillan.

Boice, R. 1991. New faculty as teachers. *Journal of Higher Education* 62(2): 149–73.

Boice, R. 1996. *First-order principles for college teachers.* Bolton, MA: Anker Publishing.

Bolton, F. E. 1907. Preparation of high school teachers. *National Education Association Journal of Proceedings and Addresses,* 600–17.

Britzman, D. P. 1986. Cultural myths in the making of a teacher: Biography and social structure in teacher education. *Harvard Educational Review* 56(4): 442–56.

Brooks, S. D. 1907. Preparation of high school teachers. *National Education Association Journal of Proceedings and Addresses,* 547–51.

Buchberger, F., B. P. Campos, D. Kallos, and J. Stephenson, eds. 2000. Green paper on teacher education in Europe: High quality teacher education for high quality education and training. Umea, Sweden: Thematic Network on Teacher Education in Europe.

Bullough, R. V., Jr. 1982. Professional schizophrenia: Teacher education in confusion. *Contemporary Education* 53(4): 207–12.

Bullough, R. V., Jr. 1987. Accommodation and tension: Teachers, teacher's role, and the culture of teaching. In *Educating teachers: Changing the nature of pedagogical knowledge,* ed. J. Smyth, 83–94. London: The Falmer Press.

Bullough, R. V., Jr. 1988. *The forgotten dream of American public education.* Ames, Iowa: Iowa State University Press.

Bullough, R. V., Jr. 1989. *First-year teacher: A case study.* New York: Teachers College Press.

Bullough, R. V., Jr. 1991. Exploring personal teaching metaphors in preservice teacher education. *Journal of Teacher Education* 42(1): 43–51.

Bullough, R. V., Jr. 1992. Beginning teacher curriculum decision making, personal teaching metaphors, and teacher education. *Teaching & Teacher Education* 8(3): 239–52.

Bullough, R. V., Jr. 1993. Case records as personal teaching texts for study in preservice teacher education. *Teaching & Teacher Education* 9(4): 385–96.

Bullough, R. V., Jr. 1997a. Becoming a teacher: Self and the social location of teacher education. In *International handbook of teachers and teaching*, ed. B. J. Biddle, T. L. Good, and I. F. Goodson, 79–134. Dordrecht, the Netherlands: Kluwer Academic Publishers.

Bullough, R. V., Jr. 1997b. Practicing theory and theorizing practice in teacher education. In *Teaching about teaching: Purpose, passion and pedagogy in teacher education*, ed. J. Loughran and T. Russell, 13–31. Washington, DC: The Falmer Press.

Bullough, R. V., Jr. 2001. *Uncertain lives: Children of promise, teachers of hope.* New York: Teachers College Press.

Bullough, R. V., Jr., and K. Baughman. 1993. Continuity and change in teacher development: First-year teacher after five years, *Journal of Teacher Education* 44(2): 86–95.

Bullough, R. V., Jr., and K. Baughman. 1997. *"First-year teacher" eight years later: An inquiry into teacher development.* New York: Teachers College Press.

Bullough, R. V., Jr., D. C. Clark, and R. S. Patterson. 2003. Getting in step: Accountability, accreditation, and the standardization of teacher education in the United States. *Journal of Education for Teaching* 29(1): 35–52.

Bullough, R. V., Jr., R. J. Draper, L. K. Smith, and J. R. Birrell. 2004. Moving beyond collusion: Clinical faculty and university/public school partnership. *Teaching & Teacher Education* 20(6): 505–21.

Bullough, R. V., Jr., and A. Gitlin. 1985. Beyond control: Rethinking teacher resistance. *Education and Society* 3(1): 65–73.

Bullough, R. V., Jr., and A. Gitlin. 1989. Toward educative communities: Teacher education and the quest for the reflective practitioner. *Qualitative Studies in Education* 2(41): 285–98.

Bullough, R. V., Jr., and A. Gitlin. 1995. *Becoming a student of teaching: Methodologies for exploring self and school context.* New York: Garland.

Bullough, R. V., Jr., S. L. Goldstein, and L. Holt. 1984. *Human interests and the curriculum: Teaching and learning in a technological society.* New York: Teachers College Press.

Bullough, R. V., Jr., S. F. Hobbs, D. P. Kauchak, N. A. Crow, and D. Stokes. 1997. Long-term PDS development in research universities and the clinicalization of teacher education. *Journal of Teacher Education* 48(2): 85–95.

Bullough, R. V., Jr., D. Kauchak, N. A. Crow, S. Hobbs, and D. K. Stokes. 1997. Professional development schools: Catalysts for teacher and school change. *Teaching & Teacher Education* 13(2): 153–69.

Bullough, R. V., Jr., and J. G. Knowles. 1990. Becoming a teacher: The struggles of a second-career beginning teacher. *International Journal of Qualitative Studies in Education* 3(2): 101–12.

Bullough, R. V., Jr., and J. G. Knowles. 1991. Teaching and nurturing: Changing conceptions of self as teacher in a case study of becoming a teacher. *International Journal of Qualitative Studies in Education* 4(2): 121–40.

Bullough, R. V., Jr., J. G. Knowles, and N. A. Crow. 1991. *Emerging as a teacher*. New York and London: Routledge.

Bullough, R. V., Jr., and J. R. Young. 2002. Learning to teach as an intern: The emotions and the self. *Teacher Development* 6(3): 417–31.

Burbank, M., and D. Kauchak. 2003. An alternative model for professional development: Investigations into effective collaboration. *Teaching & Teacher Education* 19(5): 499–514.

Carnegie Forum on Education and the Economy. 1986. *A nation prepared: Teachers for the 21st century*. New York: Author.

Carter, K., and L. Gonzalez. 1993. Beginning teachers' knowledge of classroom events. *Journal of Teacher Education* 44(3): 223–32.

Christiansen, H., L. Goulet, C. Krentz, and M. Maeers, eds. 1997. *Recreating relationships: Collaboration and educational reform*. Albany: State University of New York Press.

Clark, C. M. 1988. Asking the right questions about teacher preparation: Contributions of research on teacher thinking. *Educational Researcher* 17(2): 5–12.

Cinnamond, J. H., and N. L. Zimpher. 1990. Reflectivity as a function of community. In *Encouraging reflective practice in education: An analysis of issues and programs*, ed. R. T. Clift, W. R. Houston, and M. C. Pugach, 57–72. New York: Teachers College Press.

Clement, M., and R. Vandenberghe. 2000. Teachers' professional development: A solitary or collegial (ad)venture. *Teaching & Teacher Education* 16(1): 81–101.

Cliff, R. T., M. C. Houston, and M. Pugach, eds. 1990. *Encouraging reflective practice in education: An analysis of issues and programs*. New York: Teachers College Press.

Clifford, G. J., and J. W. Guthrie. 1988. *Ed school: A brief for professional education*. Chicago: University of Chicago Press.

Cochran-Smith, M. 2005. The new teacher education: For better or for worse? *Educational Researcher* 34(7): 3–17.

Cochran-Smith, M., and S. L. Lytle. 1999. The teacher research movement: A decade later. *Educational Researcher* 28(7): 15–25.

Cochran-Smith, M., and K. M. Zeichner, eds. 2005. *Studying teacher education: The report of the AERA panel on research and teacher education*. Mahwah, NJ: Lawrence Erlbaum Associates.

Cole, M. 1985. The tender trap? Commitment and consciousness in entrants to teaching. In *Teachers' lives and careers*, ed. S. J. Ball and I. F. Goodson, 89–104. London: The Falmer Press.

Coles, R. 1989. *The call of stories: Teaching and the moral imagination*. Boston: Houghton Mifflin.

Coles, R. 1993. *The call of service: A witness to idealism*. Boston: Houghton Mifflin.

Commission on Teacher Education. 1944. *Teachers for our times: A statement of purposes by the Commission on Teacher Education*. Washington, DC: American Council on Education.

Commission on Teacher Education. 1946. *The improvement of teacher education: A final report of the Commission on Teacher Education.* Washington, DC: American Council on Education.

Committee of Ten. 1894. *Report of the Committee of Ten on secondary school studies.* New York: American Book Company.

Connelly, F. M., and D. J. Clandinin. 1988. *Teachers as curriculum planners: Narratives of experience.* New York: Teachers College Press.

Cook-Sather, A. 2002. Authorizing students' perspectives: Toward trust, dialogue, and change in education. *Educational Researcher* 31(4): 3–14.

Cope, P., and C. Stephen. 2001. A role for practicing teachers in initial teacher education. *Teaching & Teacher Education* 17(8): 913–24.

Copeland, W. D., C. Birmingham, L. DeMeulle, M. D'Emidio-Caston, and D. D. Natal. 1994. Making meaning in classrooms: An investigation of cognitive processes in aspiring teachers, experienced teachers, and their peers. *American Educational Research Journal* 31(1): 166–96.

Cornbleth, C., and J. Ellsworth. 1994. Teachers in teacher education: Clinical faculty roles and relationships. *American Educational Research Journal* 31(1): 49–70.

Crow, N. A. 1987. Socialization within a teacher education program: A case study. Unpublished doctoral dissertation, University of Utah, Salt Lake City.

Darling, L. F. 2001. When conceptions collide: Constructing a community of inquiry for teacher education in British Columbia. *Journal of Education for Teaching* 27(1): 7–21.

Darling-Hammond, L. 2006. Constructing 21st-century teacher education. *Journal of Teacher Education* 57(3): 300–14.

Darling-Hammond, L. 1997. *The right to learning.* San Francisco: Jossey-Bass.

Darling-Hammond, L., and J. Bransford. 2005. *Preparing teachers for a changing world.* San Francisco: Jossey-Bass.

Darling-Hammond, L., and P. Youngs. 2002. Defining "highly qualified teachers": What does "scientifically-based research" actually tell us? *Educational Researcher* 31(9): 13–25.

Day, C. 1999. *Developing teachers.* London: Routledge/Falmer.

Day, C., and R. Leitch. 2001. Teachers' and teacher educators' lives: The role of emotion. *Teaching & Teacher Education* 17(4): 403–15.

Day, C., G. Stobart, P. Sammons, and A. Kington. 2006. Variations in the work and lives of teachers: Relative and relational effectiveness. *Teachers and teaching: Theory and practice* 12(2): 169–92.

Delaney, G. 1997. *In your dreams.* San Francisco: HarperCollins.

Dewey, J. 1902. *The child and the curriculum.* Chicago: University of Chicago Press.

Dewey, J. 1904. The relation of theory to practice in education. In *Third Yearbook of the National Society for the Scientific Study of Education*, ed. C. A. McMurray, 9–30. Chicago: National Society for the Scientific Study of Education.

Dewey, J. 1916. *Democracy and education.* New York: Macmillan.

Dewey, J. 1929. *The sources of a science of education.* New York: Horace Liveright.

Dewey, J. 1938. *Experience and education.* New York: Macmillan.

Dickmeyer, N. 1989. Metaphor, model, and theory in education research. *Teachers College Record* 91(2): 151–60.

Domhoff, G. W. 2003. *The scientific study of dreams.* Washington, DC: American Psychological Association.

Douglas, H. R. 1935. Subject-matter preparation of high school teachers. *Educational Administration and Supervision* 21(6): 457–64.

DuFour, R., R. Eaker, and R. DuFour, eds. 2005. *On common ground: The power of professional learning communities.* Bloomington, IN: Solution Tree.

Eliot, C. W. 1898. The unity of educational reform. In *Educational reform,* ed. C. W. Eliot, 315–39. New York: The Century Company.

Erasmus, D. 1942. *The praise of folly.* Roslyn, NY: Walter J. Black.

Erikson, E. H. 1968. *Identity: Youth and crisis.* New York: W. W. Norton.

Featherstone, D., H. Munby, and T. Russell, eds. 1997. *Finding a voice while learning to teach.* London: The Falmer Press.

Feiman-Nemser, S. 2001. From preparation to practice: Designing a continuum to strengthen and sustain teaching. *Teachers College Record* 103(6): 1013–55.

Fenstermacher, G. D. 1994. The knower and the known: The nature of knowledge in research on teaching. In *Review of research in education,* ed. L. Darling-Hammond, 3–56. Washington, DC: American Educational Research Association.

Feyerabend, P. 1975. *Against method.* London: NLB.

Flores, M. A., and C. Day. 2006. Contexts which shape and reshape new teachers' identities: A multi-perspective study. *Teaching & Teacher Education* 22(2): 219–32.

Freire, P. 1970. *Pedagogy of the oppressed.* Harmondsworth: Penguin.

Fuller, F. F., and O. Bown. 1975. Becoming a teacher. In *Teacher education: The Seventy-fourth Yearbook of the National Society for the Study of Education,* Part II, ed. K. Ryan, 25–52. Chicago: University of Chicago Press.

Garrison, J. 1997. *Dewey and eros: Wisdom and desire in the art of teaching.* New York: Teachers College Press.

Gee, J. P. 1996. *Social linguistics and literacies: Ideology in discourses.* New York: RoutledgeFalmer.

Gee, J. P. 2000–2001. Identity as an analytic lens for research in education. In *Review of Research in Education,* 25, ed. W. G. Secada, 99–125. Washington, DC: American Educational Research Association.

Gergen, K. J. 1991. *The saturated self: Dilemmas of identity in contemporary life.* New York: Basic Books.

Giles, C., and J. Wilson. 2004. Receiving as well as giving: Mentors' perceptions of their professional development in one teacher induction program. *Mentoring & Tutoring* 12(1): 87–106.

Gillum, G. 1993. *Of all things!: Classic quotations from Hugh Nibley.* Salt Lake City, UT: Deseret Book.

Glaser, B. G., and A. L. Strauss. 1967. *The discovery of grounded theory.* Chicago: Aldine.

Glass, J. M. 1993. *Shattered selves: Multiple personality in a postmodern world.* Ithaca, NY: Cornell University Press.

Goffman, E. 1959. The presentation of self in everyday life. Garden City, NY: Doubleday/Anchor Books.

Goodlad, J. I. 1990. *Teachers for our nation's schools.* San Francisco: Jossey-Bass.

Goodlad, J. I. 1994. *Educational renewal: Better teachers, better schools.* San Francisco: Jossey-Bass.

Goodlad, J. I., C. Mantle-Bromley, and S. J. Goodlad. 2004. *Education for everyone: Agenda for education in a democracy.* San Francisco: Jossey-Bass.

Goodson, I. F. 1981. Life histories and the study of schooling. *Interchange* 11(4): 62–76.

Goodson, I. F. 1992. Sponsoring the teacher's voice: Teachers' lives and teacher development. In *Understanding teacher development,* ed. A. Hargreaves and M. G. Fullan, 110–21. New York: Teachers College Press.

Goodson, I. F. 1994. Studying the teacher's life and work. *Teaching & Teacher Education* 10(1): 29–37.

Goodson, I. F., and P. Sikes. 2001. *Life history research in educational setting: Learning from lives.* Buckingham, UK: Open University Press.

Goodson, I. F., and R. Walker. 1991. *Biography, identity & schooling: Episodes in educational research.* London: The Falmer Press.

Gore, J. M. 1987. Reflecting on reflective teaching. *Journal of Teacher Education* 38(2): 33–39.

Gore, J. M., and K. M. Zeichner. 1991. Action research and reflective teaching in preservice teacher education: A case study from the United States. *Teaching & Teacher Education* 7(2): 119–136.

Gould, S. J. 1996. *Full house: The spread of excellence from Plato to Darwin.* New York: Harmony Books.

Graham, P. 1997. Tensions in the mentor teacher-student teacher relationship: Creating productive sites for learning within a high school English teacher education program. *Teaching & Teacher Education* 13(5): 513–27.

Graham, P. A. 1967. *Progressive education: From arcady to academe.* New York: Teachers College Press.

Griffiths, M., and S. Tann. 1992. Using reflective practice to link personal and public theories. *Journal of Education for Teaching* 18(1): 69–84.

Grimmett, P. P., and G. L. Erickson, eds. 1988. *Reflection in teacher education.* New York: Teachers College Press.

Grimmett, P. P., and A. M. MacKinnon. 1992. Craft knowledge in the education of teachers. In *Review of research in education,* ed. G. Grant, 385–456. Washington, DC: American Educational Research Association.

Grimmett, P. P., A. M. MacKinnon, G. L. Erickson, and T. J. Riechken. 1990. Reflective practice in teacher education. In *Encouraging reflective practice in education:*

An analysis of issues and programs, ed. R. T. Clift, W. R. Houston, and M. C. Pugach, 20–38. New York: Teachers College Press.

Guba, E. G. 1978. *Toward a methodology of naturalistic inquiry in educational evaluation.* Los Angeles: Center for the Study of Evaluation, UCLA Graduate School of Education.

Guskey, T. R. 2002. Professional development and teacher change. *Teachers and Teaching: theory and practice* 8(3–4): 381–91.

Habermas, J. 1979. *Communication and the evolution of society.* Translated by Thomas McCarthy. Boston: Beacon Press.

Hall-Quest, A. L. 1925. *Professional secondary education in teachers colleges.* New York: Teachers College, Columbia University.

Hamilton, J. L., and S. Pinnegar. 2000. On the threshold of a new century: Trustworthiness, integrity, and self-study in teacher education. *Journal of Teacher Education* 51(3): 234–40.

Hansen, D. T. 1995. *The call to teach.* New York: Teachers College Press.

Hanus, P. 1907. Preparation of high-school teachers. *National Education Association Journal of Proceedings and Addresses,* 563–77.

Hargreaves, A. 2000. Mixed emotions: Teachers' perceptions of their interactions with students. *Teaching & Teacher Education* 16(8): 811–26.

Hargreaves, A. 2001. Emotional geographies of teaching, *Teachers College Record* 103(6): 1056–80.

Hargreaves, A., and M. G. Fullan, eds. 1992. *Understanding teacher development.* New York: Teachers College Press.

Harper, C. 1939. *A century of public teacher education.* Washington, DC: National Education Association.

Harre, R., and L. van Langenhove, eds. 1999. *Positioning theory.* Oxford: Blackwell.

Hill, J. H. 1907. Preparation of high-school teachers. *National Education Association Journal of Proceedings and Addresses,* 712–23.

Hinsdale, B. A. 1910. The training of teachers. In *Education in the United States: A series of monographs*, ed. N. M. Butler, 359–407. New York: American Book Company.

Holly, M. L., and C. Walley. 1989. Teachers as professionals. In *Perspectives on teacher professional development*, ed. M. L. Holly and C. S. McLoughlin, 285–307. London: The Falmer Press.

Holmes Group. 1986. *Tomorrow's teachers: A report of the Holmes Group.* East Lansing, MI: Author.

Holmes Group. 1995. *Tomorrow's schools of education.* East Lansing, MI: Author.

Hopkins, L. T., ed. 1937. *Integration: Its meaning and application.* New York: D. Appleton-Century Company.

Howey, K. R., and N. L. Zimpher. 1999. Pervasive problems and issues in teacher education. In *The education of teachers: Ninety-eighth Yearbook of National Society for the Study of Education*, ed. G. A. Griffin, 279–305. Chicago: University of Chicago Press.

Huberman, A. M. 1989. The professional life cycle of teachers. *Teachers College Record* 91(1): 31–57.

Huberman, M. 1992. Teacher development and instructional mastery. In *Understanding teacher development*, ed. A. Hargreaves and M. G. Fullan, 122–42. New York: Teachers College Press.

Hudson-Ross, S. 2001. Intertwining opportunities: Participants' perceptions of professional growth within a multiple-site teacher education network at the secondary level. *Teaching & Teacher Education* 17(4): 433–54.

Hullfish, H. G., and P. G. Smith. 1961. *Reflective thinking: The method of education.* New York: Dodd, Mead & Company.

Hunt, D. E. 1987. *Beginning with ourselves: In practice, theory, and human affairs.* Cambridge, MA: Brookline Books.

James, W. 1888. *Psychology, briefer course.* New York: Henry Holt and Company.

Jersild, A. T. 1955. *When teachers face themselves.* New York: Teachers College, Bureau of Publications.

Johnson, D. D., B. Johnson, S. J. Farenga, and D. Ness. 2005. *Trivializing teacher education: The accreditation squeeze.* Lanham, MD: Rowman & Littlefield.

Johnston, P. 1989. Constructive evaluation and the improvement of teaching and learning. *Teachers College Record* 90(4): 509–28.

Johnston, S. 1994. Experience is the best teacher: Or is it? An analysis of the role of experience in learning to teach. *The Journal of Teacher Education* 45(3): 199–208.

Jones, M., and K. Straker. 2006. What informs mentors' practice when working with trainees and newly qualified teachers? An investigation into mentors' professional knowledge base. *Journal of Education for Teaching* 32(2): 165–84.

Judd, C. H. 1907. Preparation of high school teachers. *National Education Association Journal of Proceedings and Addresses*, 582–87.

Kagan, D. M. 1992. Professional growth among preservice and beginning teachers. *Review of Educational Research* 62(2): 129–69.

Kahne, J., and J. Westheimer. 2000. A pedagogy of collective action and reflection: Preparing teachers for collective school leadership. *Journal of Teacher Education* 51(5): 372–83.

Kaplan, S. N. 1986. The gird: A model to construct differentiated curriculum for the gifted. In *Systems and models for developing programs for the gifted and talented*, ed. J. S. Rensulli, 180–93. Mansfield Center, CT: Creative Learning Press.

Kelchtermans, G. 1996. Teacher vulnerability: Understanding its moral and political roots. *Cambridge Journal of Education* 26(3): 307–23.

Kelchtermans, G., and K. Ballet. 2002. The micropolitics of teacher induction: A narrative-biographical study on teacher socialization. *Teaching & Teacher Education* 18(1): 105–20.

Kelchtermans, G., and M. L. Hamilton. 2004. The dialectics of passion and theory: Exploring the relation between self-study and emotion. In *International handbook of self-study of teaching and teacher education practices*, ed. J. J. Loughran,

M. L. Hamilton, V. K. LaBoskey, and T. Russell, 785–810. Dordrecht, the Netherlands: Kluwer Academic Publishers.

Kemmis, S., and R. McTaggart. 1988. *The action research planner.* 3rd ed. Geelong, AU: Deakin University.

Kennedy, M. M. 2006. Knowledge and vision in teaching. *Journal of Teacher Education* 57(3): 205–11.

Klein, A. J., ed. 1941. *Adventures in the reconstruction of education.* Columbus: Ohio State University College of Education.

Knight, S. L., D. L. Wiseman, and D. Cooner. 2000. Using collaborative teacher research to determine the impact of professional development school activities on elementary students' math and writing outcomes. *Journal of Teacher Education* 51(1): 26–38.

Knowles, J. G. 1991. Journal use in preservice teacher education: A personal and reflexive response to comparison and criticisms. Paper presented at the annual meeting of the Association of Teacher Educators, New Orleans, February.

Koeppen, K., G. Huey, and K. Connor. 2000. Cohort groups: An effective model in a restructured teacher education program. In *Research on professional development schools*, ed. D. M. Byrd and D. J. McIntyre, 136–52. Thousand Oaks, CA: Corwin.

Korthagen, F. A. J. 2004. In search of the essence of a good teacher: Towards a more holistic approach in teacher education. *Teaching & Teacher Education* 29(1): 77–97.

Korthagen, F. A. J., J. Kessels, B. Koster, B. Lagerwerf, and T. Wubbels. 2001. *Linking practice and theory: The pedagogy of realistic teacher education.* Mahwah, NJ: Lawrence Erlbaum Associates.

Koster, B., F. A. J. Korthagen, and T. Wubbels. 1998. Is there anything left for us? Functions of cooperating teachers and teacher educators. *European Journal of Teacher Education* 21(1): 75–89.

Kridel, C., and R. V. Bullough, Jr. 2007. *Stories of the Eight-Year Study: Reexamining secondary education in America.* Albany: State University of New York Press.

Lacey, C. 1977. *The socialization of teachers.* London: Metheun.

Lasley, T. J., D. Siedentop, and R. Yinger. 2006. A systemic approach to enhancing teacher quality. *Journal of Teacher Education* 57(1): 13–21.

Learned, W. S., and W. C. Bagley. 1920. *The professional preparation of teachers for American public schools: A study based upon an examination of tax-supported normal schools in the state of Missouri.* New York: The Carnegie Foundation for the Advancement of Teaching.

Leitch, R., and C. Day. 2000. Action research and reflective practice: Towards a holistic view. *Educational Action Research Journal* 8(1): 179–93.

Levine, A. 2006. Will universities maintain control of teacher education? *Change* 38(4): 36–43.

Lewis, C. S. 1944/1996. *The abolition of man.* New York: Touchstone.

Lewis, L. 1990. Pilot project for portfolio assessment. Fort Worth, TX: Fort Worth Independent School District.

Lokoff, G., and M. Johnson. 1980. *Metaphors we live by.* Chicago: University of Chicago Press.

Lortie, D. C. 1975. *School-teacher: A sociological study.* Chicago: University of Chicago Press.

Loughran, J. 2006. *Developing a pedagogy of teacher education.* London and New York: Routledge.

Loughran, J., A. Berry, and L. Tudball. 2005. Collaborative learning in teaching about teaching. In *Making a difference in teacher education through self-study: Studies of personal, professional, and program renewal,* ed. C. Kosnik, C. Beck, A. Freese, and A. Samaras, 203–25. Berlin: Springer.

Loughran, J. J., M. L. Hamilton, V. K. LaBoskey, and T. Russell, eds. 2004. *International handbook of self-study of teaching and teacher education practices.* Dordrecht, the Netherlands: Kluwer Academic Publishers.

Loughran, J., and J. Northfield. 1996. *Opening the classroom door: Teachers, research, learner.* London: The Falmer Press.

Luckey, G. W. A. 1907. Preparation of high school teachers. *National Education Association Journal of Proceedings and Addresses,* 587–92.

Martin, D. 1997. Mentoring in one's own classroom: An exploratory study of contexts. *Teaching & Teacher Education* 13(2): 183–97.

Martineau, J. A. 2006. Distorting value added: The use of longitudinal, vertically scaled student achievement data for growth-based, value-added accountability. *Journal of Educational and Behavioral Statistics* 31(1): 35–62.

Mather, D., and B. Hanley. 1999. Cohort grouping and preservice teacher education: Effects on pedagogical development. *Canadian Journal of Education* 24(3): 235–50.

Mayer, D. E. 2006. Research funding in the U.S.: Implications for teacher education research. *Teacher Education Quarterly* 33(1): 5–18.

Mayes, C. T. 2001a. Cultivating spiritual reflectivity in teachers. *Teacher Education Quarterly* 28(2): 5–22.

Mayes, C. T. 2001b. A transpersonal model for teacher reflectivity. *Journal of Curriculum Studies* 33(4): 477–93.

McCall, W. A. 1922. *How to measure in education.* New York: Macmillan.

McCloskey, J. C., and H. K. Grace, eds. 1990. *Current issues in nursing.* St. Louis, MO: C. V. Mosby.

McKeon, R., ed. 1947. *Introduction to Aristotle.* New York: Modern Library.

McMahon, T. 1999. Is reflective practice synonymous with action research? *Educational Action Research Journal* 7(1): 163–68.

McNally, J., P. Cope, B. Inglis, and I. Stronach. 1997. The student teacher in school: Conditions for development. *Teaching & Teacher Education* 13(5): 485–98.

Measor, L. 1985. Critical incidents in the classroom: Identities, choices, and careers. In *Teachers' lives and careers*, ed. S. J. Ball and I. F. Goodson, 61–77. London: The Falmer Press.

Miles. M. B., and A. M. Huberman. 1984. *Qualitative data analysis: A sourcebook of new methods*. Newbury Park, CA: Sage.

Miller, S. I., and M. Fredericks. 1988. Uses of metaphor: A qualitative case study. *Qualitative Studies in Education* 1(3): 263–76.

Mills, C. W. 1959. *The sociological imagination*. New York: Oxford University Press.

Mishler E. G. 1979. Meaning in context: Is there any other kind? *Harvard Educational Review* 49: 1–19.

Monroe, W. S. 1952. *Teaching-learning theory and teacher education: 1890–1950*. Champaign: University of Illinois Press.

Mooney, R. L. 1957. The researcher himself. In *Research for curriculum development*, 154–86. Washington, DC: Association for Supervision and Curriculum Development.

Munby, H. 1986. Metaphor in the thinking of teachers: An exploratory study. *The Journal of Curriculum Studies* 18(2): 197–209.

Murphy, J. W. 1989. *Postmodern social analysis and criticism*. New York: Greenwood Press.

Murray-Harvey, R., P. T. Slee, J. F. Lawson, H. Silins, G. Banfield, and A. Russell. 2000. Under stress: The concern and coping strategies of teacher education students. *European Journal of Teacher Education* 23(1): 19–36.

National Board for Professional Teaching Standards (NBPTS). 1991. Draft request for proposals for multiple assessment development laboratories, rfp #6. Washington, DC: Author.

National Commission on Excellence in Education. 1983. *A nation at risk: The imperative for educational reform*. Washington, DC: Author.

National Research Council. 2004. *Advancing scientific research in education*. Washington, DC: The National Academies Press.

Nias, J. 1989. Teaching and the self. In *Perspectives on teacher professional development*, ed. M. L. Holly and C. S. McLoughlin, 155–72. London: The Falmer Press.

Nias, J. 1996. Thinking about feeling: The emotions in teaching. *Cambridge Journal of Education* 26(3): 293–306.

Noddings, N. 1984. *Caring*. Berkeley: University of California Press.

Oberski, I., K. Ford, S. Higgins, and P. Fisher. 1999. The importance of relationships in teacher education. *Journal of Education for Teaching* 25(2): 135–50.

Osguthrope, R. T., R. C. Harris, M. F. Harris, and S. Black, eds. 1995. *Partner schools: Centers for educational renewal*. San Francisco: Jossey-Bass.

Pajak, E. F. 1986. Psychoanalysis, teaching, and supervision. *Journal of Curriculum and Supervision* 1(2): 122–31.

Palmer, P. 1998. *The courage to teach: Exploring the inner landscape of a teacher's life*. San Francisco: Jossey-Bass.

Parr, S. S. 1888. *National Education Association Journal of Proceedings and Addresses,* 467–76.

Patterson, D. 1991. The eclipse of the highest in higher education. *The Main Scholar: A Journal of Ideas and Public Affairs* 3: 7–20.

Patterson, R. S., N. M. Michelli, and A. Pacheco. 1999. *Centers of pedagogy: New structures for educational renewal.* San Francisco: Jossey-Bass.

Paulson, F. L., P. R. Paulson, and C. A. Meyer. 1990. What makes a portfolio a portfolio? Pre-publication draft, Beaverton School District, Beaverton, OR.

Perkins, H. V. 1950. Teachers grow in understanding children. *Educational Leadership* 7(8): 549–55.

Pinar, W., ed. 1975. *Curriculum theorizing: The reconceptualists.* San Francisco: McCutchan.

Pinnegar, S. 1995. (Re-)Experiencing beginning. *Teacher Education Quarterly* 22(3): 65–84.

Pinnegar, S. 1996. Depending on experience. Paper presented at the annual meeting of the American Educational Research Association, New York, April.

Polanyi, M. 1958. *Personal knowledge: Towards a post-critical philosophy.* Chicago: University of Chicago Press.

Polkinghorne, D. E. 1988. *Narrative knowing and the human sciences.* Albany: State University of New York Press.

Pottle, F. A., ed. 1950. *Boswell's London Journal, 1762–1963.* New York: McGraw-Hill.

Prall, C. E., and C. L. Cushman. 1944. *Teacher education in-service.* Washington, DC: American Council on Education.

Provenzo, E. F., Jr., G. N. McCloskey, R. B. Kottkamp, and M. Cohn. 1989. Metaphor and meaning in the language of teachers. *Teachers College Record* 90(4): 551–73.

Randolph, E. D. 1924. *The professional treatment of subject-matter.* Baltimore, MD: Warwick & York.

Richardson, V. 1994. Conducting research on practice. *Educational Researcher* 23(5): 5–10.

Richardson, V. 1996. The role of attitudes and beliefs in learning to teach. In *Handbook of research on teacher education,* 2d ed., ed. J. Sikula, 102–19. New York: Macmillan.

Richert, A. E. 1990. Teaching teachers to reflect: A consideration of program structure. *Journal of Curriculum Studies* 22(6): 509–27.

Ricoeur, P. 1992. *One self as another.* Chicago: University of Chicago Press.

Rosenholtz, S. J. 1989. Workplace conditions that affect teacher quality and commitment: Implications for teacher induction programs. *The Elementary School Journal* 89(4): 421–39.

Roth, W-M., and K. Tobin. 2001. Learning to teach science as practice. *Teaching & Teacher Education* 17(6): 741–62.

Rothstein, R. 2004. *Class and schools: Using social, economic, and educational reform to close the black-white achievement gap.* New York: Economic Policy Institute, Teachers College, Columbia University.

Rumelhart, D. E. 1980. Schemata: The building blocks of cognition. In *Theoretical issues in reading comprehension: Perspectives in cognitive psychology, linguistics, and education*, ed. R. J. Spiro, B. C. Bruce, and W. F. Brewer, 33–58. Hillsdale, NJ: Erlbaum.

Russell, T. 1997. Teaching teachers: How I teach IS the message. In *Teaching about teaching*, ed. J. Loughran and T. Russell, 32–47. London: The Falmer Press.

Russell, T., and P. Johnston. 1988. Teachers learning from experiences of teaching: Analysis based on metaphor and reflection. Unpublished manuscript, Faculty of Education, Queens University, Kingston, Ontario, Canada.

Ryan, K. 1986. *The induction of new teachers*. Bloomington, IN: Phi Delta Kappa Educational Foundation.

Ryan, W. C. 1944. Better ways to teach teachers. *Progressive Education* 22(2): 10–11, 26–27.

Sabers, D. S., K. S. Cushing, and D. C. Berliner. 1991. Differences among teachers in a task characterized by simultaneity, multidimensionality, and immediacy. *American Educational Research Journal* 28(1): 63–88.

Samaras, A. P. 2002. *Self-study for teacher educators*. New York: Peter Lang.

Sandholtz, J. H., and E. C. Finan. 1998. Blurring the boundaries to promote school-university partnerships. *Journal of Teacher Education* 49(1): 13–25.

Scardamalia M., and C. Bereiter. 1989. Conceptions of teaching and approaches to core problems. In *Knowledge base for the beginning teacher*, ed. M. C. Reynolds, 37–45. New York: Pergamon Press.

Schmidt, W. H., R. T. Houang, and C. C. McKnight. 2005. Value-added research: Right idea but wrong solution? In *Value-added models in education: Theory and applications*, ed. R. W. Lissitz, 145–65. Grove, MN: JAM Press.

Serow, R. C. 1994. Called to teach: A study of highly motivated preservice teachers. *The Journal of Research and Development in Education* 27(2): 65–72.

Shavelson, R. J., and L. Towne, eds. 2002. *Scientific research in education*. Washington, DC: National Academy Press.

Shulman, L. S. 1987. Knowledge and teaching: Foundations of the new reform. *Harvard Educational Review* 57(1): 1–22.

Shulman, L. S. 2002. Truth and consequences: Inquiry and policy in research on teacher education. *Journal of Teacher Education* 53(3): 248–53.

Silverman, D. 1993. *Interpreting qualitative data: Methods for analyzing talk, text, and interaction*. London: Sage.

Sirotnik, K. A. 2001. Renewing schools and teacher education: An odyssey in educational change. Washington, DC: The American Association of Colleges for Teacher Education.

Sizer, T. R. 1994. *Horace's compromise: The dilemma of the American high school*. Boston: Houghton Mifflin.

Slater, P. E. 1965. Role differentiation in small groups. In *Small groups: Studies in social interaction*, rev. ed., ed. A. P. Hare, E. F. Borgatta, and R. F. Bales, 610–27. New York: Alfred A. Knopf.

Smith, W. F., and G. D. Fenstermacher, eds. 1999. *Leadership for educational renewal: Developing a cadre of leaders*. San Francisco: Jossey-Bass.

Solas, J. 1992. Investigating teacher and student thinking about the process of teaching and learning using autobiography and repertory grid. *Review of Educational Research* 62(2): 205–25.

Solomon, R. C. 1993. *The passions: Emotions and the meaning of life*. Indianapolis, IN: Hackett.

Spencer, D. A. 1986. *Contemporary women teachers: Balancing school and home*. New York: Longman.

Staff of the Division on Child Development and Teacher Personnel. 1945. *Helping teachers understand children*. Washington, DC: American Council on Education.

Stiles, L. J. 1947. Contributions of the Commission on Teacher Education to student teaching. *Educational Administration and Supervision* 33(3): 141–48.

Stokes, D. K. 1997. Called to teach: Exploring the worldview of called prospective teachers during their preservice teacher education. Unpublished doctoral dissertation, University of Utah, Salt Lake City.

Stone, B., and S. Mata. 2000. Fast-track teacher education: Are we adequately preparing teachers for California's class-size reduction? In *Research on effective models of teacher education*, ed. D. J. McIntyre and D. M. Byrd, 203–34. Thousand Oaks, CA: Corwin Press.

Stones, E. 1992. *Quality teaching: A sample of cases*. London and New York: Routledge.

Strauss, A., and J. Corbin. 1990. *Basics of qualitative research: Grounded theory procedures and techniques*. Newbury Park, CA: Sage.

Sutton, R. E., and K. F. Wheatley. 2003. Teachers' emotions and teaching: A review of the literature and directions for future research. *Educational Psychology Review* 15(4): 327–58.

Suzzallo, H. 1913. The reorganization of the teaching profession. *National Education Association Journal of Proceedings and Addresses*, 362–75.

Taubman, P. M. 1992. Achieving the right distance. In *Understanding curriculum as phenomenological and deconstructed text*, ed. W. F. Pinar and W. M. Reynolds, 216–36. New York: Teachers College Press.

Taylor, C. 1989. *Sources of the self*. Cambridge, MA: Harvard University Press.

Taylor, C. 1991. *The ethics of authenticity*. Cambridge, MA: Harvard University Press.

Tickle, L. 1999. Teachers' self-appraisal and appraisal of self. In *The role of self in teacher development*, ed. R. P. Lipka and T. M. Brinthaupt, 121–41. Albany: State University of New York Press.

Tillema, H. H. 2000. Belief change towards self-directed learning in student teachers: Immersion in practice or reflection on action. *Teaching & Teacher Education* 16(5–6): 575–91.

Tillich, P. 1967. *My search for absolutes*. New York: Simon and Schuster.

Toulmin, S. 2001. *Return to reason*. Cambridge, MA: Harvard University Press.

Troyer, M. E., and C. R. Pace. 1944. *Evaluation in teacher education.* Washington, DC: American Council on Education.

Tyack, D. B. 1974. *The one best system: A history of American urban education.* Cambridge, MA: Harvard University Press.

Tyack, D. B., and L. Cuban. 1995. *Tinkering toward utopia: A century of public school reform.* Cambridge, MA: Harvard University Press.

Ullman, M. 1987. The dream revisited: Some changed ideas based on a group approach. In *Dreams in New Perspective,* ed. M. Glucksman and S. Warner, 119–30. New York: Human Sciences Press.

Utley, B. L., C. G. Basile, and L. K. Rhodes. 2003. Walking in two worlds: Master teachers serving as site coordinators in partner schools. *Teaching & Teacher Education* 19(5): 515–28.

Van De Castle, R. L. 1994. *Our dreaming mind.* New York: Ballantine Books.

van Manen, M. 1994. Pedagogy, virtue, and narrative identity in teaching. *Curriculum Inquiry* 24(2): 135–70.

van Manen, M. 1999. The language of pedagogy and the primacy of student experience. In *Researching teaching: Methodologies and practices for understanding pedagogy,* ed. J. Loughran, 13–27. Philadelphia: Falmer Press.

van Veen, K., P. Sleegers, T. Bergen, and C. Klaassen. 2001. Professional orientations of secondary school teachers toward their work. *Teaching & Teacher Education* 17(2): 175–94.

Vavrus, L. 1990. Put portfolios to the test. *Instructor* 100: 48–53.

Veal, M. L., and L. Rikard. 1998. Cooperating teachers' perspectives on the student teaching triad. *Journal of Teacher Education* 49(2): 108–19.

Vedfelt, O. 1999. *The dimensions of dreams.* New York: Fromm International.

Walsh, D. J., N. L. Baturka, M. E. Smith, and N. Colter. 1991. Changing one's mind-maintaining one's identity: A first-grade teacher's story. *Teachers College Record* 93(1): 73–86.

Wang, J. 2001. Contexts of mentoring and opportunities for learning to teach: A comparative study of mentoring practice. *Teaching & Teacher Education* 17(1): 51–73.

Washburne, C. 1940. *A living philosophy of education.* New York: The John Day Company.

Weinstein. C. S. 1989. Teacher education students' preconceptions of teaching. *Journal of Teacher Education* 40(2): 53–60.

Weinstein, C. S. 1990. Prospective elementary teachers' beliefs about teaching: Implications for teacher education. *Teaching & Teacher Education* 6(3): 279–90.

Wenger, E. 1999. *Communities of practice: Learning, meaning, and identity.* New York: Cambridge University Press.

Whitehead, A. N. 1929/1961. *The aims of education.* New York: Macmillan.

Wideen, M. F., J. Mayer-Smith, and B. Moon. 1998. A critical analysis on learning-to-teach. *Review of Research* 68(2): 130–78.

Wildman, T. M., J. A. Niles, S. G. Magliaro, and R. A. McLaughlin. 1989. Teaching and learning to teach: The two roles of beginning teachers. *The Elementary School Journal* 89(4): 471–93.

Williams, A., S. Prestage, and J. Bedward. 2001. Individualism to collaboration: The significance of teacher culture to the induction of newly qualified teachers. *Journal of Education for Teaching* 27(3): 253–68.

Wilshire, B. 1990. *The moral collapse of the university: Professionalism, purity, and alienation.* Albany: State University of New York Press.

Wilson, S. M., and J. Berne. 1999. Teacher learning and the acquisition of professional knowledge: An examination of research on contemporary professional development. In *Review of research in education*, ed. A. Iran-Nejab and D. Pearson, 173–209. Washington, DC: American Educational Research Association.

Wilson, S. M., R. E. Floden, and J. Ferrini-Mundy. 2001. Teacher preparation research: Current knowledge, gaps, and recommendations. Seattle: Center for the Study of Teaching and Policy, University of Washington.

Wilson, S. M., R. E. Floden, and J. Ferrini-Mundy. 2002. Teacher preparation research: An insider's view from the outside. *Journal of Teacher Education* 53(3): 190–204.

Winitzky, N., T. Stoddart, and P. O'Keefe. 1992. Great expectations: Emergent professional development schools. *Journal of Teacher Education* 43(1): 3–18.

Woods, P. 1987. Life histories and teacher knowledge. In *Educating teachers: Changing the nature of pedagogical knowledge*, ed. J. Smyth, 121–35. London: The Falmer Press.

Yee, S. M. 1990. *Careers in the classroom: When teaching is more than a job.* New York: Teachers College Press.

Yin, R. K. 1989. *Case study research: Design and methods.* Newbury Park, CA: Sage.

Yinger, R. J. 1990. The conversation of practice. In *Encouraging reflective practice in education: An analysis of issues and programs*, ed. R. T. Clift, W. R, Houston, and M. C. Pugach, 73–94. New York: Teachers College Press.

Young, J. R., R. V. Bullough, Jr., R. J. Draper, L. K. Smith, and L. B. Erickson. 2005. Novice teacher growth and personal models of mentoring: Choosing compassion over inquiry. *Mentoring & Tutoring* 13(2): 169–88.

Zeichner, K. M. 1983. Individual and institutional factors related to the socialization of teaching. In *First years of teaching: What are the pertinent issues?*, ed. G. A. Griffin, 1–59. Austin, TX: Research and Development Center for Teacher Education.

Zeichner, K. M. 2002. Beyond traditional structures of student teaching, *Teacher Education Quarterly* 29(2): 59–64.

Zeichner, K. M. 2007. Accumulating knowledge across self-studies in teacher education. *Journal of Teacher Education* 58(1): 36–46.

Zeichner, K. M., and J. M. Gore. 1990. Teacher socialization. In *Handbook of research on teacher education*, ed. W. R. Houston, 329–48. New York: Macmillan.

Zeichner, K. M., and C. Grant. 1981. Biography and social structure in the socialization of student teachers: A reexamination of the pupil control ideologies of student teachers. *Journal of Education for Teaching* 3: 299–314.

Zeichner, K. M., and B. R. Tabachnick. 1991. Reflections on reflective teaching. In *Issues and practices in inquiry-oriented teacher education*, ed. B. R. Tabachnick and K. M. Zeichner, 2–21. London: The Falmer Press.

Zeichner, K. M., and R. Tabachnick. 1981. Are the effects of university teacher education washed out by school experience? *Journal of Teacher Education* 32(3): 7–11.

Zeichner, K. M., R. Tabachnick, and K. Densmore. 1987. Individual, institutional, and cultural influences on the development of teachers' craft knowledge. In *Exploring teachers' thinking*, ed. J. Calderhead, 21–59. London: Cassell.

Zembylas, M. 2002. "Structures of feeling" in curriculum and teaching: Theorizing the emotional rules. *Educational Theory* 52(2): 187–208.

Zembylas, M. 2003. Emotions and teacher identity: A poststructural perspective. *Teachers & teaching: Theory and practice* 9(3): 213–38.

Index

Randolph, 28
research,
    clinical faculty conceptions of and
        resistance to, 90, 92, 96–97
    collaborative, 86

Sarte,
    bad faith, 59
Scardamalia, 133
self-study, 9, 63
Shulman, 9, 15, 16, 22, 27
Solomon,
    on emotions, 106–107, 111, 118
Smith, 4
Stones, 28
Student learning
    and poverty, 4
Suzzallo, 23, 24

Taubman, 62
Taylor, 73
Teach,
    learning to, 108–118
Teacher education, 5
    academic training, 22
    cohorts, 7
    conditions of, 6
    and general education, 37–38
    normal schools, 17, 18, 19, 23, 24,
        25
    pedagogical training, 23
    and public school/university partner-
        ships, 6, 30, 33, 70, 86–87
    professionalizing subject matter con-
        tent, 27
    purposes of, 24
    reform of, 31, 38
Teacher educators,
    and clinical faculty, 85–102
    identity formation, 51–68, 69–84
        identification and membership,
            55, 56–60

self-expression and enactment, 55,
    64–66
subject location, 55, 61–64
persona, 53, 54
subject positions, 57, 68
temperament, 56, 63
Teacher research, 9
Teachers
    anger, 112–115
    beginning, emotions of, 110–118
        illness, 116
    dreams of, 159–174
        analysis of, 162
        and emotions, 159–160
        rhythm of, 170
        themes, 162–170
        and vulnerability, 162
        and work conditions, 171
    development of, 119–131
        school context, 130
    developmental stages, 123–126
        weaknesses of, 131
    emotional labor, 112, 113
    growing responsibilities for teacher
        education, 69
    guilt, 115–117, 144
    identity formation, 126–127
        emotions and, 105–118
        life cycles, 124–126
    life history, 129, 130, 180, 196
    love of students, 110–112
    metaphors, 127, 180, 193–204
        analysis of, 194–196
            value of, 203
        examples, 196–202
        and identity, 195
        and self-understanding, 194
        problems of, 124–127, 170
    philosophy as living, 227
    status, 60
    subject position, 65, 68
    vulnerability, 69, 117, 162
    work, 5